LINA CAVALIERI

LINA CAVALIERI

The Life of Opera's Greatest Beauty, 1874–1944

Paul Fryer *and* Olga Usova

McFarland & Company, Inc., Publishers

Jefferson, North Carolina, and London

LIBRARY OF CONGRESS ONLINE CATALOG

Fryer, Paul, 1955–
Lina Cavalieri : the life of opera's greatest beauty, 1874–1944 /
Paul Fryer and Olga Usova.
p.   cm.
Includes bibliographical references (p.) and index.
Discography: p.
Filmography: p.

ISBN 0-7864-1685-8 (softcover : 50# alkaline paper) ∞

[1.] Cavalieri, Lina, 1874.   [2.] Sopranos (Singers)—Biography.
[I. Title.]
ML420.C388F7   2004   782.1'092B—dc22   2003023691

British Library cataloguing data are available

Cover photograph: Cavalieri as Violetta in Verdi's *La Traviata (Reutlinger Studio,
Paris 1901, from the collections of the author and Svetlana Vlasova)*

Manufactured in the United States of America

McFarland & Company, Inc., Publishers
Box 611, Jefferson, North Carolina 28640
www.mcfarlandpub.com

To Andrei, Gleb, Danila and Nigel

ACKNOWLEDGMENTS

The authors would like to acknowledge the financial support of the Historic Singers Trust: and the invaluable assistance of Emilia Rudaya, Mikhail Talalai, Alexander Pozdnyakov (of *Lenfilm*), Mike Mashon (*Library of Congress*), Robert Tuggle (*Metropolitan Opera Archive*s), Amedeo Gigli, Marvin Lyons, Ulla Tillander-Godenhielm, Dr.William McRae, Erio Tripodi, Anna Shoulgat, Tom Kaufman, Bob Kosovsky (*New York Public Library Performing Arts*), Barbara Karn, Stella Wright (*Massenet Society, London*), Kevin Brownlow, Edward Morgan, Pierre Vidal (*Biblioteque Musee de l'Opera*), Alice Bloch, Charlotte Revollon-Lubert (*Opera Monte Carlo*), Marcella Ilari, Patrizia Lazzari, Svetlana Vlasova; the staff of the British Library Newspaper Library; the staff of the State Museum of Theatre and Music, St.Petersburg; and the staff of the Music and Motion Picture Divisions of the Library of Congress, Washington D.C.

CONTENTS

PREFACE

Even the most casual observer who happened across a reference to "the most beautiful woman in the world" might be intrigued enough to find out who she was. The authors of this, the first English-language biography of Lina Cavalieri, certainly were. Starting from entirely opposite points, they became captivated by the rags-to-riches' story of this woman who rose from the streets of Rome to international fame as a cabaret singer, an operatic diva and a silent movie star. Lina Cavalieri became an icon of beauty and fashion: a media personality whose image appeared on postcards all over the world, who enjoyed notorious love affairs, entering into a scandalous liaison with a Russian prince and marrying into one of the world's richest families. And yes, as the numerous photographs published here prove, she was very beautiful.

Cavalieri was one of the greatest stars of her era: Her reputation filled theaters from St. Petersburg to London and Paris. She shared the stage of New York's Metropolitan Opera House with Enrico Caruso and was the first major opera star to appear in a feature-length film. Yet today, she is almost forgotten.

Distinguishing between fact and fiction in the examination of such a colorful life story has been a problematic task. Much of what has been previously written about Cavalieri originates from unreliable, anecdotal sources: Her self-styled autobiography, *Le Mie Verità* (Rome, 1936), littered with inaccuracies, has provided the major source for most previous accounts. This book attempts the first scholarly assessment of her life and career, accessing, for the first time in English translation, a wealth of material relating to her hugely successful career in pre–Revolutionary Russia. For example, the largely adulatory accounts of her stage personality and performance technique which exist in several sets of memoirs and later in studio-generated publicity material have been replaced in this study by the far more probing critical assessments of some of her colleagues and the many writers who dismissed the force of her sheer physical presence to provide us with a vivid picture of a singing actress of distinction and considerable potential. Some questions about her life remain unanswered, but this has only added to the intrigue, and knowledge of the star suggests that this is exactly what she would have wanted. Here we can witness again the opera star that so impressed Puccini in the New York premiere of *Manon Lescaut* and of whom Massenet conceded the value of her beauty gave her the right to make mistakes from time to time.

In an era in which crossover performances from one genre or medium to another

1

are expected, in which it seems that every singer must also act, every actor must also sing, every opera star aspire to film stardom and every movie star prove their credentials as a serious dramatic actor—it is easy to forget that in the golden decades between 1890 and 1920, when gramophone recordings, moving pictures and even experimental radio broadcasting revolutionized every part of the entertainment industry, stars such as Lina Cavalieri became the true pioneers of crossover performance.

It is hoped that this biography will provoke renewed interest in a creative artist whose contribution to and influence upon the culture and society of her time have long called for a critical reevaluation.

Paul Fryer and Olga Usova
November, 2003

I.

BEGINNINGS

Throughout most of her life, Lina Cavalieri was widely acknowledged as one of the most startlingly beautiful women of her time. But that distinction clouds some of the more important details of a vividly extravagant life often lived in a blaze of publicity. An extraordinary range of achievements that took her from the modest beginnings as a café chanteuse to the dizzy heights of sharing the stage of New York's Metropolitan Opera House with Enrico Caruso also saw her become the first opera star to make a successful transition from the lyric stage to the silent screen.

It was always her beauty, however, for which she was applauded and remembered:

> Over the years, hundreds of journalists have asked me whom I regarded as the most beautiful woman in the world. Invariably I replied, "Lina Cavalieri." Why? She was tall and extremely slender—a rarity among turn-of-the-century prima donnas. Her classically pure features were enhanced by dark hair and eyes, and a long swan-like neck. Yet her beauty was not cold. Her expression was full of animation, and she moved with grace and authority. Cavalieri's most dominant quality however was her extraordinary charm. What is charm? I would define it as a quality of mind and soul which finds expression in a person's physical appearance and behavior. Cavalieri expressed it to a superb degree. Although her voice had its limitations, she worked so diligently on its development and handled it so deftly that she emerged from her debut in Milan's La Scala—a theatre which attracted the most sophisticated, discriminating and critical opera audiences in the world—as a full-fledged star. I had first seen Cavalieri at the Conservatorium Theatre in St. Petersburg when I was about fourteen. During the next few years I heard her sing every role in her repertoire. One day I made a portrait of her from memory—a pastel— and sent it to her. I was thrilled when it was presented to her onstage, along with a great number of baskets and bouquets of flowers. The next day I received a charming letter from her, together with a beautiful autographed photograph. But it was not until 1929 that I finally met her. It was at the opening of a new production of Edmund Rostand's *La Princesse Lointaine* at the Sarah Bernhardt Theatre, for which I had designed the costumes and settings. Cavalieri congratulated me on my success, and I told her the story of our one-sided romance, which amused her. Although she was then over fifty, she was still as beautiful as when I first saw her."[1]

In 1912, at the age of 19, the artist and designer Erté, from whose memoirs this passage comes, was leaving St. Petersburg bound for a new life in Paris. He recalled, "As I entered my carriage, I was thrilled to see that my idol, the soprano, Lina Cavalieri, was also Paris-bound. Surely this meant that luck was with me."[2] Erté later claimed that during a year in which he lived in America (1925–26), he was interviewed 197 times. On 138 occasions he was asked who he thought was the most beautiful woman he had ever met. He always answered, Lina Cavalieri.

A similar story is told by the Canadian historian Marvin Lyons: "As for Lina Cavalieri, I first became aware of her about 30 years ago when I saw her photograph among the papers and souvenirs of my now deceased friend Cyril Narishkin in his home in Paris. She was extraordinarily beautiful, wearing no jewellery or makeup, and obviously very pure and virginal. I learned a great deal about her from him because she was his first lover and he still had very strong feelings for her, even though she was much older than he was and at the time he was only a boy. When I knew him, 70 years later, he still adored her and preserved her memory in his heart."[3]

It is difficult to reconcile what appears to be a rather small and carefully produced voice, captured on a handful of gramophone recordings which Lina Cavalieri made for the Columbia company between 1910 and 1913 with the reputation of an operatic singer whose New York stage appearances included Giordano's *Fedora*, Cilea's *Adriana Lecouvreur*, and the first performance at the Metropolitan Opera of Puccini's *Manon Lescaut*, in which Enrico Caruso played Des Grieux. Cavalieri's operatic talents were evidently of a very specific nature.

Rupert Christiansen surmises that "her art was a fragile thing … an insubstantial but pretty little voice that went well with her diaphanous beauty. As a singer she could not be taken very seriously, but as a late manifestation of the courtesan—a courtesan with a career and a press agent—she was magnificently successful."[4] This view is largely supported by the many press reports and reviews of her performances, especially in New York, which clearly indicate a performer whose acting and physical presence on stage were frequently considered to be of greater and more enduring impact than her singing. The Russian baritone and opera commentator Sergei Levik spoke briefly but incisively of Cavalieri in his memoirs: "She had the attributes of a first-class operetta singer or, more precisely, of a diseuse who knew how to make the most risqué material attractive through a sort of naiveté. A graceful dancer, she was able to make the most suggestive movements and gestures with such innocence, child-like simplicity and charm that their pornographic nature was ignored."[5]

Levik was fairly dismissive of Cavalieri's musicianship, expressing the clear opinion that her voice was of average quality. He was impressed, however, by her ability to work hard to achieve her ambitions, both operatic and otherwise: "The enormous work that Cavalieri had done on herself under the supervision of good teachers turned a weak, smallish voice … into a completely tolerable professional instrument … even exacting conductors considered her capable of performing demanding roles."[6]

That she was possessed of both the temperamental capriciousness and the disarming charm that so befit a star performer in any field is amply illustrated by a story retold by Levik in his book: "In the prison scene in *Faust* she once doubled the tempo.… The conductor was confused for a moment but realised that any disagreement would only increase the confusion and followed her.… When we were in her dressing-room after the performance, the conductor came in gloomily in order to deliver a dressing down, but Cavalieri sweetly presented him with a box of chocolates and in the end it was the conductor who felt guilty."[7] On that occasion Levik recalled that the conductor reminded the assembled company of the comment made to Cavalieri by Jules Massenet after he had heard her sing the title role in his opera *Thaïs*: "Your beauty gives you the right to make mistakes sometimes."[8] Levik also recorded a conversation he had with the great baritone Mattia Battistini, who claimed that Cavalieri would often "do something different where you least expect it and put you out."[9]

Perhaps Cavalieri might be accused of a lack of professionalism, perpetrating cheap tricks at the expense of her fellow artists, but one might just as easily attribute such wilful behavior to one who thrived on spontaneity in her performances. Many would defend this approach as being an essential component of the great performer. After all, Caruso was generally considered to be one of the most prolific practical jokers in operatic history, but there is no suggestion that his high spirits made him any less of a consummate professional; indeed, it is likely that the contrary is true. So, what kind of operatic stage performer can we assume Cavalieri to have been?

In a profile of the singer, published at the height of her Metropolitan Opera career in 1908, William Armstrong addressed the question of her acting technique: "The dramatic side of her art Mme. Cavalieri has never studied, in the traditional sense of the word. Her somewhat daring theory is that one should act naturally, and that study of the accepted sort only results in acting unnaturally.... She forms her conceptions not so much by reason as by instinct—the instinct of a woman's sympathy and psychological power.... Mme. Cavalieri tries to get at the key in which a character is written. For Carmen she goes to Merimee's book; for Thaïs, to the novel by Anatole France; and from these ground tones she builds up the scale of the character. Then her research is ended, and for the rest she follows her own emotions as the music of the opera, and the sequence of its episodes, may guide her."[10]

This natural, instinctive approach to acting was a characteristic shared with her colleagues and rivals Geraldine Farrar and Mary Garden, both of whom had faced the same censure for their spontaneity, yet achieved the same, often startling, results in their stage performances. The spontaneous performer is also frequently the least predictable. But it is that very lack of predictability that invests their performances with that added excitement which makes them truly memorable. Whether we can assess Lina Cavalieri as a great performer, or rather, as Rupert Christiansen suggests, a notably beautiful woman of limited talents but an immense skill in deploying them, is one of the most intriguing aspects of an examination of her career. That process, however, is far from straightforward and, as in all of the best romantic sagas, requires a degree of tolerance and the occasional suspension of disbelief on the part of the reader.

Truth is often found to be far stranger than fiction, and it would appear that Mme. Cavalieri sometimes experienced significant problems in clearly differentiating between the two. Certainly, for the serious researcher, distinguishing the factual from the fictional in a biographical study such as this can often present major difficulties. Ironically, the principal reason for this confusion is the existence of a book titled *Le Mie Verità* (*My Truth*), which purports to be an autobiography but is actually a collaboration between Cavalieri and Paolo D'Arvanni and was published in Rome in 1936. The first mention of memoirs penned by Cavalieri is in a book by Jarro (G. Piccini), *Viaggio Umoristico nei Teatri,* published in 1903. In the chapter, "Le *'Memorie'* di Lina Cavalieri" the author wrote: "Generally books by artistes are the work of famous writers who had frequent occasion for exploring them…. La belle Lina Cavalieri … who is a model beauty … and who is in universal good grace, has written her own *Memoirs.* Various writers offered her their co-operation: such a pleasant woman as Lina Cavalieri never lacks collaborators."[11] It appears from this book that Cavalieri's memoirs of 1903 were a collection of anecdotes often far from being true and that some of these were later used again in the book that appeared in 1936.

Information about these memoirs also appeared in the Russian press: "One of our provincial newspapers found in the Italian press the memoirs of Lina Cavalieri and published an extract from them. Cavalieri told about one Russian aristocrat who fell in love with her who dressed like a coachman and conveyed her to her home and was always tipped with some money. Then he presented her with diamonds and other gifts…. These love affairs … are interesting to the public."[12] In the 1936 memoirs this person is identified as Duke Raimondo di T, who apparently served as her driver when she sang *La Traviata* at the Pagliano Theatre in Florence.

The majority of published material on Cavalieri's career appears either to emanate from versions supplied by herself, often from this unreliable "autobiography," or from subsequent studio or journalistic reinterpretations of the same material. It is extraordinarily difficult to extract accurate factual information from such potentially unreliable sources. For example, the apparently simple matter of putting her later silent film career into straightforward chronological order presents considerable difficulties.

Giorgio Vecchietti's article, "La famosa Cavalieri," originally published in the Italian film magazine *Cinema* in March 1937 is based upon an interview he carried out with the retired star. In this interview, Cavalieri stated clearly that she had made her first two films for the Tiber Studios in Rome in 1915 and 1916. In the autobiographical *Le Mie Verità,* Cavalieri expanded on this version of the story: "In Rome, I owed the possibility of work in films to Mr. Menchari. I shot with him my first two films, *Sposa nella Morte* and *La Rosa di Granata,* in which I worked with my husband Muratore … Emilio Ghione … was the director. From Italy I returned to the U.S. and signed for the Players Film Company in New Jersey. There I shot *Gismonda … L'eterna Tentatrice … and Le due Spose.*"[13]

If this is accepted as an accurate version of events, how are we then to deal with what we might consider to be Cavalieri's most interesting film, the screen version of *Manon Lescaut,* which, according to Vernon Jarratt's *Italian Cinema,* was made by Cavalieri in America in 1914. This film, which, according to the listings of the *American Film Institute Catalogue,* was partly shot on location in France—in Paris, Amiens and Le Havre—suggesting the possible involvement of a European producer, was directed by Herbert Hall Winslow, costarred Cavalieri's husband at the time, the French tenor Lucien Muratore, and featured an American supporting cast. Produced by the Playgoers Film Company and released in the United States in May 1914, the film was reviewed by *Moving Picture World* in June of that year.

Read in conjunction with the dates and information given by Cavalieri, the definitive dating of *Manon Lescaut* clearly suggests that it was indisputably her first film. Yet Jarratt states that she had begun making films in Italy before 1913. Where is the truth? Does the truth of Cavalieri's autobiography prove to be the same truth as that offered about her life by other sources, and how far do the records of her public career in the theater, cinema and opera house go toward providing an answer to this dichotomy? There are many unanswered questions still remaining about the intriguing life of la belle Cavalieri.

Lina Cavalieri was born on Christmas Day, December 25, 1874, into a poor Italian family in the old town of Viterbo, not far from Rome. In honor of the day, she was named Natalina, *natale* being the Italian word for Christmas. A year later she was taken to be baptized in the cathedral of Santa Maria in Trastevere in Rome on December 26, 1875.[14]

Being the oldest child, Lina helped her mother look after the other children: her brothers Nino and Oreste and her sister Julia. In her childhood, along with the usual fairytales told to all children she heard stories about her father's noble lineage, of a rich family in former times whose coat of arms was decorated with a margrave's coronet. Florindo Cavalieri's noble origins are impossible to substantiate, but there is no doubt that his eldest daughter possessed a great dignity in her bearing and an elegance in taste and manners that seem entirely uncharacteristic of her humble origins. The family fortune had apparently been lost as a result of an unsettled legal case fought among relatives to secure an inheritance. In several publications Cavalieri's father was represented variously as a traveling merchant dealing in olive oil[15] and as a newspaper salesman.[16] Marcella Illari claimed that "he found work as a domestic in the house of a stone-cutter, Constantino Santori … perhaps with the help of Vincenza Cavalieri who was living in the same house."[17] The author confirms this with reference to a passage in the registry of the church of Santa Maria, Trastevere, in 1877.

All prospects of good fortune, however, were in the distant past; the present provided a very different picture. The unstable financial situation in Italy had caused the loss of many jobs, and Lina's father, working as an assistant in an architect's office, was among the many to suffer. This was a particularly painful blow to the young girl. For all of her life Lina idolized her father. Their spiritual connection was so strong that more than twenty years later, as she traveled on the ship which took her to fame in New York, she had a premonition, which she related to her brother, then acting as her business manager, that their father had died: A telegram awaited them on their arrival, confirming the sad news. For a perceptive and intelligent child, the family's poverty must have been hard to bear. Every day Lina witnessed the sadness in the eyes of her siblings, her mother's growing exhaustion and the desperation of her beloved father, faced with the knowledge that he could not even adequately feed his family. Although she had very few options open to her, Lina's determination to help her family grew stronger with each succeeding day. Later she was to sum up her own determination: "When I wanted something badly—I always achieved it."[18] But what could she hope to achieve?

Even in these early childhood years, Lina displayed an enviable strength of character and a fiery temperament that often manifested itself when she played street games with the boys in the local Italian Cossacks brigade. Many people envied her courage, her great physical vigor and bravery. She would take part in impromptu raids on local kitchen gardens, steal from fairground booths, and enter into the spirit of rough-and-tumble war games with her companions with a frightening relish. On many occasions she would return home with her dress torn or the soles falling off her shoes, to the despair of her troubled parents. The days of carefree childhood, however, were almost at an end: Inevitably, perhaps, it was decided that Lina must find work to help the family's strained finances. At first she was sent to learn the trade of a dressmaker, but the girl didn't display any inclination toward this craft, and her restlessness and independent temper soon put an end to her training. However, as the oldest child in the family, Lina had to earn money somehow. She then worked as a flower girl, selling bunches of violets in the streets, but such seemingly romantic employment could also hold many dangers for a young girl, and it was soon abandoned for a factory job, packing copies of the Roman newspaper *Forum*.

For a creative child, such a life was soul destroying; and Lina's natural creativity had now begun to surface. She began to sing to express her sorrows and her joys, even the burdens of her housekeeping chores, in song. A music teacher who lived in the neighborhood overheard her impromptu vocalizing, and he offered to give her a few free lessons. He earned his living by accompanying and coaching would-be diseuse, who hoped to make a living as performers in the café chantant, which were becoming very popular at this time. Here was the very first indication of Lina's future path to the fame and good fortune that she craved. After a few lessons, it

ROMA. Piazza Navona.

The Piazza Navona in Rome.

seemed to her teacher that the young Lina, now nearly 14 years old, was a little more gifted than many of his similar pupils, and he decided to promote his protégé by introducing her to the host of a café chantant in the Piazza Navona. Having learned three fashionable Neapolitan songs Lina auditioned to best of her abilities, trying to remember the advice of her teacher, and was offered an engagement. Although this café was hardly a fashionable establishment, it was a paying job, and was far preferable to the spirited young performer than her previous employments.

In order to get to her new place of employment, Lina had to walk virtually from one side of the town to the other; a tram ride was an unaffordable luxury. Her mother escorted her to the café every day, waited for her behind the scenes, and after midnight once again they walked from Navona's square through the dark Roman streets to their home. In this modest theater-restaurant Lina signed her first contract: Her fee was one lira for each evening's performance. In line with the traditional practice of the time, after her performance, she went around the audience with a plate, collecting gratuities.

When she received her first payment, she was obliged to spend the money on a suitable dress and shoes to wear for her performances. The dress was homemade and the shoes were bought at a sale. Although Lina was never to experience such difficult circumstances again during her professional life, she remembered vividly the fear that she felt on the evening of her debut: "I saw nothing around me. I was trembling with fear. I didn't dare to take the first step. The melancholic accompanist had already played the prelude twice. From back-stage peremptory hissing was heard: 'Begin!… Begin!…' Trembling hands picked at the plain dress on my poor shivering body. My mouth refused to open. My throat squeezed with terror uttered a sound. At this terrible moment I seemed to sense the miserable place in which we found ourselves: need! Almost instinctively I began to move my lips. When the music finished I trembled because of the noise of applauding hands and almost automatically, crying, literally fell behind the scenes."[19]

Cavalieri's memoirs indicate that the year was 1887, and her career in the public spotlight had begun.

THE QUEEN OF VARIETY

Paolo Guzzi has left us the following description of the kind of venue in which Lina Cavalieri began her performing career:

> The café-chantants were of two sorts at the beginning of the 19th century: one of them was rich, spacious, with an international cast of performers of the various variety turns, the other poor, with restricted space, designed for the close circle of local habitants. The public attended the luxurious cafés-concerts especially for the variety of entertainments. The bourgeois audience came there to show themselves and to see others. The female spectators rivaled the actresses in refined and splendid dresses and costumes. The evening in the café-chantant consisted of two parts and the variety turns went on in order of the *crescendo* [increasing level] of importance. Firstly there were singers, male and female, of modest fame—*chanteuse* or *gommeuse*—and their male homologues. Those singers were dressed with exaggerated elegance, designed rather to make the audience laugh than to excite general admiration. The second part of the real concert program began when its very *habitués* made a tardy appearance. The *vedette* or *étoile*, the star, closed the performance and it was the crowning touch to the evening's entertainment. The *vedette* could be also an actor, a famous stand-up comic.[1]

If we are to believe Cavalieri's affirmation in her autobiography that she had debuted at the age of 14, in a venue such as those described by Guzzi, it is reasonable to suppose that she would have been the chanteuse of the first part of the variety bill, until April 8, 1894, when her name appeared twice—as the 4th and 13th acts on the program—on the playbill of the Concerto delle Varietà, in the Via Due Macelli in Rome.[2] Throughout this time she took lessons in voice and dance and increased her celebrity by taking part in the beauty competition that was staged at the Teatro Constanzi as part of the Roman carnival. A talent such as Cavalieri's would not go unnoticed for long. Patrons and employers alike recognized the original beauty of the "disguised princess" who appeared to blossom more magnificently the more she was noticed.

She was engaged to perform in more splendid cafe chantants, and her fee grew from 1 lira to 15 lire for each evening. As her fame spread, in 1895 she was employed to appear at such important establishments as the Grande Orfeo and Diocleziano in Rome and for an increasingly distinguished audience. Wearing fashionable dresses, embroidered with the best costume jewelry that she could afford, Cavalieri scored her first real successes and rapidly became one of the most popular entertainers in the Italian capital. Although it seems certain that the young performer would have been denied such chances without the assistance of an influential patron, it is not easy to identify who this person actually was. Taburi offers some suggestions: "Who was the first to launch the name of Lina Cavalieri, a marvel of the Piazza Navona, in the halls of *Scacchi* (Chess) or *Caccia* (Hunting)? Possibly, it was the Prince Maffeo Sciarra Colonna, who succeeded in discovering ... the most splendid women of the epoch and offered them, with ease, the pearls and emeralds that he bought by selling, clandestinely, the pictures from his famous collection. Or Ladislao Odescalchi, the Prince in Rome and the Magnate in Hungary, with his red beard reaching to his waist and whose generosity grew into a proverb on the tongues of men. Or Giovanni Savorgnan of Brazzà. Or one of the Theodoli. It is unknown: perhaps it was a collective discovery."[3]

Taking advantage of the new opportunities given to her, Cavalieri developed her repertoire of songs to include some of the most popular of Mario Costa's compositions: "Ciociara," "Funiculi-Funicula" and "Frangesa." Her popularity continued to grow, and as a result, she was invited to Naples, one of the most fashionable centers for music and the arts and home of many of the popular songs that she had incorporated into her stage performances. Paliotti suggests that the management of the Salone Margherita engaged her in 1895 without much enthusiasm and contracted her actual name, Natalina, to the shorter form, Lina, so that it might show up more noticeably among some of the more exotic stage names of the time. "However that may be, this young girl was so exuberantly beautiful and she had a voice so sensual that Marino and Caprioli [owners of the Salone Margherita at this time] didn't hesitate for an instant, after her debut, about placing her name with the local celebrities like Carmen Marini and Diego Giannini. She quickly outclassed both and she stayed for a while in Naples passing from the *Salone Margherita* to the *Circo delle Varietà*, to the *Eldorado* and to the *Eden*. And there her successes were repeated inasmuch that Marino and Caprioli wanted to sign a contract with her again."[4] Naples became the jumping-off point from which Cavalieri made the next major leap of her burgeoning career; across the Alps to arrive, at last, on the stage of the renowned Folies Bergère. Although some Neapolitans had dismissed the young Cavalieri as a provincial upstart, within less than a year the "village girl" became a star not only of the Folies but also of London's Empire Theatre.

The Parisian audience would be the deciding factor in the establishment of Cavalieri's international career, for to achieve genuine star status here would guarantee for her not only the highest fees, but also the most prestigious engagements upon the most elite variety stages of Europe. The Folies Bergère's press advertising proclaimed at this time: "Ask Russians, Americans or even Japanese where they meet again in Paris? They will answer you: 'At the Folies Bergère!'"

Cavalieri's success in Paris was staggering, and it is hardly an exaggeration to claim that on the morning after her Paris debut, she woke up as a star: She later recalled that the critics "littered [her] with recognition, flowers and gifts."[5] Within a few days, she recorded, "I was surrounded with many impresarios with top hats in their hands, and innumerable gardenias in their buttonholes, owners of many bank drafts, and three splendid signed contracts—on excellent conditions!—London, Berlin, Petersburg."[6] The management of the Folies Bergère renewed their contract with a young star for the autumn of 1896. "October came quickly and with autumn more fulsome praises of the public came. A new ephemeral queen of the Folies Bergère was born. My rises increased still to 5,000 lire a month. My name in the programmes which are distributed in the stalls by servants dressed in scarlet, was of the same dimension as the names of Loie Fuller, Lyane de Pougy, Carolina Otero."[7] Later Cavalieri noted, "When I wanted something badly, I always achieved it."[8]

The engagement at the Folies also helped to launch Cavalieri's career in other European capital cities. In May 1897 she performed at London's renowned Empire Theatre, singing the songs of her country with the accompaniment of six mandolinists in the costumes of Neapolitan fishermen. She vied with other stars of the Folies Bergère, including de Pougy, Gaby Deslys, la Tortojada, Cleo de Merode and even with "la belle Otero," the reigning queen of "chanson animée." This was the era later named "la belle époque," a time of beautiful women, seductive sirens, women as unattainable, dreamlike creatures, their beauty likened to that of butterflies or exotic flowers. Performers were especially renowned as much for their physical beauty as for their singing, acting or dancing talents. The playbills of that time list the names of the many "incomparable," "beautiful," "divine" mesdames or mesdemoiselles. It seemed that few of them, however, could hope to equal the rising popularity of Lina Cavalieri. This was nowhere more noticeable than in Russia.

The famous critic Yuri Belayev, wrote of her, "Her appearance always created a furore, for she was 'heroine of the day.'"[9] Anastasia Tsvetayeva, sister of the famous Russian Silver Age poetess Marina Tsvetaeva, in a chapter of her memoirs which details a family trip to Italy in winter 1902–1903, recalled: "I remember the greatest restaurant hall, a lot of light, glass ... brilliance, table d'hôte, a lot of people, strange, among them our company was lost. Wines, fruits. Music, sounds of waves. The prettiness of Italian speech ... Music! Fiddlesticks, strings, the enchanting sight of the orchestra. Suddenly something happens at the end of the hall, a flare up of general emotion, running with restrained hissing—but possible to restrain?—and the eyes of all turn to the doors. May be *everyone stands up*? [*sic*] A precious name sounds, restless on the lips of both Italian and foreigner. The name belonging to the Beauty beyond comparison, because she is the First in the world! La signora Lina Cavalieri!... She entered the hall, surrounded by her suite, and I remember a chiselled profile of a majestic and beautiful woman, famous actress ... Pearled. Dark-haired. Dark-eyed."[10]

Gabrielle D'Annunzio's claim that Cavalieri was the most perfect personification of Venus on the earth was only one of the many descriptions, littered with superlatives, which have survived from those who saw her at this time. One said, "Yes, she was original, beautiful! A slim figure, the face of a Madonna, charming smile," and others added, "The eyes of a gazelle and lithe stature." The Russian actor Rostovtsev wrote: "She had a not very strong but very pleasant voice as a singer. And she really merited to be admired! Her elegant figure and pretty face resembled an expensive porcelain statue."[11] Even the women could not be indifferent to her appearance: "Oh, my Lord! How could such beauty be born! A parting in the middle of her beautifully coiffured hair. And her hair shows off a face of childlike innocence.

58. - PARIS. - Les Folies-Bergère

The Folies Bergère in Paris at the time of Cavalieri's appearance there.

Her eyes are saintlike. And a deep *décolleté* shows her fragile shoulders, her impeccable bust and her neck of perfect form.... It is impossible to keep cool, she is so beautiful!"[12] "A loving, poetic creature gifted with rare beauty and rare sensibility." In the memorable words of the Russian opera singer Leonid Sobinov, "a marvelous flower, loving, fragrant with spring orchids."[13]

Cavalieri became "the most beautiful woman in the world," and the world was apparently enchanted by her grace and original beauty, her angelic face and gorgeous figure, appearing frequently in public in enviably luxurious gowns and jewels, increasingly familiar through the circulation of a million picture postcards and photographs published in newspapers and magazines. Gradually Cavalieri was becoming not only an ideal model of the fashionable 1890s for the advertisements of the wares of the most eminent couturiers, but also an original symbol for her time, a widely recognized ideal of female beauty. And, unlike many of her competitors, her fame was based on classic beauty rather than novelty. Accompanying the publication of one of the famous Reutlinger photographs of the singer which had gained great popularity at this time, *The Sketch* noted that "She dances ravishingly, and if she has not the universal renown of her colleague of the Rue Richet, Loie Fuller, it is that she has not sought to be novel, but only to perfect herself along the old lines of art."[14]

The belles of the Belle Epoch; Mérode, Otero and other variety artists.

Cavalieri arrived in Russia for the first time on June 16 [old calendar] 1897,[15] and her fame rapidly spread. Her name first appeared in the Russian press on June 8, when the following announcement was published: "The Krestovsky Theatre on Krestovsky Island: In June there are new debuts. The renowned beauty, Mlle. Gignory; the noted first star of Paris, Mlle. Paula Brebion; the famous Italian beauty La Cavalieri."[16] The *Petersburg Newspaper* recorded that the Krestovsky's new star was not particularly noted as a singer "but is a remarkable beauty. At least in Paris she was recognised as a beauty. The people are talking about her in the fashionable restaurants and on the islands."[17]

Cavalieri's first performance on the summer stage in the pleasure garden of Krestovsky Island was originally scheduled for June 20, but finally took place on the following day. The contract, which she had signed in Paris on October 20, 1896, was for two months: from July 1 to September 1, 1897. *The Petersburg Leaflet* reported: "For the last two years all the newspapers of Paris and London cried out about Mlle Cavalieri, that is why yesterday's appearance of this Italian 'little star' at the Krestovsky theatre much interested our Petersburg public. The electric garlands, thrown across the stage, were lit, the transparency with the name 'Cavalieri' illuminated by the many-coloured small lights. The six mandolin-players and guitarists came onto the stage and following them, at last, the debutante herself darted out. Mlle Cavalieri is very young, graceful, her appearance resembles a little La Seniorita Otero and justified entirely the epithet joined to her name in the Parisian newspapers—'la belle.' Mlle Cavalieri sang exclusively Italian songs with great animation, gaiety and fervour…. [H]er fresh and pleasant voice made a fine impression. The mandolin-players accompanied her and joined in her songs."[18]

At the same time, on the same stage, the entertainment featured "Grande étoile, the first star of Paris, Paula Brebion; the first beauty of Spain, la belle Espagnole, Mlle. Tortojada; la belle Napolitaine, Mlle. Dora Parnes." Additionally the gardens offered the diversions of a Romanian orchestra and Russian military orchestra, an Italian band and "The most extraordinary show ever seen! The real African village of 60 men, women and children, direct from Africa! You can see their houses, a school for children, the place for military action, a kitchen for cooking. You can see the fabrication of different national crafts and buy articles of gold or silver, African sculpture, textile etc."[19]

All of St. Petersburg, it seemed, talked of the extraordinary beauty who had already been acclaimed by the newspapers in Paris and London, who had acquired a substantial following at the Folies Bergère and who had just arrived from London, where she was described as "the hit of season" at the Empire Theatre. Those who saw the famous beauty noted that la belle Cavalieri rightly bore this epithet— she was young, graceful and very elegant, her spectacular dresses and stunning hats could not fail to be noticed equally by the women and the men. Society ladies noted, with a certain degree of condescension, "Elle a du chien..." (She is spirited). The patrons at the Krestovsky, who formed the league known as "cavalerists," gave their new idol a standing ovation every evening, covering her with flowers and showering her with ever more valuable gifts to express their admiration. The management rubbed their hands with delight as the public forced its way into the theater to see the new star of the Krestovsky and after the evening performance many would make their way to the garden restaurant in the hope of a supper with or at the very least near such beauty.

A reporter from *The Petersburg Newspaper* wrote an appreciation of the new "heroine of the day": "She is very elegant, graceful and dressed with a rare taste. I have travelled much across Italy, but I have never seen so refined an Italian woman

Cavalieri in tarantella costume, early 1890s.

A portrait from the Reutlinger studio, early 1900s.

as Cavalieri. She is an Italian of Paris, who is able to combine the Italian simplicity and the French stylishness. She is so beautiful that she can inspire the painter
to depict her on the canvas, the poet to glorify her charming figure and the pleasure garden's aesthete—to fall in love. If you ask me about the genre of the singer
Cavalieri, I'll give an answer in one word: 'a sweetheart!'"[20]

Only one week into her phenomenally successful run at the Krestovsky Gardens, however, an unexplained scandal broke out, and the name of La Cavalieri disappeared from the playbill. In the theater it was announced: "Through unforeseen
circumstances Miss Cavalieri will not take part in the concert." She didn't appear
on the stage for a second and then a third day. As a result, the director of the pleasure garden applied to the courts accusing his new star of breaking her contract. The
case was finally heard on August 11, and the court found in favor of the Krestovsky
management. Cavalieri was required to pay a fine and costs—the equivalent of a
month's salary, 5,000 French francs (1,812 rubles). The details of the incident were
published by *The Petersburg Newspaper*: "Yesterday one Italian at the Krestovsky theatre suddenly refused to appear on the stage because she was put on the last place
in the concert programme. Wishing to make things difficult for the director of the
theatre this quick-witted lady, affecting an illness, left the stage and sat in the theatre
box with a number of her supporters.... The scandal was great. A great many of the
public stood up and left their seats and insisted on the return of the entrance fee.
This demand was met, the sum was large."[21]

On her return to Paris, Cavalieri informed the press about the barbarous customs in Russian cafés chantants. In particular, she was indignant that after a concert,

it was her duty to have supper with unknown patrons in the restaurant of the Garden and to encourage these patrons to order expensive dishes and drinks. According to Cavalieri, she refused to do this, and, as a punishment, the management began to place her act at the end of the concert, when the public was tiring and beginning to leave the hall, preferring to go to the restaurant or to another establishment to continue their evening's entertainment. Cavalieri claimed that she refused to appear on the stage, in spite of the persuasions of the director and the manager of the Garden. Cavalieri's public condemnation of her treatment by her Russian employers received coverage in the Russian press, which seemed divided as to their reaction to the singer's complaints. Her assertion that in the cafés chantants of Petersburg performers were expected to do more than sing in order to earn their salaries was largely supported by a report which appeared in the following year: "The owner of the pleasure garden addresses a theatrical agent: 'You, brother, translate to her,

Cavalieri in an Italian folk costume for the variety stage, late 1890s.

that I could raise the price by two or three hundred roubles, if she could drink the champagne better!' One of the 'specialities' of 'stars' is the capability to pull a tablecloth at the right and proper time in order to spill the wine so that customers order more. It is necessary for an artiste to know to 'faire danser le commerce' [to force the commerce to move] and not to forget herself because—alas!—The salary of one thousand is not sufficient for the fanciful toilettes, accessories and town dresses, besides the first-class 'étoile' [star] is obliged to have jewels to a value of 10 or 15 thousand. 'What do I need you for, "bebeshki," if they drink only seltzer water?'—said one Petersburg impresario."[22]

After this less than happy experience, Cavalieri passed the autumn in Paris, where she had returned to take part in the spectacular productions on the stage of the Folies Bergère, appearing with the acknowledged star of café chantant, la belle Otero. The Russian newspapers responded to her version of her experiences in St. Petersburg by asking the question, would Cavalieri come to Russia once more? She had signed a contract with the Moscow impresario Charles Aumont for September and October, but perhaps, they speculated, she would prefer to default and to pay the fine again. The St. Petersburg scandal, however, only served to increase Cavalieri's popularity, and her salary grew from 5,000 to 8,000 francs. Impresarios came from St. Petersburg to invite her to return for a season at the city's most celebrated cabaret venue, the Aquarium. The manager was a particularly adroit showman who recognized the value of such a notorious star: He also invited la belle Otero to appear at the same time. This would be a really explosive combination. Carolina Otero was six years older than Cavalieri[23] and more experienced both on stage and in life. She had appeared in Russia for the first time in 1893 with great success on the stage of one of the more important pleasure gardens in Petersburg, the Arcadia. Her salary for the summer season of 1898 was 15,000 francs, considerably more than that offered to her new co star.

Whether Cavalieri's return was an act of revenge or not, when she suddenly appeared at a performance of a French drama in the Mikhailovsky Theatre in St. Petersburg, to all intents and purposes she had every appearance of being a victor: It seemed as though every pair of opera glasses was directed toward her box, examining her beauty, her wonderful silk dress, "gris perle" trimmed, with fine black lace, elegant hat with one ostrich feather and an abundance of diamonds and pearls at her neck. The Mikhailovsky hosted a permanent French company that was considered among the finest in Europe. The play that night was a new vaudeville titled *Le Pigeon*, and one journalist noted that during the intervals "all the opera glasses of both men and women were directed to Box N9 of the dress circle," where Cavalieri sat.

For the next two months, Cavalieri appeared in every popular and fashionable venue in St. Petersburg. On October 18 her presence was noted at the Mikhailovsky Theatre once again, and it may be that she was the guest of Prince Alexander Bariatinsky, who was shortly to play such an important role in her personal and professional life. She attended a performance of the ballet *La Belle au Bois Dormant*, with the famous ballerina Mathilda Kshessinskaya at the Mariinski Theatre, and performances in the Ciniselli Circus, at the most fashionable restaurants and pleasure palaces. Reporters of the Petersburg newspapers noted that all opera glasses, like steel needles, were directed toward the seemingly irresistible magnet in the person of "la belle Cavalieri." When she appeared in the city, shopping, a crowd of curious people would gather in front of the shop window to watch her. At a café, a waiter offered her the comfort of a private room, but she refused, claiming that the experience reminded her of the American bar in Monte Carlo.

Apparently unaffected by the professional misfortunes of her season at the Krestovsky Garden the previous summer, Cavalieri now set out to conquer Moscow. She was engaged to appear in the variety theater owned by the French entrepreneur Charles Aumont. In truth, Aumont was little more than a former French tavern keeper who had opened a fashionable restaurant in Moscow that also presented its customers with a live revue each evening. This venue had attained a certain popularity with a particular group of wealthy Moscow patrons who enjoyed the high life, and Aumont had therefore been able to employ some of the leading café chantant stars. In time Aumont's establishment had become one of the leading variety venues in the city: An offer from Aumont to appear in Moscow could be a very important step for any performer.

Cavalieri's debut was fixed for November 29, 1897, but her luggage, which included all of her costumes and music, was delayed by customs, and the long-awaited first appearance did not finally take place until December 13. *The Moscow Leaflet* reported: "She was given an enthusiastic welcome and a storm of applause. The singer performed some Italian songs and one Russian romance, "Black Eyes," badly articulating the Russian words of the song.... The public filled the stalls, stood up from their seats and, applauding, went to the footlights and called for the artists. Mlle. Cavalieri had a sensational and well-deserved success; two baskets of flowers were presented to her."[24] Another reviewer confirmed the success, adding that Cavalieri was a "graceful and refined Italian with a nice, pretty voice."[25]

During the winter season Aumont's productions were housed on the site now occupied by one of Moscow's leading theaters, while in the summer, performances took place in a hall of the Aquarium on Sadovaya-Triumphalnaya Street. An evening's entertainment usually began with an operetta, which was followed by a variety bill, often featuring imported foreign stars. One such guest star was Lina Cavalieri, performing the popular Neapolitan songs of the day, accompanied by an "Italian" ensemble comprising two fiddles, four mandolins and guitars, and dancing the tarantella beating time with a tambourine. It seemed that all Moscow flocked to Aumont's to see Cavalieri in the flesh, probably wishing to see her far more than actually hear her sing. Almost every photographic studio in Moscow displayed her portrait in their windows, and postcards featuring her in various poses were sold in stationery and tobacco stores all over the city.

There seems little doubt that Cavalieri possessed at least some of the attributes of a first-class singer of satirical songs, what we might describe as a "diseuse." She differed from some of the popular French performers of this time, relying not simply upon the wit and incisiveness of their material, but rather on her own particular brand of gracefulness and a certain evident air of naivety, her dancing not overtly physical but rather possessing a "childlike simplicity and elegance." She also

Portrait photographs by the Reutlinger studio, Paris, late 1890s–early 1900s.

Portrait photograph by the Reutlinger studio, Paris, late 1890s–early 1900s.

seems to have been able to invest her material with a certain nobility and poetry that may have been absent from the stage personas of some of her competitors. Aumont ran three venues in Moscow: his own Aumont's Theatre, the Chicago and the International. At Aumont's Theatre, Cavalieri shared the bill with Maria Labunskaya, a famous dancer who had also achieved stardom in Paris. It was rumored that as a member of the corps de ballet at the Mariinski Theatre, Labunskaya had formed a liaison with the future Tsar Nicholas II, and as a result, she was deported from Russia and lived in France, where she began her solo career. Labunskaya was famous as one of the most beautiful women on the Paris stage. She was booked in Russia as a very expensive French star with the title of "la belle et célèbre" (beautiful and famous). Aumont presented some variety concerts at the International Theatre with Labunskaya and Cavalieri, and the theater was always filled beyond capacity.

Cavalieri also shared the stage in Moscow with many less distinguished artists: In Aumont's concerts at Shelaputin's Theatre these included Chernov with his performing dogs and a chorus of French gypsies. *The Moscow Leaflet* made the following highly pertinent comments about one such concert: "The artists of Mr. Chernov knew their job perfectly and in contrast to their two-legged rivals. They always know their roles excellently, don't quarrel with the impresario, don't bring an action against him and never break a contract. They have one more perfect quality, very rare in artists, they never drink other than pure water and neither can an admirer stand them a cognac, though attempts were made."[26] Cavalieri continued to appear

Photographs taken in Paris, early 1900s.

in Moscow until the end of January 1898, when she returned to Paris for a further engagement at the Folies Bergère. Many distinguished Russian visitors were in the French capital that spring: Labunskaya; Suvorin, owner of the Maly Theatre in St. Petersburg; the critic Skalkovsky; the opera singers Medea and Nikolai Figner; notable among Cavalieri's admirers, Jacob Rubinstein, son of the Russian composer; and, significantly, Prince Alexander Bariatinsky. Cavalieri's presence was noted at many of the most fashionable Parisian venues and at the races at Longchamps, always surrounded by a crowd of enthusiastic admirers.

Late in July, Cavalieri returned to St. Petersburg to undertake a short season at the Aquarium for the impresario George Alexandrov. Knowing how difficult it could be to fill theater seats during the summer months in

St. Petersburg, Alexandrov cleverly contracted both la belle Otero and la belle Cavalieri for this period, thereby maximizing the chance of healthy business. Cavalieri's box office appeal, guaranteed by the previous year's scandal at the Krestovsky, was considerably enhanced by the intriguing competition that existed between the two stars. The Aquarium on Kamennostrovsky Avenue was patronized by gentlemen and officers rather than the rich merchants who more frequently made up the Moscow audiences: The two leading ladies competed with each other for the attention of their audience—Lina Cavalieri, the personification of angelic beauty and naivety singing "scabrous songs" and almost apologizing for their indelicate content; Otero, the epitome of a Spanish woman, lively, brisk, and seductive.

Caroline Otero had established her reputation not only as a singer of café chantant, but no less famously as a very expensive courtesan, described thus by Coco Chanel: "The real collection of spangles, gems and plates, flowers and plumes, contented armours of this priest of delight. You see the performer quite alone. But it isn't true. She is never alone; she is always like a shadow escorted by grand gentlemen; bald shadows with monocles and in swallowtails. The shadow in a swallowtail knows what her hats and castanets will cost. To support her is the same as to control property. To undress her is just the same as to move to a new place. Otero! Look how she protrudes her bust. Look how she slightly measures her 'colleagues' ... from under drooping eyelashes. Look at how her black eyes throw sparks of fire. Look at her challenging toreadors."[27]

The Petersburg Newspaper covered the first appearance of the two stars:

Cavalieri's great rival on the variety stage, Caroline Otero.

Yesterday the Aquarium was extraordinarily animated. "All of Petersburg" had gathered for the debut of Mlle Cavalieri. In addition to the already existing star in the local sky—"la belle" Otero—another "la belle"—Cavalieri—had settled. Both are reputed beauties, both sing and they both dance. The Petersburg public who witnessed this extraordinary concert and at the same time the competition of two beauties had divided into two parties: "oterists" and "cavalierists." Otero was the first to appear on the stage and she was met with loud and prolonged applause. Foreseeing the competition, Mme Otero decided to put on a good show and to uphold her reputation as "unconquerable."... There was much life and fire, much grace and unfeigned gaiety— those are all concentrated in this really fascinating artiste, who performed some Spanish songs and in conclusion—the notorious "March Otero." It was not a success but a triumph for the artiste. After some of Otero's encores, la belle Cavalieri appeared accompanied by 9 Neapolitans. This young, really very beautiful Italian was literally strewn with brilliants: her smart and rich appearance was in the best way in keeping with her marvellously pretty face. Mlle Cavalieri sings nicely and dances gracefully. If she has more cheerfulness and more ease, then Mlle Cavalieri doesn't leave much to be desired. They forced her to sing encores endlessly and she agreed very amiably. Four colossal flower baskets were the deserved reward for this likeable artiste. It is unnecessary to add that the theatre was over-crowded.[28]

Alexandrov's plan proved highly successful. *The Petersburg Leaflet* confirmed it: "The participation in divertissement of two 'notorious beauties' Mlles Otero and Cavalieri has had so great an influence on the Petersburg public that already, the third day, it is impossible to obtain a vacant seat in the theatre. The Spaniard, Otero, became unrecognisable: her slipshod attitude towards the performing of her songs and dances has disappeared, and now she presents herself in all her glory. The rival of Otero is the Italian Cavalieri, who is not a serious competitor ... but never the less, she represents that attractive magnet by which usually the metropolitan impresarios 'catch' our public. Mlle Cavalieri is young, beautiful and has a pretty voice of which she makes the best use—these are all the cafe-chantant star needs for success."[29]

Both stars resorted to tricks in order to score points over each other. When either was unable to appear, ostensibly through poor health, the other would monopolize the evening's entertainment in such a way as to secure the maximum amount of local press coverage. On one evening, Otero was scheduled to appear on the bill after Cavalieri, to which she took exception. The interchange between the star and the stage manager was recorded in *The Petersburg Newspaper*: "'But the Italian is ill'— the stage manager persuaded the Spaniard—'it is bad for her health to go on stage after 11 o'clock in the evening'—'I know her, *it is bad*' answered the Spaniard—'it is bad not for her, but for her diamonds, which must lose in brilliance after mine!'"[30] Otero left the theater refusing to perform.

On August 13 a special benefit performance was staged at the Aquarium. The gardens were decorated with 10,000 electric light bulbs, and, on stage, each of the performers changed their repertoire: The Spanish Otero sang in Italian, the Italian Cavalieri sang in Spanish, the Russian Miliketti sang in French and the French Debriege, in Russian. Cavalieri scored the greatest success of the evening, performing gypsy songs and dances; one critic recorded that "The heroine of the evening was la belle Cavalieri who performed with great ardour.... Her success grows more and more every day."[31] A special benefit performance for Cavalieri was announced for August 25. The advance publicity for this event stated that she would perform both solos and duets of Neapolitan, French and gypsy songs accompanied by a gypsy chorus. Three days before the concert, patrons of the Aquarium received a booklet that announced that the event would commemorate the fifth anniversary of Cavalieri's stage career. After stating that all tickets for the performance were sold, *The Petersburg Leaflet* announced that Cavalieri's gown, made especially for the occasion, had cost more than 40,000 rubles and was studded with diamonds and pearls: "Before her entree on the stage, more than 10 colossal flower baskets were brought there. The Gypsy chorus conducted by Nikolaj Shishkov was placed around the stage. The theatre shook with applause when the benefit artiste appeared on the stage. Her gown of light-lilac-coloured gauze was literally covered with gems…. Having sat in the middle of the Gypsy chorus Mlle Cavalieri sang perfectly well some Gypsy romances. The rapturous delight of the public exceeded all bounds. Every couplet was accompanied by loud and incessant applause. All in all, Mlle Cavalieri had such an extraordinary success that every European star would like to be in her place. In one of flower baskets there were emeralds as a present to the benefit artiste. In one connoisseurs' opinion they costs more than 150,000 roubles."[32] It is not at all surprising that after this performance the press announced that the management of the Aquarium had offered Cavalieri a further contract for the following year.

Shortly after this memorable evening, Cavalieri left for Paris, now accompanied by an entourage suitable for a star: two ladies' maids, two manservants, a cook, ten musicians and her personal hairdresser. She also left with rubies said to be worth 40,000 rubles, a further present from admirers at her benefit performance. From Paris, she traveled to Monte Carlo to renew her acquaintance with Prince Bariatinsky: They shared some considerable success at the roulette wheels, where, it was rumored, the Prince won 80,000 francs, and Cavalieri won enough to help her to purchase a villa on the Champs Elysées, one room of which she decorated in the Russian style.

Cavalieri as a tarantella dancer and singer, 1890s.

On December 12, 1898, Cavalieri returned once again to St. Petersburg, causing much interest by her appearances at a ballet performance at the Mariinski Theatre and at a masquerade ball at the Pavlova Hall. She also sang at two important charity concerts: the first, on December 30, at the Pavlova Hall, the second, on January 2, 1899, organized by the Princess Shakhovskaya. Amongst the many representatives of Petersburg high society in attendance, by now predictably enough, was Prince Bariatinsky.

Many impresarios attempted to lure Cavalieri back onto the variety stage in

Cavalieri as a tarantella dancer and singer, 1890s.

St. Petersburg. Her reluctance to accept their lucrative offers appears to have stemmed from the influence of a new wealthy and influential lover who had entered her life and who would shortly help to irrevocably change the pattern of her career. In a rather desperate attempt to exploit Cavalieri's ascendant celebrity, Alexandrov announced the appearance of a "new Cavalieri" at the Aquarium. This turned out to be a certain Mlle. Persico, about whom very little appears to be known. *The Petersburg Leaflet* reviewed her first performance: "Mlle Persico appeared with the notorious musical company Gramegna, in this way imitating Mlle Cavalieri and her company. The debutante had a large voice, beautiful looks and performs national songs with particular brio."[33] Such attempts at exploiting Cavalieri's stage persona, however, were to become redundant with the news that broke in the St. Petersburg press a matter of days after her imitator's debut appearance. On January 31, *The Petersburg Newspaper* had run the following deliberately ambiguous story: "The beautiful Italian [Cavalieri] having performed last summer on the stage of one of our pleasure gardens, united with the bonds of Hymen with her true and generous protector. They say that her protector ... has consented to give her his name on the condition that the Italian would not perform any more on variety stages."[34] Eight days later, *The Petersburg Leaflet* followed with further news: "Previous misalliances have been repeated more and more often. Earlier rumours in society about marriages between two brilliant representatives of old noble families and Gypsy girls haven't stopped, yet they have started talking again about a new marriage of one of

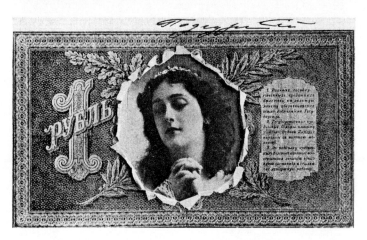

Novelty postcards showing Cavalieri's head transposed onto Russian banknotes.

the most popular of the 'golden youth,' bearer of an old historic family name with the 'little star' of the canvas sky. They say that the other day the stag party was celebrated and the friends of the fiancé brought their congratulations to the betrothed.... It is supposed that their wedding will be celebrated abroad."[35]

To complicate matters further, on March 4, another press report claimed that rumors of a recent marriage were entirely unfounded: "One of those heroines … didn't marry the young aristocrat as the false rumours had been set about. She has continued to live on the Neva's banks only because one of our 'great' professors of singing uncovered in her such a voice, which must supposedly eclipse the fame if not of Mme Sembrich, at least of Mme Arnoldson!!! The beauty is now in the hands not of one but of three professors, not counting Mr. Battistini, who is also interested in the success of the future diva. One has told me that la belle des plus belles will make her debut next season in the role of Mimi in the opera *La Bohème* by maestro Puccini."[36]

With the mystery of the supposed marriage to Bariatinsky still unresolved, Cavalieri continued to appear at major society functions, many of which were also attended, coincidentally, by her supposed husband. Also, at this time, she purchased a house in her own name in St. Petersburg, although it is not clear how she raised the money to finance this. And, meanwhile, the popular press continued to refer, often obliquely, to a marriage between a star of the café chantant and a wealthy nobleman. A return engagement at the Aquarium was hinted at in mid–June, but this did not materialize. In late June and early July, Cavalieri was in Paris once again; she performed at the Ambassadeur and served as a member of the jury for a beauty competition. By the middle of July, however, she had returned to St. Petersburg, and stories of her marriage returned with her. In September, *The Petersburg Leaflet* published the following surprising revelation: "All the rumours about a supposedly forthcoming brilliant marriage of Cavalieri were myths. The Italian beauty—alas!— according to recent information, has been married for a long time and is mother of two charming babies. It is another eloquent testimony to the unreliable biographical information of our café-chantant stars!"[37]

After a further spell in Paris, Cavalieri came back to Petersburg once again in November 1899 and announced that she would no longer sing on the variety stage. She continued to lead a very luxurious lifestyle in the capital, and, although no longer on the public stage, she continued to remain clearly in the public's eye: Her activities were widely reported. In December, she attended the opening of a grand new society restaurant in Koniushennaya Street, wearing such dazzling jewelry that the press instantly dubbed her "this queen of diamonds."[38] Whether princess or commoner, on stage or off, Cavalieri retained the same overwhelming fascination both for journalists and for those who eagerly consumed their popular society columns.

Although in her memoirs, Lina Cavalieri passed over the more unpleasant aspects of her first visit to Russia, there is no doubt that Russia had made a considerable impression on her. She described the first real Russian winter that she experienced, with boundless snow and cruel frosts. The great capital of the Russian Empire impressed her with its noble beauty and genuine sense of imperial luxury. With regard to her first appearances at the theater on Krestovsky Island, she particularly noted that among foreign guest artists, Italian performers were especially popular with the Russian public. This is not surprising as Italy's reputation as a "country of singing, cradle of melody, nursery of singers" was as clearly recognized in Russia as it was all over Europe. From their earliest recorded appearances in 1737 until World War I, Italian companies and soloists alike were given the most enthusiastic of receptions in Russia, not only in the principal cities, but also equally in the provinces.

By the close of 1898, as we have seen, Cavalieri had become the center of attention, drawing full houses to her performances and accepting the invitations of a seemingly endless list of handsome officers, all of whom courted the "divine

Linochka" with eager rivalry. At one such party, it appears, Cinderella had met her prince. He was a handsome, romantic figure: blonde hair, big blue eyes edged with long eyelashes, an enchanting smile set off by a chestnut-colored mustache. In addition to this he was a distinguished military officer, adjutant to Duke Leuchtenberg, a prince in his own right and the heir of an ancient and noble family.

Shortly after their first meeting, the popular press now supposed, our Cinderella became a princess: la Princesse Lina Bariatinsky, as she styled herself in her memoirs, *La mie verità*. Exactly how this ennoblement was achieved remains something of a mystery. A public alliance between a popular, even notorious, café-chantant singer and Prince Alexander Bariatinsky would seem improbable. Yet, in her memoirs, Lina Cavalieri claims that the couple were married by an orthodox priest in a private chapel. According to her account of the events, Bariatinsky laid a noble crown upon her head, and she voluntarily relinquished her crown as "queen of variety." The newly "married" couple apparently embarked on a foreign trip. Accompanied by her "husband," Lina traveled around the whole of Europe impressing all with her beauty. She later described her experiences: "This was the epoch of my extravagant behaviour. Sasha didn't leave any of my wishes unfulfilled. General admiration surrounded me, intoxicated him and made us both happy.... He felt himself to be master of a beloved treasure and, not counting money, bedecked his idol with magnificent jewels.... And I was so proud of myself ... I felt myself more beautiful than any other woman, more than any other fascinating charmer, unapproachable siren. At balls I was the queen. It was I who was devoured by eager eyes."[39]

She contrasted the almost mythical luxury of the Romanov imperial court with her own original beauty and freshness. She no longer wore the café-chantant gowns; as befitting the consort of a prince, her dresses were now of more a severe and irreproachable style, her splendid jewels no longer serving as an irresistible attraction to her theater audiences, but only to set off the beauty of her features. Nevertheless, this dream like "marriage" did not survive; the evidence suggests that it was either dissolved or declared invalid. The unfortunate Cavalieri was portrayed as a foreign femme fatale, who had bewitched an unsuspecting Russian prince and ensnared him in order to acquire both his title and fortune. In some quarters those very same people, who had so readily applauded her on stage, now rewarded her with nicknames of intrigante and libertine, although her only social crime appears to have been her humble origins as a star of the variety stage. Nevertheless, she had been bold enough to fall in love with a prince. The marriage "was nullified by the Tsar (Nicholas II) on the grounds that the prince had married beneath his station."[40] Some sources suggest that Cavalieri received a very generous financial settlement, possibly emanating from the imperial family: "Throughout her career she was famous for her jewels, many of which were gifts of the Czar himself and other royalty."[41] Certainly, such a settlement might explain her sudden ability to purchase an expensive property in the Russian capital.

Cavalieri claimed that her love for her art far outweighed her love for any man, even so ideal a husband as Prince Alexander Bariatinsky. Furthermore, she claimed that she was inconsolable after their separation and that this contributed to his early death before the age of forty. Which elements of this rather romantic tale are true and which pure fabrication is almost impossible to establish for certain. There appears to be no legal record of such a marriage having ever taken place, and there is every reason to believe that, in fact, it was never formalized. The Bariatinsky family was powerful and influential. They owned grand houses in both Moscow and St. Petersburg and maintained estates in several different regions of Russia and a luxurious villa in Yalta on the Black Sea coast. Members of such families were unlikely to marry cabaret singers, no matter how beautiful or talented and particularly not one who had already, it was widely supposed, frequented the beds of several other men. Certainly, by this time Cavalieri had borne what appeared to be an illegitimate son, possibly by the Marquis di Rudini, an influential member of the Italian government. Rich and aristocratic men might take singers and dancers as their mistresses, almost without comment, but not as their wives.

Prince Alexander Bariatinsky

What seems to add to the unlikely nature of this marriage is the fact that the Bariatinsky family had already weathered a similar embarrassment. A year earlier, the youngest son of the family, Vladimir, had married a dramatic actress, Lydia Yavorskaya, the daughter of General von Hubbenet, governor of Kiev. In view of this undesirable situation, it would have been considered an impossibility to allow the eldest son, successor to the family title, to marry a café singer of such low origin. Alexander's father had been tutor to the sons of Tsar Alexander III, and after the death of the emperor, he remained a close friend of his widow, the Empress Maria Feodorovna. Such a close connection with the Imperial family would only have added to the Bariatinskys' reluctance to support such a questionable liaison. After Alexander and Lina ended their relationship, his parents found him a more obviously suitable bride: the Princess Yurievsky, daughter of Tsar Alexander II and his morganatic wife, Catherine Dolgorukaya.

Even though her liaison with Bariatinsky was to end in such unhappy circumstances, the possibilities that opened up as a result of Cavalieri's new status were to bring about the next development in her career as a performer. In happier times, the new "Princess Bariatinsky" hospitably opened the doors of her private residence in St. Petersburg to fellow artists, members of the Italian opera who enjoyed such success in the city. They were the idols of many Russian ladies, the baritone Mattia Battistini, the enchanting tenor Giuseppe Anselmi, the famous soprano Louisa Tetrazzini, and many others, among whom, two are worthy of particular note— Francesco Marconi and Maddalena Mariani Masi. Although Cavalieri had declared that she now had a distaste for her former career in café chantant she still possessed an evident desire to sing. Now, however, she aspired to an entirely different genre of performance—she wanted to become a singer of opera. This new ambition appeared to occupy most of her thoughts, and after she had sought the advice of several established performers, the tenor, Marconi, finally convinced her that she might realize her dream.

The same purposefulness, diligence and simple insistence that Cavalieri had already displayed in her previous endeavors would now be brought to bear on transforming Cavalieri, the queen of variety, into Cavalieri, *prima donna* of the opera.

The Opera Star I

To St. Petersburg

Lina Cavalieri's early singing experience, as we saw in the previous chapter, was far from the classical repertoire in which she was later to make a comparatively brief but notable impact, having begun her professional life as a street singer, graduating to cafés and cabarets and finally making her way to the stage of the celebrated Folies Bergère.

Her notorious liaison with Prince Bariatinsky in St. Petersburg led her to become a regular attendee of Italian opera performances in the city. Italian singers were very popular in Russia at this time, where they commanded extravagant fees, and the roster of star performers appearing regularly in the city included Anselmi, Battistini, Marconi, Tetrazzini, Tamagno, Sembrich, Caruso and Scotti. Cavalieri noted: "As an Italian and a singer I asked to be introduced to these Italian singers, who began to visit my house. I sang for them and they sang for me. Naturally I told them of my youthful dreams and that my role as a queen of the variety stage did not satisfy all my aspirations. Marconi and Tetrazzini explained to my husband that the treasure of my voice should not have been wasted."[1] Faced with such distinguished advocacy, Bariatinsky had apparently agreed to finance lessons with Maddalena Mariani Masi, who was living in St. Petersburg at this time and running a singing school in the city. Although retired, Masi had enjoyed a fairly distinguished stage career. Amilcare Ponchielli had written the role of *La Gioconda* for her, and she had sung it at the premiere at La Scala in 1876, in a cast that also included Julian Gayarre.

Because Cavalieri now possessed considerable experience as a performer of light musical material, it might reasonably be assumed that both she and her new teacher would wish to develop her talents within the more approachable repertoire of the Opéra Comique and operetta. But Cavalieri evidently had other ideas, expressing a high opinion of her talents and potential: "I had such an agile voice that she [Mariani Masi] could train it as she pleased: soft soprano, lyric soprano, dramatic soprano. As all great singers of the past, I did not hesitate to sing all types of operas, I was ready for all challenges.... [A]ll the repertoire of the light soprano was easy to me, but it was not what I wanted to sing. How could I use my dramatic temperament, give vent to my acting impulses in such operas?"[2]

After some lessons with Mariani Masi, Cavalieri traveled to Lisbon, accompanied by her teacher, and made an ill-judged and evidently premature operatic debut at the Teatro San Carlos on January 29, 1900, singing the role of Nedda in *Pagliacci*, with a distinguished cast that included Fernando De Lucia, Alfonso Garulli, and Mario Sammarco. But such an ambitious debut was destined to be a disaster, and, as Robert Tuggle suggests, the response was far from encouraging: "The first night the public endured the performance, the second night its protests chased the whole company from the stage."[3]

The operatic bass, Andreas De Segurola, had been engaged for the season in Lisbon and recorded in his memoirs that José Pacini, director of the San Carlos, announced that he had contracted Enrico Caruso to sing *Rigoletto*, *Fedora* and *Pagliacci* in the forthcoming months and that Lina Cavalieri would make her debut opposite Caruso in Leoncavallo's popular opera.[4] De Segurola described Cavalieri as "a superbly beautiful Italian demimondaine ... sponsored by the president of the most important navigation company in Italy."[5] He later identified Cavalieri's sponsor as an Italian millionaire, Ignazio Florio, president of the Florio e Rubattino Compagnia de Navigazione.[6] He recalled, vividly, his first meeting with the singer: "From Milan, Manager Dormeville wrote me asking me to assist and help as much as possible, Lina Cavalieri.... She took living quarters at the same Hotel Breganca and, of course, spurred by great curiosity I immediately called on her to put myself at her disposal as my friend wished, and as I was anxious to do. And Holy Mother! Holy Smoke! And all the Holy's in the world—what a beautiful woman she was! I had never before seen, and I have never since, seen so perfect a head planted on so beautiful a pair of shoulders. And no ivory or alabaster in the four corners of the earth could emulate the lusciousness of her skin. And as to her figure, we had better not comment on that if we want a good night's sleep!"[7]

However, as De Segurola also recorded, Cavalieri's great physical beauty could not compensate for her evident lack of vocal skill. "So, to the murmurings and expressions of admiration which greeted her entrance on the stage, followed harsh demonstrations of disapproval after her singing of the difficult Nedda's bird song. I personally, who heard her from the audience, don't think she was as vocally deficient as all that, and certainly her alluring looks and fascinating appearance could justify all the jealousies and all the stabbings between all the Canios and Tonios on the stage or off."[8]

Cavalieri's own recollection of the events corroborates this, although in somewhat qualified terms. After describing the first night as a triumph, Cavalieri suggested that the reason for the subsequent failure was mostly nerves. She claimed that members of the Portuguese royal family were present, as were several spectators, sitting in stage boxes, who had apparently done everything in their power to distract her by copying her gestures and mimicking her facial expressions. She further suggested that these disruptive elements were deliberately planted by her manager, Petrini, who had threatened to ruin her performance if she did not accede to his advances. Cavalieri left the stage, feeling unable to continue, and her role was taken by a substitute singer that the theater management had, with considerable foresight, already told to stand by.

The St. Petersburg public, who had taken Cavalieri so readily to their hearts, was apparently unaware of her new venture on the opera stage. It was certainly unheard of at this time that a singer of the variety stage would become an operatic prima donna. *The Petersburg Leaflet* reported:

> Lina Cavalieri, not long ago having brilliantly failed in Lisbon where she had taken it into her head to sing in opera, cannot get rid of her strange pretension. "I want sing in opera!" ... She even made up her own repertory: Puccini's *La Bohème* (Mimi), *Cavalleria Rusticana* (Santuzza) and *Pagliacci* (we are imagining this will be Nedda!). One of these days she will perform in Warsaw, in the Great Theatre, on the same stage where, not long ago, the ear of the Warsaw public was being charmed by our general favorite Mattia Battistini's singing. The very mediocre chansonette singer (who doesn't remember this apology for her songs and dances?) Cavalieri is not fitted even for the operetta, but it is a real impudence on her part to undertake the roles of Mimi, Santuzza, Nedda! Whereas all the Warsaw houses are gay with her name printed in the biggest letters on monstrous size playbills! That is what the beauty and the diamonds mean![9]

Whatever the actual circumstances of Cavalieri's failure in Lisbon, it seems certain that she was not properly prepared vocally for such exposure. There is considerable uncertainty as to the true nature and extent of her serious vocal training. She claimed that she had studied the role of Nedda with Mariani Masi for nine months prior to her ill-fated debut in Lisbon, later adding that she had studied with the baritone Guiseppe Kaschmann, in Russia. On her return from Europe in the autumn of 1909, she stated, "My voice has developed considerably in volume. M. Jean de Reszke, with whom I did some work recently, told me that he would never have believed it could have grown as it has."[10] Later, however, she contradicted this claim in an interview with Elise Lathrop: "I only saw Jean de Reszke in passing through Paris. I did not work with him.... I have been working with Victor Maurel. He is a wonderful teacher. I study all my roles with him."[11]

Whether met by success or failure, this newfound career on the operatic stage was incompatible with her recently acquired status as the consort of a Russian prince. Cavalieri claimed that she and Bariatinsky were divorced as a direct result of her new stage career. "My second debut in theatre coincided therefore with my first divorce.... It is true that everything has a price, because I had to pay for every conquest by giving up part of myself."[12]

Contrary to the appearance of fragile beauty so strongly suggested in many of her early portrait photographs, Cavalieri was bred of resilient stock, and after the disappointment of her failure in Lisbon, she returned to Italy and resumed her studies with Mariani Masi. On March 4 she made an equally ambitious but this time far more successful second operatic debut as Mimi in Puccini's *La Bohème*, at one of Italy's foremost houses, the Teatro San Carlo in Naples. *The Petersburg Newspaper* reported on the event, claiming that the soprano had been "showered with flowers" by a most appreciative audience. [13] The report also stated, incorrectly, that Cavalieri would travel directly from Naples to undertake further operatic performances in London.

Il Mattino included a long and detailed review of the San Carlo performance, in which the critic noted that although the majority of the audience was deeply prejudiced against the singer for her sheer temerity in presuming to appear in such an august house, "soon their fears were cleared away and they were convinced that this was actually a serious and courageous artistic experiment. Even the most perverse and malevolent person who had been in no mood to hear her burst into cheers."[14] Congratulating the singer for succeeding in carrying off such a dangerous gamble so effectively, the critic noted that the audience's praise seemed to be both unanimous and entirely spontaneous. That Cavalieri's voice should have developed so much in so short a time was considered a remarkable feat and attributed as much to the singer's own efforts as to the effective teaching of Mariani Masi and was indicative of the promise of a highly successful career to come. The review continued,

> She put her heart and soul into her interpretation. Her playing is facile and unstrained. She acts with an expressive intuition of Mimi's character, reproducing her various moods from careless vivacity to touching melancholy. She behaves on the stage like a skillful artiste. She had to encore the story aria, performed with refinement. At the end of the first act she had three calls to the footlights. In the second act her nervousness had already disappeared and the audience changed its sentiments towards the singer. In the third act her success was yet increased and La Cavalieri was constrained to encore the whole second half of the act. Four curtain calls at the end of act. In the last act ... she sang reputably, with a dragging feeling of sorrow. Five stormy curtain calls. The simple, sincere and elegant chronicle of applause and encores indicates the warm and enthusiastic welcome that La Cavalieri had this evening and that indicates also the seriousness of the success she has achieved.[15]

How much of her success was the result of her indisputable beauty and how much to her vocal prowess remains a difficult question to answer. Even at this early stage in her career, the critics were divided on the subject of her vocal abilities. Under the headline "Cavalieri without Puritans," the music critic of *Il Pungolo*, provided a somewhat more reserved appraisal than his colleague, setting the pattern for contrasting critical summaries of the same performances that was to become a feature of Cavalieri's entire opera career:

> Presently setting aside the female fascination of this famous woman and judging Lina Cavalieri like an ordinary mortal making her first appearance on the opera stage, I should mention that her small voice needs to be strengthened with more persistent exercises and demands more mature studying.... Lina Cavalieri has sincere aptitude for the stage; she possesses a spontaneous ease, she acts intelligently: her elegance is reflected in her dramatic acting. The small voice ... has a certain prettiness. She phrases with taste and coloration, normally and opportunely. Her intonation is well schooled but her phrasing sometimes has a slowness ... and it becomes monotonous when it is not appropriate to the music. The high sound, by contrast, is displeasing. She forces them.... All told, if the perseverance that Cavalieri has demonstrated does not abandon her and her studiousness teaches her aspects of the music that she now ignores, she could continue her opera career for which she has a natural predisposition.[16] This observer, however, could not resist the temptation of questioning, at the very end of the review, the singer's serious intent in this new profession: "It might be ... a caprice, just for the fun of it, a freak and nothing else."[17]

Writing almost twenty years later, when Cavalieri had made yet another new career, on the silent screen, Jerome Shorey suggested that, even at this early stage in her legitimate career, Cavalieri's physical appearance made an immense contribution to her success: "She was a success only partly perhaps through her singing, for with her beauty one could allow other prima donna a considerable handicap and win handily."[18] Conversely, however, Cavalieri claimed that, though her beauty and growing reputation were both of considerable help in certain circumstances, they could equally be a tremendous handicap. She was to make the point on a number of subsequent occasions that her physical appearance often prevented her audiences, fellow artistes, theater managers and composers from accurately assessing her true abilities as a serious performer. She quoted a specific instance involving one of the most influential figures in the Italian musical establishment: "Giulio Ricordi, father of Tito, was one of them. Despite his son's requests, he absolutely refused to come and listen to one of my performances, as he was sure that he would have been bewitched by my beauty and would not have given an objective opinion of my voice.... As there was no way of convincing him, I had to give up any support from him. Even Puccini, who had been initially distrustful, but had become one of my admirers, could not convince his old publisher."[19] This story is corroborated by the fact that when Cavalieri was contracted to sing in *La Bohème* in Palermo, Ricordi would only grant permission if she agreed to sing the opera first at Ravenna, to establish her ability to perform the role to his satisfaction.[20]

It is indicative of the over riding fascination with the singer's appearance, shared by critics and audiences alike, that in the same edition of *Il Mattino* that included the review of her performance, an almost equally lengthy article by Matilde Serao appeared detailing the costumes that the singer wore:

> The costumes are supremely elegant and scrupulously faithful to the epoch (1830). First act: a dress of a gray half-woolen fabric, a skirt decorated with three white pipings, the corsage with opened neck and with a bow of black ribbon on it; an apron of black silk, a long neckerchief of an azure woolen fabric. Second act: the same dress as the 1st act with a hood of rose gauze decorated with strips of rose coloured bands. Third act: a woolen dress of aubergine colour, a tight corsage with colorette and cuffs of white lace and with a bow of black ribbon, a long neckerchief of a black woolen fabric. Fourth act: an extremely beautiful dress of a *pompadour* fabric, yellow with little roses, a skirt decorated with pipings of black velvet, the collar with triplicate volant bordered with black velvet band, a long ribbon of black satin around the waist-line knotted at the back and flowing like wings on her skirt. Like the costumes, the hair dresses and shoes are of the epoch.[21]

Within months of Cavalieri's successful Italian debut, her international opera career began to develop. In October 1900, the *Warsaw Journal* announced the forthcoming debut of Cavalieri in the city: "The Warsaw theatre administration is carrying out talks about an engagement at the opera with the singer Lina Cavalieri, who is allegedly possessed of exceptional beauty and of rare talent."[22] Several leading Russian newspapers also carried the story. The *Petersburg Newspaper* added, "Can it really be true that in the Warsaw opera theatre one can sing the chansonette?"[23]

Cavalieri's contract in Warsaw lasted just over a month. She made her debut in Puccini's *La Bohème* on December 21, in a cast that included Hofman, Khodakovski, Sillikh and Skulskaia. Four days later she appeared in *Pagliacci*, with Mario Sammarco, and on December 29 added *La Traviata* with Sammarco and Hofman to her repertoire. In a total of eleven appearances, *Pagliacci* was given three times, *La Traviata*, five times, there was a single performance of *Faust*, again with Sammarco, and an appearance at a charity gala concert held at the Redoubt Hall. On the night of her debut, the Great (Bolshoi) Theatre was sold out, with almost 100 people standing. The *Warsaw Journal* carried a long and detailed assessment of the event: The critic, writing under the suitably theatrical pen name Poor Yorick, was evidently far more impressed by the efforts of the new Mimi than of her Rudofo: "On Thursday, in Puccini's *La Bohème*, Mlle Cavalieri and Mr. Hofman debuted. It recalled the conservatory performances ... where everybody was following with strained attention the first steps of young debutants and debutantes, trying to recognise in them the future, complete artists. Such an impression was made by the performance of *La Bohème*. The same shy steps on the stage, the same strained attention of the audience. We should state right away that as much as Mlle Cavalieri is a gifted, promising and interesting debutante, so Mr. Hofman is not."[24] The critic went on to discuss Cavalieri's performance in considerable detail, providing us with one of the most complete assessments of her stage performance from this early period of her operatic career. The inconsistencies in her vocal production noted in this review, which would become a persistent cause for concern, suggest strongly that, in terms of pure technique, Cavalieri may still not have been ready for such a demanding role, although the reviewer expressed only praise for what he recognized as the quality of Cavalieri's vocal training.

> Mlle Cavalieri cannot be considered a polished actress... she is only learning, but this is a good school, a thorough school, which, together with her voice and stage presence, could give a pledge of future success. Mlle Cavalieri does not have a strong lyric soprano voice, but has quite a good range, not yet quite even. Her head register is the best: it is more sonorous and pure; the middle is weaker, especially the transition from the middle to the chest register: this part of her range still has a dark tinge, while the chest register is more sonorous again. Her voice is perfectly well trained; her attacks, especially of the head notes, are sure. There are no fluctuations in the adjacent semi-tones and her intonation is pure, which proves the musical ability of the artiste. The breath, observation of phrasing, diction and style of singing—all of these qualities are the results of the teaching of Mme. Mariani, and whatever may be said, there is no other singing school than the Italian one."[25]

The physical aspects of Cavalieri's performance were also examined in detail, suggesting the same consideration of acting technique that was later to contribute so importantly to her success in front of the film cameras: "Undoubtedly the part of Mimi had been carefully studied by Mlle Cavalieri.... The young debutante was hindered by an unfamiliar set and alien styles of performance and gesticulation. She refrained from superfluous gesture, being helped by her little pinafore dress with pockets. But this is better than overdoing it. The nervousness of her first entrance in front of a strange audience obviously had an effect on her acting. In the death scene there was no complete realism, no tragedy, but there was simplicity of a touching nature. In general, Mlle Cavalieri has made a most advantageous impression upon everyone and made a highly attractive Mimi, a very good performance for a debut."[26] This notable, if qualified, success, seems to have been achieved in spite of the severe shortcomings of Cavalieri's stage partner, of whom the same critic recorded, "it would be better for him not to sing at all."[27] In Cavalieri's second Warsaw performance, as Nedda in Pagliacci, Sammarco, who was making his debut in the house, proved to be a far happier partner and was so much applauded for his performance of the prologue that he repeated it. "Mlle Cavalieri (Nedda) was a little nervous in the first act but then, having regained self-control, she sang her aria very well and was also much applauded."[28]

In November, *The Petersburg News* had announced, "next Summer the famous Cavalieri will come to Petersburg to perform in the capacity of opera singer, with the company of the Baron Gunsbourg, who has leased the Aquarium Theatre."[29]

As had already become evident from the coverage of her Naples debut, Cavalieri's physical appearance, including the elaborate costumes and glittering jewelry that she wore for many of her appearances, was becoming an important aspect of her public persona. It would also seem that the singer was keenly aware of the importance of her image and had already discovered the value of self-publicity. Writing of her third appearance in the Polish capital, on December 29, as the tragic heroine of Verdi's *La Traviata*, the generally perceptive critic of *The Warsaw Journal* opened his review with the following observation: "The theatre was over-full, and this was definitely caused not only by the audiences' intention to enjoy the opera ... but also to estimate Mlle Cavalieri's costumes and diamonds, about which the hundred-mouthed goddess was, by this time, giving many interesting details. And really, so beautiful a Violetta has not yet appeared on theatre stages.... [H]er natural beauty and grace ... have created the ideal image of a woman with whom one could fall in love to distraction."[30] This performance, however, was not simply a triumph for physical glamor: "On the vocal side, Mlle Cavalieri has made a very advantageous showing. Being familiar with her vocal abilities already no one, of course, was waiting to hear astonishing coloratura or exceptional trills, but there was some apprehension as the role of Violetta presented some great difficulties. Having taken the decision to sing La Traviata, Mlle Cavalieri has come out of the situation with credit and given pleasure to her audience with her singing. The actress was able to use her voice wonderfully.... Mlle Cavalieri is exceptionally musical ... with only one shortcoming—that was a lack of warmth in her singing and of sincerity in her acting. But that will come when the actress, performing opera for a comparatively short time, is more at home on the stage and more familiar with the parts that form her repertory."[31]

The first day of the New Year, 1901, saw Cavalieri give her second performance of *La Traviata*, once again to a packed house. "This time Mlle Cavalieri sang more confidently and in the 4th act she played with great dramatic effect."[32] It was also noted, however, that the luxurious and elegant new costumes that Cavalieri wore for this performance, including a silver fox cloak and an ermine wrap, were not entirely in keeping with her character's reduced circumstances in the final act of the opera. Sammarco repeated his performance as Germont pere to great acclaim, being compelled to encore his second act aria. The interest generated by the scandalous stories of the soprano's lifestyle, and in particular, at this time, of her liaison with Prince Bariatinsky, fueled even greater interest in her stage performances. It was announced that she would sing Marguerite in Gounod's *Faust* on January 6; however, her illness prevented her appearance, and she was replaced by Yanina Vajda-Korolevich. Two days later she was well enough to sing Nedda again, and on January 9 gave her third performance as Violetta. In this performance, Hofman, who had failed to make any impact on Warsaw audiences, was replaced by Florianski. *The Warsaw Journal* critic considered this to be a major improvement in the production and also noted: "Mlle Cavalieri got rid of some sense of shyness.... [S]he was playing more unconstrainedly and singing more easily than during previous performances.[33] After stating categorically that he would not give any description of Cavalieri's costumes in his review, the critic felt compelled to mention that her appearance was so "uncommonly luxurious and elegant, all the ladies' opera glasses could not be torn from her for the whole evening."[34] He also praised the addition of some particularly effective stage business that Cavalieri had incorporated into her performance in the final act: "sinking from the armchair to her knees, and only then falling to the floor—very real and produces a strong impression."[35]

Such comments suggest that, in addition to gaining far greater confidence on stage, Cavalieri was also beginning to experiment with some of the more adventurous and evidently effective stage business that was to be frequently noted in

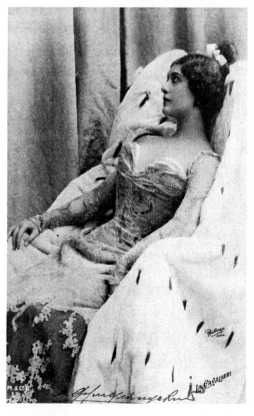

Cavalieri as Violetta in Verdi's *La Traviata* (photograph by Reutlinger Studio, Paris 1901, from the collections of the author and Svetlana Vlasova).

reviews of her later stage appearances. On January 16, she made her delayed debut as Marguerite in Gounod's *Faust*. Singing to another packed house, she was not as well received as she had been in the Puccini and Verdi roles in which she had previously been heard. *The Warsaw Journal* critic noted, "a lack of power and an unevenness in scale, especially in transitional notes, caused faulty intonation sometimes, although this unevenness was not evident to all listeners.... [I]n the famous "Air de bijoux," Mlle Cavalieri was, I think, the best."[36] The suggestion was clearly made that Cavalieri's appearance in the role was far more effective than her singing of it.

On January 18, Cavalieri sang at a gala benefit concert to raise money for inexpensive canteens to help feed the homeless. The concert, held at the Redoubt Hall, was sold out. Her final performance during this season was on January 27, when she again sang *La Traviata*. By now, her appearances were drawing extraordinarily large and enthusiastic audiences. *The Warsaw Journal* reported that Cavalieri nights were now guaranteed sellouts and that, for this last opportunity to see her, tickets had changed hands at three times their normal face value. The performance was treated as a gala event: "The actress was presented with an elegant flower basket by the directors of the Warsaw Great Theatre and she was showered with flowers from above."[37] It was also announced that the management was so delighted with its new guest singer that it had already decided to offer her a return engagement in the next season. The St. Petersburg press continued to keep its readers up to date with Cavalieri's success in Warsaw, and in March, it was confirmed that Gunsbourg had contracted the singer to appear with his Monte Carlo company during their forthcoming season at the city's Aquarium Theater.

In the succeeding months, prior to her return to Russia, there followed performances at some of the leading opera houses in Italy: On October 3, 1901, she made her Florence debut at the Teatro Verdi, as Violetta in *La Traviata*, which was followed in February and March of 1902 with appearances in *Manon* and *Fedora*. She chose Manon once again as the vehicle for her Milan debut in May 1902 at the Teatro dal Verme, while October and November were to witness further performances in Florence, in *Andrea Chenier* and again as *Fedora*.

In the spring of 1903, she was invited to return to Milan, this time at the Teatro Lirico, where she appeared in a run of eight performances of *Fedora*. At the same theater on October 17 she made her debut appearance in the title role of Massenet's *Thaïs*, with the composer in attendance. This role was to form an important and sometimes controversial part of her later career. Massenet was said to be much impressed by the new prima donna, who was already proving to be ideal casting for several of his most important heroines. In his biography of Massenet, James Harding quotes a review of this Milan performance that credits "her beauty, her admirable physique, her warm and colourful voice, her passionate acting [which] enthralled the audience who praised her to the skies."[38]

Cavalieri's Italian career continued to develop with the aid of a few carefully chosen roles, designed to show the singer at her best, physically and vocally. The next step was achieved in January of the following year, when she made her Genoa debut at the Teatro Carlo Felice, in the now familiar leading role of Giordano's *Fedora*. The following month she appeared at the Teatro Il Communale, Trieste, once again in Massenet's *Manon*. Although many of her Italian engagements at this stage of her career were confined to single performances or short runs, Cavalieri had begun to build not only a recognizable profile as an operatic performer, but also a small but respectable repertoire of some of the lighter lyric roles of the Italian and French repertoire. This, in one of the world's most critically aware arenas of the opera world, was, in itself, a considerable achievement, particularly considering the point from which Cavalieri had launched her assault on the operatic establishment. Perhaps surprisingly, however, she now expressed a marked preference for more vocally demanding roles: "I have always sung in dramatic operas because they made me feel I had complete control over my voice. Exceptionally, only because I could perform all three roles owing to the range of my voice, I sang in *The Tales of Hoffmann*. I also performed as Mimi in *Bohème*, but it was not a role that perfectly suited my character, as she was too passive. *Manon, Fedora, Tosca, Andrea Chenier, Adriana Lecouvreur, Siberia, Traviata, Carmen* and *Thaïs*, those were my operas."[39] In addition to these she also sang Marguerite in Gounod's *Faust* and Gilda in Verdi's *Rigoletto*. As her repertoire widened, so did the number of foreign houses that showed an interest in engaging her.

In May 1901, Cavalieri returned to St. Petersburg, the site of so many of her former successes on the variety stage. This time, however, the satirical numbers and Neapolitan songs of the past were to be replaced by a repertoire that consisted of *La Traviata* (in which she made her debut on May 16), *Faust* and *La Bohème*. Her arrival was covered in detail by the press. Cavalieri, with her two ladies' maids, and escorted by a crowd of her admirers, went to the Grand Hotel Europe on Mikhailovskaya Street, at the corner of the Nevsky Prospect. Tickets for the Aquarium opera

A postcard celebrating Easter (from the collection of Svetlana Vlasova).

Left: **The queen of hearts, one of a series of playing cards, early 1900s.** *Right*: **A greeting postcard from the late 1890s.**

season were selling very quickly. The florists were overloaded with orders for flower baskets and bouquets. Very few people, it seemed, seriously believed in Cavalieri's intentions of becoming an opera singer, as, to many, it was considered so completely inappropriate for a performer of such humble origins to aspire to such high art. Her affair with the wealthy and influential Prince Bariatinsky equally was now common knowledge, however, and it was thought that his money and connections probably explained the new career of this prima donna.

This skepticism also surfaced in the press. The satirical diarist Buyanov provided the following example: "She will sing in the opera. Oh, my Lord, how fortune has endowed this lady with a variety of talents! She alone has so many lines of business: at first she played the role of 'Beauty,' then the role of 'The Queen of Diamonds,' and now that of 'Opera Diva'.... I knew a Hungarian man who came into my courtyard and he was endowed with even more talents! He played the pipe with his lips, the violin with his hands, he was ringing little bells with his head, he was beating a drum with his right leg and a kettledrum with his left. In addition, he was hitting the triangle with his elbow. However, la Signora Cavalieri will develop her talents even more. They say that now she is studying ballet dancing, and in addition she is sculpting in clay. It seems that it is a bust of Raoul Gunsbourg. But it is turning out to look like Napoleon."[40]

Cavalieri as Violetta in Verdi's *La Traviata* (photograph by Dupont, New York, from the collections of the author and Svetlana Vlasova).

Much to the chagrin of her many detractors, Cavalieri's debut with Gunsbourg's company as Violetta, with Garret as Alfredo and Soulacroix as Germont père, met with distinct, if qualified, approval by the Petersburg critics. "Mlle Cavalieri accomplished, if not a labour of Hercules, then at least an arduous step, meriting sympathy and encouragement.... [W]e were not expecting such success from her; if she is not yet a finished actress in every respect, undoubtedly she has promise — she had many of the dispositions to make a good actress. We will not speak of her well known beauty and youth, which are of great importance for any stage career.... [S]he must do some more work on her voice ... but she has, already, some very successful moments in her singing. Her musicality is one of her undoubted qualities..."[41] The critic also issued a note of warning, appropriate to many similar young singers at this early stage in their careers: "She must study more and not get carried away by surface successes, which she will not be short of."[42]

On the night of Cavalieri's debut, the Aquarium was filled with a glittering audience, virtually all of whom had come to see if the café singer would fail. *The Petersburg Leaflet* noted that many in the audience were skeptical and highly prejudiced against the singer. In the event, however, its critic was also impelled to state sympathetically that "yesterday's Cavalieri is not the same we saw and heard two years ago at the same Aquarium.... Now, she has a nice voice.... As to her coloratura, it is still far from perfection.... But one cannot be strict with the young singer for the first time. Her nervousness is natural and quite clear: next time, undoubtedly, she will feel more easy."[43]

Not all observers, however, were either so enthusiastic or encouraging of Cavalieri's newly revealed talents. The critic of *The St. Petersburg Gazette* provided very clear evidence of the diametrically opposed opinions which were to constantly surface throughout Cavalieri's Russian career, loved by many, but equally ridiculed: "The serious part of the audience ... treated Mlle. Cavalieri's singing with more restraint. Of course, her performance of Violetta's role does not stand up to criticism; the absence of any coloratura, the always faulty intonation, a style of singing revealing an absence of any training or method, the striking lack of skillfulness in the mastery of breathing (in the impressive dramatic passages, Mlle. Cavalieri was really cutting short her singing and loudly inhaling the air)—all of this strikes anyone who has had occasion to hear the masterly Italian singing from Patti to Sembrich and Arnoldson.... [T]he timbre of her voice is not very agreeable.... Her acting was not notable for its refinement and she kept up the bad habit of swinging her arms about furiously."[44]

It might be fair to note that the support that Cavalieri received for her debut was not entirely of the highest quality. Although Soulacroix received much praise for his performance as the elder Germont, Garret's Alfredo "was out of tune all the time"[45]; Elsewhere, he was described as "a mediocrity, his stage appearance is not attractive, his voice has an unpleasant timbre, tired and often false in the high notes."[46] The orchestra, under Grelinger, was described as "scanty even for the operetta ... really insufferable."[47]

Perhaps the most balanced assessment of this debut came from Soloviev, who, writing in *The Exchange Gazette*, seemed to recognize both the strengths and weaknesses of the singer and be able to place in context the achievement of carrying off, with reasonable success, an operatic debut in a well-known and much-loved role in front of a largely skeptical, if not downright hostile, audience, many of whom would have delighted in Cavalieri's complete failure. "The fact is that thanks to her iron will and indestructible energy Mlle Cavalieri has developed her voice and her gift which were, not so long ago, on the smallest scale.... [A]nybody might study singing through boredom, as though one is going in for some sport. But, the fact is, Mlle Cavalieri had intended a great transformation for herself, and realised it.... [I]n most cases Mlle Cavalieri controlled her singing very well, attacking her notes surely: in her singing there is sincerity, expression, a lack of sugariness and the exaggerations that strive after cheap effect.... In spite of her great and sincere success, Mlle Cavalieri, being endowed with an artistic nature, will not consider her performance as a culminating point in her artistic career and will not say *c'est arrivé*."[48]

Whatever the critical assessment of her achievement, Cavalieri the opera star was an instant popular success, and the theater was sold to over capacity for all eighteen of her performances that season. If success could be measured by the volume of floral tributes that were showered on the soprano on her first night, then Cavalieri should have been accounted the greatest hit of the season. No less than twenty-five baskets of flowers, the gift of her many admirers, were delivered to the stage door of the Aquarium in eight taxicabs. It was said that, throughout the run of performances, she received between sixty and eighty bouquets every day.

When, on May 18, she repeated her performance as Violetta, the music critic of *The New Time*, was in attendance and commented in detail on the quality of her singing, also noting that imperfections, though evident, could be resolved: "Her intonation is perfectly right, her trill is very good. Her breath is not entirely secure and her sense of rhythm is weak. Nevertheless, Mlle Cavalieri has all the potential to achieve serious success on condition of her subsequent persevering work."[49]

In a lengthy interview, published in *The Petersburg Newspaper* on May 20, Cavalieri talked of her new career: "The first person to give me this idea was a singer well known to you, Marconi. Once he had heard me sing he advised me to busy myself seriously with my voice. I respect Marconi's opinion very much and that is why I applied to Mme Mariani Masi as a singing teacher. I am indebted to her for my formation as an opera artiste.... Even in childhood I found I had an aptitude for singing."[50] In response to questions about her humbler origins, Cavalieri was quick to point out that she was by no means the first performer to make such a transition: "There were many examples of this. Maybe you remember Blanche Lescault, who sang, I remember, at the Nemetti Theatre? That is the very Blanche Lescault who now sings, like me, in the opera and besides in Paris."[51] On the matter of her attitude toward the skepticism displayed by her audience on the first night, Cavalieri's physical reaction, described by the interviewer, was as demonstrative as her reply: "'There are apparently quite a lot of curious people who want to see if the former café concert singer can change into an opera singer.' And Mlle Cavalieri started roaring with laughter and showed a row of blinding white and even teeth."[52]

Cavalieri's second operatic challenge in St. Petersburg was Gounod's *Faust*, in which she first appeared on May 25. This opera enjoyed great popularity with the

Above and opposite: **Some of the glamorous postcards which were published in the late 1890s and early 1900s, some from the Reutlinger Studio.**

St. Petersburg audience, and they had enjoyed many distinguished singers in the leading roles. At least one critic recognized the scale of the challenge that Cavalieri had now set for herself, suggesting that Marguerite was a far more difficult and potentially dangerous proposition for an inexperienced singer and noting that, in spite of her relative success thus far, many would still enjoy witnessing her downfall: "We remarked in the stalls the presence of musicians and professors of singing, apparently anticipating with pleasure the opportunity of showing the operetta diva her place."[53] The evidence suggests, however, that they may well have been disappointed. "Mlle Cavalieri's first appearance in the second act was not the entrance of a frightened debutante but of an actress who was fully aware of her charm. Maybe this was too much the unpretentious Marguerite, but in the third and more important act of the opera, the singer adopted a more simple, more free and easy tone."[54]

Once again, however, Cavalieri found little worthwhile support from her fellow performers. Garret was criticized for the sentimentality of his performance and also for singing out of tune: Bouxman's Mephistopheles was considered to be lacking both in power and demonic quality, and, although Soulacroix's Valentine was generally well received, the orchestral playing was again singled out as well below an acceptable standard. *The New Time* recorded that the poor quality of the company had an obvious effect on the leading lady: "In ensembles, and even in duets it seems that the company is not prepared to perform, especially in the quartet in the third act, when all of the characters in the opera were trying to confuse each other and not to sing what was written or how it was written. Such a rare quartet was not heard in Petersburg for a long time. When Mlle Cavalieri sings alone, all runs smoothly, her natural good ear for music and her innate gift help her, but when other voices entered ... she became flustered and lost her place."[55] The critic went on to suggest that some of the instruments were actually missing from the orchestra, which meant that some passages of the score could not be played, resulting in occasional curious and comical silences that Gounod could never have conceived in his composition.

The critic of *The News and Bourse Newspaper* recorded that Cavalieri sang the famous Jewel Song "with easiness and distinctness,"[56] and that her performance was one of "dramatic expressiveness and … great enthusiasm."[57] Furthermore, the general inadequacy of the supporting singers and players was noted as "insipid … weak … out of tune … badly rehearsed…,"[58] confirming the impression that Cavalieri had more than merely a skeptical audience to overcome in this potentially difficult role. The general skepticism of the St. Petersburg press continued. The following satirical poem appeared in *The Petersburg Leaflet*:

There any many different events,
Important and unimportant, in the world:
In the Caucasus there was a noise
The unprecedented, heavy shower of hail,
A hurricane penetrated the houses,
Stripping off roofs and doors …
And in the Aquarium a cry was heard:
"Cavalieri! Cavalieri!"

It is not known for what
Important reason
There was mortal combat
In the glorious town of Tan-Tszin.
The Europeans from two sides
Were grappling like beasts …
And in the Aquarium a cry was heard:
"Cavalieri! Cavalieri!"

Having taken upon her
The heavy care of her people
And of her native land,
The wife of Botha
Is going to Europe.

Will this glorious Boer daughter
Succeed in her undertaking?
And in the Aquarium a thunder was heard:
"Cavalieri! Cavalieri!"

Sad news is coming
About a drought in Sevastopol;
Poor men again will be
Pinched with hunger –
If only there was bread
For children at least …
And near us there are celebrations:
"Cavalieri! Cavalieri!"

"Cavalieri is beautiful!"
"Cavalieri is incomparable!"
"Our entire soul
Could fly to meet la Cavalieri!"
"She is truly the gift of heaven!"
"She is a nymph! She is a fairy!"
"She is a miracle of miracles!"
"Cavalieri! Cavalieri!"[59]

Certainly most of St. Petersburg seemed to be obsessed by its new star. Her name on the posters outside the Aquarium guaranteed a full house at each performance, and at each performance she was greeted with ovations and calls for ever more encores. After her fourth performance as Violetta, on May 30, it was announced that she would appear as Gilda in Verdi's *Rigoletto*. Unfortunately, however, this performance never took place, although no reason was given for its abandonment. She continued to appear until the end of June, with a series of Violettas, Mimis and Marguerites, and each seemed stronger and more confident than the last.

The press, however, continued to be equally as interested in the glamor of this new star as they were in her musical progress. At the beginning of June, *The Petersburg Newspaper* ran a rather frivolous feature on the subject of kissing on stage, and it would have been an unforgivable omission if Petersburg's most glamorous and romantic diva of the moment had not been consulted on the matter. Cavalieri's comments were revealing both of her attitude toward stage performance and of her insight into the growing influence of her own public image:

> The vocation of an artiste is to charm the public. That is the reason that she must resort to all technical methods allowed by the conditions of the stage to hypnotise the audience. The kiss, if demanded by the role, is necessary.... The scenic kiss is none other than the execution of the request of the author of the piece. That is why every jealousy on the part of the artiste's husband is absolutely stupid. The artiste's vocation, I repeat, is to charm her public, she must try to please and if she has admirers they are worshippers of her talent and nothing more. If one forbids kisses in order to avoid scenes of jealousy, why not forbid graceful dressing and beautiful hair styles—all of that excites even more attention. When one kisses behind the scenes, that is blameworthy, but a kiss on stage is insignificant. Generally speaking, the artiste's husband must foresee all consequences. A woman and an artiste are two different creations![60]

The author of the article could not resist adding that already, outside of Russia, Cavalieri had been given the nickname of "the kissing prima donna."

Extensive press coverage was given to Cavalieri's first performance in Puccini's *La Bohème* on June 12. Noting that this was the best production of Gunsbourg's season so far, the critic of *The Petersburg Newspaper* stated that, "Mlle Cavalieri as Mimi is better than Violetta or Marguerite, for which one needs a complete singing technique. Puccini's heroine can be managed without it."[61] Cavalieri sang her role in Italian, while the remainder of the company sang in French, a not uncommon practice at this time, but one that served to emphasize any shortcomings in the ensemble, and, once again, the supporting singers and the orchestra were criticized for their substandard performances. Cavalieri's second appearance in the role, on June 14, was greeted with great enthusiasm by the now standard packed audience. Her reading of this role, which combined the qualities of simplicity, sincerity and a great enthusiasm for the music, thoroughly delighted the audience. The critic of the *News and Exchange* recorded Cavalieri's considerable achievement in transforming herself from the cabaret singer to a credible performer of major operatic roles: "Mlle Cavalieri's success is growing with each performance.... [She] undoubtedly possesses a great talent and an artistic flair.... To become a beautiful singer within one and a half years is a rare and wonderful phenomenon and, up to now, almost unique."[62] Although the sentiments expressed by this writer seem representative of the general feelings of critics and audiences alike, it is important to remember that journalistic assessment can be as partisan and as fickle as can the support and affections of an opera house audience.

In the case of Lina Cavalieri, however, far more expert critical assessment of this stage of her performing career also exists from the pen of a fellow singer, the distinguished Russian lyric tenor Leonid Sobinov. Sobinov wrote to E. Korneva on June 20:

> A lot of impressions ... First of all that it is a tender, fragrant moving gift.... I have never seen her before when she had been singing Neapolitan chansonettes accompanied by dancing of dubious grace and that is why those images I have seen now are not darkened by recollections of recent times which have gone, fortunately never to return.... That rather bad singer who had sung Marguerite's story, probably under stress, must die for everybody. Now a star is rising, having broken out of the darkness, who is going, victoriously into the light ... for it is impossible not to have respect for that talent ... all in her is so touchingly pure, so endlessly fresh, that one would like to believe that her soul

Above and opposite: Cavalieri as Nedda in Leoncavallo's *Pagliacci*.

is also pure and fresh in spite of everything in her past. If one comes to know the particulars of her performances one could cavil at many things, and it can be said that the advertising exaggerates. That may be; on the other hand, it is impossible to treat her talent otherwise. It is a wonderful flower, a delicate spring fragrant orchid.... You may have doubts as to my impartiality because everyone knows that Cavalieri is very beautiful ... but her beauty is only one trait of her gift.... I have seen *La Bohème* (twice) and *La Traviata*. How much intellect there is in each of her stage movements, how much musicality and temperament in her phrases! How wonderful is her facial expression! Her voice is delightful ... easily yielding to coloratura, her crystal-clear piano, her chest register wonderful in recitatives! And besides this, she possesses wonderful rhythm and general musicality! Down with the sceptics and hard-hearted men and long live and bloom this marvellous flower!! Cavalieri is my best and strongest impression."[63]

Sobinov attended all of Cavalieri's performances and was also present at her benefit on June 23, when *La Traviata* was given to an audience that also included the ballerina Mathilda Kshessinskaya, the actress Lydia Yavorskaya (Prince Bariatinsky's sister-in-law) and the highly distinguished operatic tenor Nikolai Figner. Cavalieri's first entrance was greeted with a storm of loud and prolonged applause, and, after the first act, she received a standing ovation while the stage was almost buried in flowers. The evening was a triumph and one of the greatest successes that the Aquarium had ever witnessed. *The New Time* reported, "endless loud ovations of the overcrowded theatre ... the audience charmed and dizzied by admiration and

delight."[64] They claimed that the total value of the diamonds and other valuable gifts presented to the singer exceeded 20,000 rubles.

Interviewed by *The Petersburg Leaflet* a few days after the benefit, Sobinov was, once again, lavish in his praise: "I am one of her most ardent admirers.... She has an extraordinary tender gift, breathing youth, but at necessary moments she shows an exceptional power of tragic animation.... Lina Cavalieri is an artiste with an undoubtedly great future."[65] On the day following the concert, anyone walking near the corner of the Nevsky Prospect and Malaya Morskaya Street might have been surprised by the sight of a very large open-topped motor vehicle approaching the main entrance to one of the houses. It was full of flower baskets, garlands and bouquets. The management of the Aquarium had arranged to have all of the flowers presented to Cavalieri during the performance delivered to her apartment. *The Petersburg Leaflet* reported having counted at least twenty baskets of flowers as they were unloaded from the car.

Cavalieri gave her last performance of the St. Petersburg season on June 26. All of her performances had sold out, and after her departure, the theater was almost deserted. *The Theatre and Art* reported that Gunsbourg's financial affairs were seriously undermined by the loss of his new star. The impresario had a very high reputation in Russia at this time; it seemed that every enterprise in which he engaged was a success. It would appear, however, that Gunsbourg's only real trump card for this season at the Aquarium was the engagement of Cavalieri. Virtually every newspaper report and review suggested strongly that the majority of soloists, the chorus and the orchestra were of a fairly mediocre standard and that it was hardly an exaggeration to claim that only the star quality of the new diva had saved the season. *The Petersburg Leaflet* recorded that the eighteen performances in which Cavalieri took part realized 54,000 rubles at the box office and that the soprano's fee for the season was 17,200 rubles.[66] *The Theatre and Art* was uncompromising in its assessment of the season: "Abominable, voiceless singers, a nasty little orchestra and the same chorus, frayed scenery, a poor repertoire.... The beauty of Mlle Cavalieri came to the rescue.... If one believes the delights of the public and some music critics, at present she is one of the greatest artistic figures of Petersburg."[67]

Although Cavalieri left St. Petersburg shortly after her concluding performance, her newly minted image as one of the most prominent performing artists of the moment remained in high profile: The most popular coiffure of the day, for example, was described as *a la Cavalieri*. The fashion spread so quickly that one wit looking through his opera glasses at the many ladies in the stalls and boxes was said to have remarked, "How many Mlles Cavalieri are there tonight?" It was also claimed that around one million postcard photographs of the star had been sold.

It seemed that each new actress and singer who appeared in St. Petersburg was compared to Cavalieri. But perhaps the most significant result of Cavalieri's successful transition from variety theater to opera house stage was the inspiration she provided for other, similar performers to achieve the same transition. Among these was the singer of gypsy romances and operetta star, Anastasia Vialtseva, a beautiful and popular performer who built an opera career in both St. Petersburg and Moscow and included Carmen and Delilah among her roles.[68] Predictably enough, the gossip surrounding the new star also continued. The press had reported prominently that Cavalieri's former lover, Prince Bariatinsky had left the capital for Biarritz in preparation for his forthcoming marriage to the Princess Yurievskaya, and, a few weeks later, *The Petersburg Newspaper* ran a short but provocative story claiming that an Italian industrialist had presented the singer with a pearl necklace worth a million lire as a token of his admiration.

After completing her engagement in Russia, Cavalieri enjoyed a three-month break from performing. Much had now been achieved, and success in the Russian capital, for all of its critical reservations, would strengthen the singer's credentials for a new and more difficult stage in her career: a further attempt to achieve recognition in her native Italy. In the almost two years since her Lisbon debut, she had given only five performances in Italian houses. In October 1901, she returned to the stage for the first of a sporadic series of appearances that occupied her for the next two years, mostly in Italy. Although most of these engagements were for single performances, they did serve the important purpose of allowing the singer to extend her rather restricted repertoire.

In the first two years of her operatic career, Cavalieri had sung only four roles, Nedda, Mimi, Violetta and Marguerite. Before she returned to her adoring St. Petersburg public in February 1904, she would double this repertoire, adding what would become her most significant roles: Massenet's *Manon* and *Thaïs* and Giordano's *Fedora* and *Andrea Chenier*. Although at these early performances she did not make a significant impact in any of those roles, they would later help to serve to bring her to prominence in some of the world's leading opera houses. On October 3, 1901, she made her Florentine debut at the Teatro Verdi in a single performance of the familiar role of Violetta. She returned to the same house in February and March, giving her first readings of *Manon* and *Fedora*. She sang Manon again, at the Teatro dal Verme in Milan in May and, in the autumn, returned to Florence for single performances of *Andrea Chenier*, her debut in this work, and *Fedora*. In 1903, she sang only in Milan: In April she gave eight performances of *Fedora* at the Teatro Lirico and returned to the same house in October for a single *Thaïs*.

Possessed of great self-confidence, enviable poise and a rare degree of glamor, Cavalieri acquired many admirers and supporters in these early stages of her operatic career. But the positive response to her evident charms was not entirely universal. Such early success also has a tendency to breed arrogance, and this was one of the less attractive qualities with which Cavalieri was later to accuse her younger self. She was never invited to sing at the Opéra Comique in Paris, a house that might have been expected to be keenly attracted by her talents. She attributed this to an incident early in her career, when she was invited to perform the second act of Puccini's *Tosca* for a charity gala at the theater. She had discussed her portrayal of the character with Albert Carre, the director of the Comique, and it was obvious that they did not see eye to eye in several important respects. Diplomacy would have dictated that Cavalieri should follow the advice and suggestions given to her to modify her assumption of the role to suit the taste of the theater's distinguished director, a highly influential figure in Parisian musical circles. She declined to do so, however, and also stated, with an even greater lack of diplomacy, that she had agreed to appear at the Opéra Comique only because it was a charity event.

A similar event occurred at the Teatro Pagliano (Verdi) in Florence in 1902. Cavalieri had made a very successful debut there the previous year as Violetta in a single performance of *La Traviata*, in a production that became as celebrated for the glamorous costumes and jewels worn by the singer, as for the vocal quality of her performance. The managers of the theater, Scalaberni and Secchi, acutely aware of the box office potential of the singer, eagerly offered her a further contract to perform *Manon*, *Fedora* and *Andrea Chenier* the following year. At this time the Teatro Lirico in Milan was viewed as one of the testing grounds for two of the world's most important opera houses, the Teatro alla Scala, Milan, and the Metropolitan Opera in New York. This was mostly due to the influence of Edoardo Sonzogno, head of the publishing house, Casa Sonzogno, who controlled the rights to the works of many of the most prominent and influential opera composers of the day, including Mascagni, Leoncavallo, Cilea and Giordano, including *Fedora*.

Cavalieri strongly wished for her developing Italian career to lead from the Pagliano to the Lirico and viewed the title role in *Fedora* as being potentially her best calling card. She was frustrated by Sonzogno`s apparent indifference and his reluctance to watch her perform the role. Signor Cavaciocchi, an agent of Casa Sonzogno, came to see Cavalieri's performance in Florence and subsequently arranged for Sonzogno himself to attend one of the forthcoming Paris performances, though he did not inform Cavalieri of his intentions.

At the dress rehearsal, Cavaciocchi, eager that his employer should share his enthusiasm for this newly found interpreter of his client's work, came to Cavalieri's dressing room and made a few brief observations on her performance, criticizing, in particular, her tendency to convey a feeling of nervousness in one scene by shifting her weight from one foot to another. He felt that this action was inappropriate and likely to be misinterpreted by the audience. Cavalieri, however, did not receive his observations kindly and dismissed them out of hand, seemingly unconcerned that the disapproval of the Casa Sonzogno could result in her being refused permission to sing not only *Fedora*, but also the role of Stephania in Giordano`s *Siberia* and Maddalena in his *Andrea Chenier*, both of which were key to her repertoire.

On the following evening, Cavaciocchi accompanied Sonzogno to the premiere. Before the performance began, he visited Cavalieri once again, in the hope that he might persuade her to alter certain parts of her performance. Again she refused, until, out of desperation, Cavaciocchi blurted out that if she did not modify her approach to the role she would risk the disapproval of Edoardo Sonzogno himself. Cavalieri was certainly quick enough to realize what such disapproval might mean and the effect that a negative impression might have on her future aspirations to appear in Milan. Displaying a necessary pragmatism, she rethought her portrayal and adjusted her performance to comply with the Sonzogno agent's suggestions. After the second act Edoardo Sonzogno came to her dressing room and, after praising her performance, invited her to sing the title role in Massenet's *Thaïs* at the Teatro Lirico.

Jules Massenet had first heard Cavalieri in his *Thaïs* at the Teatro Lirico in Milan in October of 1903. It was after this performance that Gabriele D'Annunzio had sent Cavalieri a book of his poems inscribed with the following dedication: "To Lina Cavalieri, who was able to combine with her talent an unusual harmony between the beauty of her body and the passion of her voice—from a grateful poet."[69] Massenet had been equally impressed by "her beauty, her admirable physique, her warm and colourful voice."[70] Shortly after the performance, the composer invited her to lunch at the hotel where the great Giuseppe Verdi had died two years earlier. He was full of praise for her performance and they became friends.

In January 1904, Cavalieri's return to St. Petersburg was announced. The month-long season at the Conservatory Theatre was to feature Sigrid Arnoldson, Leonid Sobinov and Giuseppe Anselmi. So great was the public interest that all tickets for the season were sold out in three days. Sobinov was a highly popular figure at this time, and audiences were eager to see what kind of a stage partnership he would form with Cavalieri. Sobinov enjoyed tremendous popularity at this time and was among the most highly paid of Russian singers.[71]

The St. Petersburg season had been scheduled to begin on March 2, but Cavalieri's eagerly anticipated arrival was delayed by an invitation to appear in Monte Carlo. On March 1, 1904, she replaced Lise Landouzy in Raoul Gunsbourg's new production of Offenbach's *The Tales of Hoffmann*, singing all three soprano roles. The performance was given as a benefit in aid of Russian casualties in the Russo-Japanese War, and this important opportunity might be viewed as Gunsbourg's way of thanking Cavalieri for rescuing his season three years earlier in St. Petersburg. In a distinguished cast that included Alvarez, Renaud and Deschamps, Cavalieri scored a major personal success. This was considered to be a Russian season in Monte Carlo and the resort was patronized by many leading figures from the Russian nobility, to whom Cavalieri would already have been a familiar figure. It appears, however,

Cavalieri in one of her most celebrated roles as Massenet's *Manon*.

Cavalieri in one of her most celebrated roles as Massenet's Manon.

that Cavalieri may have owed this opportunity as much to the influence of noble patronage as to her suitability for the role or the beneficence of Raoul Gunsbourg. In a letter which the singer wrote to Prince Albert of Monaco on the day following the performance she acknowledged his support, stating, "Knowing how much you wish to help me, I have no words to suitably thank you."[72] A Monte Carlo debut was certainly an important progression for any opera singer. Cavalieri's absence from St. Petersburg, however, caused considerable concern among both the public and her fellow artists. Sobinov wrote to Ostrovskaya: "As to me, I began my new season very successfully. Arnoldson and Cavalieri are very late.... Cavalieri ... is still in Monte Carlo and sends a cable that she is ill. Her coming is not expected in less than ten days."[73] This diplomatic illness, created, no doubt, to cover the conflict in obligations, was also announced in the press: *The Petersburg Newspaper* told its readers that the singer had a cold and a throat infection. Her belated arrival was finally announced on March 6, and she gave her first performance three days later as Massenet's Manon—the first opportunity that Russian audiences had to hear her in this role.

Partnered with Giuseppe Anselmi as Des Grieux, Cavalieri as Manon proved doubly interesting to the Petersburg audiences: first as the opera was virtually unknown in Russia at this time, and second, as this was their first opportunity to see her perform on stage in almost three years. The opera itself was not well received by the critics. One noted that it was "very monotonous. If some more or less expressive music appears, it is quickly dispersed in a torrent of pinkish water.... The love duet ... is very nice at the beginning but after one or two dozen bars it sounds like a sweet Kissel [a kind of starchy desert]."[74] Critical response to Cavalieri's performance was mixed, but, as had so often occurred in the past, the most heated part of the debate was reserved for discussion of her physical appearance.

The Petersburg Leaflet was complimentary, the critic describing the evening as a great success and taking time to commend the added strength and flexibility of her voice as "able to produce all possible gradations ... from the pianissimo to the fortissimo."[75] Although the review which appeared in *The Petersburg Newspaper* agreed that Cavalieri's voice was stronger than it had been, in every other way it was highly critical of both her performance and her appearance: "First of all, the theatre was not full, and the illustrious beauty was met without a single clap. It is no wonder as during the three years that St. Petersburg has not seen her, she has grown so much plainer that the audience would not have known her again.... The grave shortcomings are now met in her singing as well (such as swallowing and dashing off entire phrases etc.). Furthermore, it is difficult to imagine a more cold singer.... She sang the famous 'addio' in the second act without the least sign of feeling.... No wonder that the audience rather treated the singer with restraint.... In general, the public looked disappointed and the performance went off rather sourly."[76]

The description of Cavalieri offered by the same paper on the following day painted a very different picture from that which was suggested by the volume of photographs and postcards which were still on regular sale: "Before me was an emaciated woman, straight like a pole, with a sallow and wizened little face and with some scars on her cheeks. Her forehead is small and flat, her mouth, when she is smiling, produces an unpleasant impression of emptiness.... Her hair is thin.... Is it really Cavalieri herself?... What has happened that, so soon, not a trace remains of her truly divine beauty?"[77] The writer attributed this serious decline to the illness that Cavalieri had suffered the previous year. This apparent change in the singer's appearance became a major topic both in the press and in the fashionable salons of the city. The subject drew serious analysis from several writers, touching on the very nature of the transience of physical beauty itself: "They are not talking about her voice or her talent, but they are discussing whether she has lost her good looks or not,"[78] wrote Ossip Dymov. "The obituary notices having, by mistake, buried Cavalieri, have sincerely and deeply mourned not a singer, not a votary of the stage, but just a beauty, just a bearer of human beauty. Look intently at this face and this figure. Hundreds of photos reproducing Cavalieri's image well enough are at your service. It is impossible to invent such a face even with the richest and purest imagination."[79]

The debate on Cavalieri's humble origins and the sensibility of her move from cabaret to opera continued to rage in Petersburg more than four years after the singer's operatic debut. Alone among the critics, E. A. Stark in the *St. Petersburg Journal* seriously questioned the sense in continuing such an apparently fruitless debate: "I found that around the Cavalieri name too many opinions are interlaced, being partial from both sides: some people were abusing her with might and main, jeering at her aspiration to reach such heights, and others literally were dying of delight, seeing in Cavalieri almost the 8th miracle of the world.... The stage is a very treacherous magnifying lens, in consequence of that, all of Cavalieri's shortcomings were brought out in relief, at times making her even ridiculous.... From my point of view, I can tell you that she could simply be a good opera singer and not a scandalous celebrity—that is just fine!"[80] In the same newspaper, the music critic considered that her "Manon is too sharp for the sweetness of Massenet's music.

Giuseppe Anselmi, Cavalieri's frequent stage partner in st. Petersburg, as Des Grieux in Massenet's *Manon*.

In the love duet in the 3rd act Cavalieri showed herself as a passionate Italian woman but not a graceful Frenchwoman making ... a declaration of love."[81] The matter of her singing voice continued to provoke contrasting opinions: one critic claiming that she had sung "subtly and expressively,"[82] another stating that she had "to her credit, a strong voice, good for dramatic parts ... but it is not particularly charming, its timbre is not captivating."[83]

Following the pattern of her previous seasons, however, her second performance as Manon on the following night was far better received. The house was full, with standing room and gangways all occupied, and the response was so enthusiastic that she was impelled to give an encore of her act two aria. One of the most influential of all Russian theater journals, *Theatre and Art* had been highly critical of Cavalieri on her first opera appearances at the Aquarium; now M. Nesterov felt moved to write a lengthy and highly complimentary assessment of Cavalieri's progress:

> The actress is an example of what results one could achieve with persistent work. It is astonishing how Cavalieri, who only some years ago had sung for the first time on the opera stage before the Petersburg audience, could form herself into an undoubtedly useful opera singer? Where has her squeaky voice disappeared? Where has her cheerless feebleness of movements and gestures vanished?! The voice of Mlle Cavalieri has developed, got stronger, perfectly regulated in all registers. The intonation, observation of phrasing, rhythmic sense, are impeccable. The role is worked in minute detail. In a word, in front of you is the last word in vocal and acting technique. Now Mlle Cavalieri has to take care to wipe the traces of effort off, which she had expended for the realisation of her chosen career. More feelings, more sincerity! The art achieves the perfect illusion.... It does not show the least strain. The artist knows, of course, how much work and trouble this ease and natural behaviour on the stage costs her.... Meanwhile, each note, each gesture of Mlle Cavalieri are shouting of many years' work the actress had done to achieve such a note and such a gesture. The presence of Mlle Cavalieri's talent is before our eyes. We hope to applaud the actress not only for her impeccable performance of the 2nd act aria, but also for the whole truly artistic pleasure![84]

In an interview that Cavalieri gave to *The Petersburg Newspaper*, she claimed that her operatic repertoire was now in fact much larger than the one that she would perform during this season. She declared her favorite role to be Fedora, which she had first sung in Florence two years earlier, but which, at this time, was virtually unknown to Russian audiences. When asked if she would actually be given the opportunity of singing with Leonid Sobinov, she replied that "she would like it very much, but that the directors of the Italian opera would scarcely agree because it was not in their interests. The actress thinks, however, that she will succeed in persuading the directors to 'allow' her to sing 'one time at least' with Sobinov."[85] This optimism proved ill founded, and the opportunity was not to occur until the Italian season at the Maly Theatre in the spring of 1908, when the singers finally appeared together in *Manon*, *La Traviata* and *Faust*.

The distinguished critic, writer and playwright Yuri Beliayev provided a lengthy and poetic appraisal of Cavalieri in *New Time*. He declared that her performance of Manon was the only one that he ever wanted to see, describing her as an "impressionist…. Some moments receive, in her musical performance, a new and original interpretation. She is also a beautiful stylist. In the first act, Cavalieri appeared in her hood, the colour of withered grass, like a genuine old print, gently touched with colour. She approached the stairs—it was a print, she sat on a bench—it was another print. *Une gravure animée.*"[86]

For her second role in the season, Cavalieri returned to Violetta, with which she had made her St. Petersburg debut for Gunsbourg in 1901. She was partnered once again with Anselmi and Kashman, and it was observed once again that her acting was far stronger than her singing, and at least one critic complained that something better ought to be expected, "especially when the prices of seats were being trebled for her performances."[87] *The Petersburg Newspaper* criticized her for "exaggerations, misplaced impetuosity, crude Italian stresses, affected bombast."[88] In spite of this, however, the critic was also moved to admit that "she has a voice, she has a temperament, she has a good ear for music, she has musicality."[89] Beliayev alone noted in the performance qualities that others evidently did not: "This opera is very convenient for making the acquaintance of Mlle Cavalieri's gifts and her vocal strengths. Her voice is, undoubtedly, a dramatic soprano, which nobody had expected. And because there are not many dramatic sopranos now, a high road will be opening up before Mlle. Cavalieri. The role of Violetta is partly coloratura, but mostly it is lirico-dramatic…. The first act is not advantageous for her, not because she is not proficient in its vocal difficulties, but because the very treatment of her voice has such a character that now it is not worth it for her to think about the coloratura. On the contrary, the rest of the opera is good for her and gives her opportunities to show what energetic and persistent work means. We remember keenly her operatic debut in the same La Traviata at the Aquarium Theatre. These two performances are worlds apart"[90]

Naturally, Cavalieri was also observed attending social engagements such as the theater: among these performances was a benefit for Sobinov, at which he performed Massenet's *Werther*. This triumphant evening concluded with numerous encores and a stage covered in flowers. Sobinov himself noted that Cavalieri sent a basket of lilacs, which contained the inscription "To the divo Sobinov—with admiration." Later that same evening, she attended a charity market, organized by the French ambassador, to raise funds for the widows and children of Russian soldiers

Genoa, 1905 (from the collection of Svetlana Vlasova).

killed in the war against Japan. Needless to say, the stall that she manned sold out of its goods very quickly indeed.

After a benefit performance of *Traviata* on March 31, this short season concluded with a final performance of *Manon*. On the following day, Cavalieri joined an impressive roster of performers in a charity concert at the home of one of St. Petersburg's wealthiest residents, Dmitri Poliakov. Once again, the beneficiaries were the families of Russo-Japanese war casualties. Ticket prices were high, and, when combined with charitable donations, the event raised a total of 5,000 rubles. The stars of the evening were Cavalieri and Anselmi, confirming the singers' undiminished popularity.[91] Cavalieri left St. Petersburg on the Sud-Express to Milan, where she stopped for only one day before proceeding to Paris to appear yet again with Gunsbourg's Monte Carlo company at the Theatre Sarah Bernhardt in what was to be one of the highest profile charity gala performances of the season. La Société des Grandes Auditions, under the auspices of the Contesse Greffulhe, had arranged for a performance of Verdi's *Rigoletto* to be given in aid of the Russian hospital train of the Grand Duchess Maria Pavlovna and the Russian soldiers wounded in the Russo-Japanese War. Cavalieri would be joined by Enrico Caruso as the duke, with Maurice Renaud in the title role, casting described in *Le Monde Illustré* as "a magnificent trio."[92]

This highly prestigious occasion also marked Caruso's Paris debut and his only performance in the French capital that year, an event that Pierre Key was later to describe as "the start of a Caruso furore in Paris, which never abated.... Peasants, wearing overalls, appeared at the box-office of the Sarah Bernhardt Theatre, holding 100 franc notes in their hands. They wished to hear the tenor, even at the, to them, terrific price."[93] *The Petersburg Newspaper* confirmed that "Prices are very high, but tickets are selling like hot-cakes."[94] *Le Monde Illustré* noted that Paris was now able to see Cavalieri, "whom we have applauded only at the Folies Bergère ... in a new capacity, a no less appreciable side to her talent ... more than enough to get the entire Parisian public running to see the performance. How unfortunate, at the same time, that we are obliged to a war for this artistic luxury."[95]

The performance itself, which began with the playing of both the French and Russian national anthems, was a triumphant success: The three leading artists received ovation after ovation, and Caruso had to repeat the Duke's fourth act aria no less than three times. *Le Journal de Monte Carlo* recorded that "The enthusiasm provoked by the admirable interpreters of Verdi's masterpiece was beyond description."[96] Notable audience members included Madame Bernhardt herself, the singers Adelina Patti and Jean de Reszke, and the composer Massenet. The Grand Duke Paul and the Russian ambassador to France had also been expected to attend but had been obliged to withdraw due to the official mourning for the loss of the battleship *Petropavlovsk* and the death of Admiral Makarov. A profit of more than 75,000 francs was recorded, with benefactors including the president of the French republic and many of his most prominent government ministers.

During her stay in Paris, Cavalieri lived in her own private residence, dec-

PARIS - Théâtre de la Renaissance

Theatre Sarah Bernhardt (Renaissance), Paris, 1900s.

orated in the Renaissance style, and was accompanied by her singing teacher, Mariani Masi, who continued to coach and advise her. Cavalieri's collaboration in this gala performance was public confirmation of her new legitimate status as an operatic star of note and a highly significant development in her burgeoning international career. Her next important move in that career was also to be achieved under Gunsbourg's management.

In February 1905, Cavalieri created the role of Ensoleidad in the world premiere of Massenet's opera *Cherubin* in Monte Carlo, one of the most important operatic events of the season. Mary Garden sang the title role, and the supporting cast included Marguerite Carre, Blanche Deschamps-Jehin and Maurice Renaud. Interest in the new opera was high, and the dress rehearsal on February 12 was attended by more than thirty leading critics from all over Europe. The premiere, two days later, was attended by Prince Albert and other members of the Monegasque royal family sharing their box with the composer. The critical response was generally very favorable, Gabriel Fauré declaring that the work shared some of the grace and spirit of Mozart. Garden was to repeat her performance at the Paris premiere at the Opéra Comique in May of that year, with Lucien Fugère in place of Renaud, and Cavalieri replaced in her role by Aline Vallandri. For the Monte Carlo premiere, Gunsbourg mounted a lavish production with scenery designed by Visconti. *Le Journal de Monte Carlo* considered that Cavalieri "achieved a great success.... She proved herself a match for Mlle. Garden; she interpreted her role with verve and gave life to her performance, especially in the scene of the *aubade* in the third act, where her superb voice thrilled the audience."[97] André Charlot, writing in *Le Monde Illustré*, attributed her success to "her effulgent beauty and her double talent as a dancer and a singer."[98]

Cavalieri's association with Massenet's work, which had begun with performances as Manon in Florence and Milan three years earlier, was to continue throughout her career: She was later notably to score a great personal success as Salome in *Herodiade*, at Oscar Hammerstein's Manhattan Opera House in New York in November 1909.

As early as June 1904, Cavalieri's forthcoming return to the St. Petersburg stage was announced, with the promise, never to be fulfilled, that she would soon be seen as Tatyana in Tchaikovsky's *Eugene Onegin*. It was also widely rumored that the singer had paid an unidentified composer the sum of 25,000 rubles to write an opera especially for her, but this project also failed to materialize. A further publicity stunt

'hoto P. Boyer,   L'ENSOLEILLAD (Mlle Lina Cavalieri)   Décor de M. Visconti

ACTE II. — La Posada

Cavalieri as L'Ensoleillad, in Act 2 of Massenet's *Cherubin* (by permission of the State Museum of Theatre and Music, St. Petersburg).

708. - MONTE-CARLO. - *Théâtre et Terrasses*

Edition Gilletta, phot., Nice

The Monte Carlo opera house, where Cavalieri appeared in the world premiere of Massenet's *Cherubin* in 1905.

involved the announcement that the singer had written her memoirs and that these would include an unexpurgated version of her life and many adventures. This caused considerable interest among the young noblemen of the Russian capital, who formed the hard core of the singer's romantic admirers. No less a figure than Medea Mei Figner, the great star of the Mariinski Theatre, was asked her opinion of Cavalieri: "I think it is necessary to be possessed of a strong will to achieve what Cavalieri has achieved. She has good vocal qualities, she has temperament.... If it were not for her former café-chantant career, she could make a great artist."[99]

The year 1905 in Russia began in the most inauspicious way. The first of the revolutions which would eventually see the demise of the tsarist regime and the rise of communism, was sparked when a group of protesters in the square in front of the winter palace were fired upon by panicking soldiers in a tragic event which became known as Bloody Sunday. Only a few days after this historic event, the Italian Opera Season at the Maly Theatre was announced, featuring Cavalieri, Arnoldson, Masini, Anselmi and Battistini. Although many of Cavalieri's friends advised her to delay her arrival in Russia to avoid the very real possibility of becoming caught up in the volatile political situation, she honored her contract with the impresario Guidi. The Maly season was staged in direct competition with a second Italian opera season at the Conservatoire Theatre, under the management of Prince Tsereteli, whose company was led by Sobinov. On the night that the Maly season opened with Bizet's *The Pearl Fishers*, opera lovers could also choose to hear Sobinov in *Rigoletto*.

Cavalieri made her first appearance of the season on March 21, singing

Massenet's *Manon* opposite Anselmi. According to the *Petersburg Leaflet*, "The talented couple had a sensational success."[100] Although the majority of journalistic comment and coverage of Cavalieri's presence in St. Petersburg continued to be centered on her physical appearance and personality, one critic consistently showed far greater insight. Yuri Beliaev's articles on the singer have left us with a far more insightful, vivid and informative picture: "She has a beautiful voice and is now singing with ease, which she did not do before…. She sang very well and played much better. And the best of all was that, on stage there was a fairy tale, a live fairy tale. Everybody believed it…. Before our eyes, all this time, there stood a beautiful fairy tale, now cheerful, now melancholy, who was singing. And in the last act the sight of her brought tears to everybody's eyes, as if it was not Violetta who was dying, but the singer herself…. She reminds us of some fragile, wonderful plant decorated with an even more wonderful flower … the face of a smiling angel from an old Roman fresco. There seems to be something abstract and mystic in this beauty."[101] Not everything written about the singer praised her beauty or the skill of her stage performances, however. She also became a target for humorous and satirical writers, as have so many prominent personalities before and since. One such article made a comparison between Cavalieri and her namesake, who was also forging a public career, largely upon the established credentials of the famous name: "There are two Cavalieris—Lina Cavalieri and Maria Cavalieri. The difference between them is that Lina Cavalieri was always Cavalieri and Maria Cavalieri became Cavalieri not long ago. Because of Lina Cavalieri, seven have shot themselves. Because of Maria Cavalieri no one has yet shot themselves but they say that one is about to and will do it as soon as he can borrow 10 roubles for a pistol."[102]

Maria Cavalieri appears to have shared some early experiences with the more famous Lina, having also begun her career as a cabaret singer, later studying roles such as Santuzza and Tatiana with a foreign teacher. Her voice was described as "a not bad dramatic soprano."[103] Another journalist noted: "Instead of one Cavalieri there will soon be two singing in opera. Well-known Maria Cavalieri takes lessons from Mr. Tomars [*sic*] a famous tenor…. Everyone is attracted for some reason to the opera career. They seek to sing in the opera from café-chantant, from the operetta and even from the drama. Now, next in line is the ballet. There are already dancers performing on the dramatic stage; quite possibly, soon, they will sing."[104]

Inevitably, perhaps, comparisons were also made between Cavalieri and Anastasia Vialtseva, when the latter turned from her usual repertoire of Russian gypsy romances to operatic material for the first time at a charity concert in aid of war orphans in January 1906. The concert, held at the Mariinski Theatre, featured Vialtseva in an aria from *Samson and Dalila*, and, although it was suggested that other artists from the imperial theatre were reluctant to appear with her, they had little choice as Vialtseva enjoyed the sponsorship and protection of several influential patrons.

The popular press continued to fuel interest in the details of Cavalieri's lifestyle. Even the delicate state of her health would become the subject of several column inches. It was suggested that she was sensitive to changes in temperature, dampness, cold drafts, excess food and drink, or even boring conversation. In an interview published later that year, when Cavalieri had returned to her Paris home, she lamented the press's obsession with her physical appearance: "I am especially upset over the constant mentioning by Russian music critics of my notorious beauty. I am very pained that I have the reputation of 'a beauty.' When an actress is beautiful everybody thinks that her success is due to her good looks.... I am sure that a good appearance is advantageous to an ungifted actress ... but for the true actress beauty is a misfortune which forces one to think worse of her than she merits."[105]

During this current stay in St. Petersburg, Cavalieri spent the majority of her time in her suite at the Grand Hotel Europa, only venturing out to rehearsals and performances in the comparative safety of a heated glass carriage. In spite of these evident precautions, apparently the singer caught cold. Elsewhere, in complete contrast, it was suggested that she enjoyed a particularly robust constitution, enjoyed keeping fit and slept every night with the window open, even in the depths of winter. Perhaps, therefore, her reluctance to appear as publicly as she had on previous visits may be ascribed to a certain understandable nervousness, brought about by the recent, violent political unrest in the city. On April 10, a benefit performance was given for Cavalieri of *La Bohème*, in which she was partnered with the Rodolfo of Anselmi. A full house included many of the most distinguished names in St. Petersburg society. On the day of the performance, both the stage and Cavalieri's dressing room were covered in flowers. An equal number of letters and messages were received, ranging in content from romantic poetry to pleas for a private meeting to the inevitable requests for autographs. Victor Abaza provided a detailed assessment of Cavalieri's performance in *La Bohème*:

> At the first appearance of Mlle. Cavalieri you see in front of you a *grisette* Mimi with her childish, naive beauty. You see a fragile and ailing creature—and involuntarily, this makes us think that her untimely death will take away with it this charming creature. It is necessary to recognise that in *La Bohème* Mlle. Cavalieri is really on the top of her vocation. She is the central personage of the opera and she creates a fascinating image of the heroine of the old, refined novel by Murger. The graceful, pallid, slender *fleuriste* from the Latin Quarter, falling in love with a poor young poet, manifesting coquettish joy and sufferance and dying a poetic, sad death, she was clearly represented in front of us in the image of Mimi-Cavalieri. It is impossible to reproach Mlle. Cavalieri with excessive gesture, emphasis or using of some scenic effects that other actresses abuse. The genuine art, intensity, veracity and beauty of the performance and moreover the voice, these are the merits of Lina Cavalieri's talent. The scene of Mimi's death in the last act draws tears of regret for the young, only just having blossomed, and inspires the audience to a touching melancholy. I doubt whether we will see a more suitable performer of Mimi's role than Lina Cavalieri. The public, who welcomed her enthusiastically in *La Bohème*, will retain in their memory this fascinating image."[106]

The level of public interest in the singer was by no means either unusual or reserved for the night of her benefit. Whenever she appeared at the theater, and for whatever reason, she attracted a crowd. During the season she attended the benefit performance given for Battistini of Herold's opera *Zampa*. During the intermission, she visited the baritone in his dressing room. This occasion, remembered by the theater critic Yuri Elets, a good friend of Battistini's, provides a vivid impression of such a marked public reaction:

The last act of *Zampa* had already begun when I went out into the corridor to accompany the diva back to her box. A whole throng of people were waiting for her, in which the female element was prevalent. "Divine, charmante, adorable!" the exclamations were heard from all sides, and she was surrounded by a dense wall of people. I was observing facial expressions: One could read on them many different senses—delight and envy, and something like idle curiosity.... Quite a young man, a student of the school of jurisprudence, kept repeating in a desperate, pleading voice: "Ah, nom du ciel, when could I find you at home at least? I was there seven times!" ... The prima donna returned the same stereotyped smile to all questions and supplications, but her bouquet became more and more depleted, and she carried only two flowers into her box. Two or three of the boldest women admirers burst into the entrance hall of her box.... I decided to address them myself, "You have seen and that is enough!" Cavalieri sighed loudly and fell into a chair.[107]

One popular paper repeated a conversation supposedly overheard between two members of the Maly Theatre audience: "'I did not expect to see you here today.... Cavalieri is not singing today'—'Yes, I know she is not, but she is sitting in a box.... They told me by telephone and I came especially to admire her.'"[108] The writer proceeded to suggest, perhaps not entirely flippantly, that, in order to ensure full houses, on nights when the soprano was not singing, the management ought to overprint the playbills with an announcement that Cavalieri would be in the audience instead.

The final performance of the Maly Theatre season had been scheduled as *Il Barbiere di Siviglia*, with Olimpia Boronat as Rosina. However, Boronat was taken ill and Cavalieri was called upon to repeat her now familiar Violetta, partnered with Florencio Constantino and Battistini. The ovations went on for such a long time

that the three stars eventually returned to the stage and sang, to the accompaniment of a rather poorly tuned piano, a further half-hour of encores. The management certainly enjoyed a considerable financial success with the season, in spite of the relatively high fees paid to the star singers. Both Masini and Battistini demanded 1,000 rubles per performance, and Cavalieri's fee of 1,500 rubles was more than justified by the demand for tickets that her appearances generated.

Cavalieri spent her last few days in the Russian capital visiting friends and bidding them farewell, while she waited for suitable deluxe accommodation to be available for her return to Paris. After four

At left and opposite: **Cavalieri in the title role of Giordano's *Fedora* (photograph by Dupont, New York, from the collections of the author and Svetlana Vlasova).**

days she departed via Warsaw and Vienna, taking the Orient Express on the final leg of her journey to Paris. The reason for her hurried departure was yet another very special engagement at the Theatre Sarah Bernhardt: performances of Umberto Giordano's *Fedora*, under the management of Sonzogno, with Enrico Caruso and Titta Ruffo, conducted by Cleofonte Campanini. Sonzogno's Italian season was already in full swing by the time Cavalieri joined the company. The Milanese impresario had extended the season by a further two months to present eight additional operas: These would include *Adriana Lecouvreur, Siberia, Andrea Chenier, L'Amico Fritz* and *Zaza*. The Paris premiere of *Fedora* was one of the most eagerly social awaited events of the season. As the impresario Nicola Daspuro later recalled, "As soon as the performances were announced, all tickets disappeared as if by a miracle."[109] In his biography of Caruso, Ybarra adds that "everybody who was anybody in Parisian political, artistic, aristocratic and wealthy circles was on hand—and the spectacle of beautiful women in extremely expensive jewels was breathtaking. Lina Cavalieri, that dazzling apparition of loveliness ... sang excellently ... But—Caruso! It was his night."[110] The demand for encores at each performance was so great, that the conductor, Campanini, was compelled to make an announcement to the audience asking for a few minutes extra gap between acts to allow his exhausted orchestra the chance to regain their strength.

The cream of Parisian society was in attendance: Ravel, Debussy, Massenet and Saint-Saens, politicians and businessmen alike. Also in the audience was the soprano Frances Alda, the wife of the director of the Metropolitan Opera, Giulio

Gatti Casazza, who made a particular note of Cavalieri's performance: "I remember going to the first performances thinking she would be laughable, instead of which I was impressed by her singing and acting. And she was unbelievably beautiful."[111] Alda was both a good judge of talent and an uncompromising commentator on the events that she witnessed. She left a vivid portrait of Cavalieri in her memoirs: "I remember, too, seeing Cavalieri once in St. Petersburg. I was dining at that famous restaurant on the island in the Neva. Suddenly a hush fell over the place, the chatter of voices died away.... Every head was turned to watch the progress of a woman in a gown of pale yellow satin that was moulded over the most beautiful figure I had ever seen. Above the low décolletage rose a small, proud, dark head with classic features.... It was Lina Cavalieri."[112]

Not for the first time in her career, Cavalieri had overcome major obstacles in order to be seriously considered for the role of Fedora. When the performances were announced, Umberto Giordano contacted Victorien Sardou, upon whose novel the opera's libretto had been based, to give him details of the casting.[113] Sardou was delighted by the prospect of hearing Caruso and Ruffo in the principal male roles but expressed severe reservations as to the ability of Cavalieri to carry off the title role, which had originally been portrayed in the play by the great Bernhardt herself.[114] Eventually, however, Sardou was prevailed upon to give the singer a chance, and Cavalieri recalled that on the first night the author came to visit her in her dressing room at the end of the first act, declaring that he had been wrong to prejudge her so harshly and that she was one of the best Fedoras that he had ever seen. She also claimed approval from Bernhardt herself, stating that after one performance the great actress came to her dressing room and said, "I came to tell you Madam Cavalieri ... that I could not have performed Fedora any better."[115]

Although several critics considered *Fedora* to be inferior musically to Giordano's *Siberia*, they were in no doubt as to the main attractions of the production: Caruso and Cavalieri. One critic at least also suggested that Cavalieri was the equal to her more distinguished partner. Boisard, reviewing the performance for *Le Monde Illustré*, declared that the soprano received "a real ovation.... She has a nobility of face and vocal expression, and she combines her acting, full of ardour and sincerity, with the skill in singing already experienced.... M. Caruso and his beautiful partner, who was wonderfully equal to him at this moment, performed so marvellously the duet in the second act that Loris suddenly resembled Tristan madly in love with Yseult in expectation of her embrace."[116]

After this latest high-profile triumph, Cavalieri remained at leisure in Paris for three months before traveling south to Orange in August to appear at the Theatre Antique in Boito's opera *Mefistofele*, in which she shared the stage with one of the greatest singing actors of his generation, the Russian bass Feodor Chaliapin. The restored Roman arena, situated on the south side of the town, which housed the theater, now accommodated up to 12,000 patrons. The summer opera season offered two productions, Berlioz's *The Trojans*, with the Russian soprano Felia Litvinne as Didon, and Boito's opera with Cavalieri and Chaliapin. The productions were directed by Raoul Gunsbourg and conducted by Eduard Collonne. Chaliapin had been delayed in London and arrived late for rehearsals but left a vivid description of the performance in his memoirs: "It was a beautiful southern night, the bright stars burned in the darkest of blue skies, and on the stone steps of the ancient amphitheatre sat a multitude of people.... I, as Mephistopheles, stood high in the niche of a half-ruined wall.... The atmosphere itself was eerie.... The orchestra opened. A cold beam from the spotlight fell on me.... With the ending of the Prologue the applause was frenzied.... Bowing to the audience, I felt myself back in the theatre again."[117]

Cavalieri remembered the evening as "exceptional," noting that the grandness of Boito's operatic creation was greatly enhanced by the extraordinary setting of the Theatre Antique.[118] "I spent the time before my entrance in an improvised dressing-room, twilit with candlelight.... I thought about those marvellous Greek productions that became genuine manifestations of perfect art due to the creations of Aeschylus, Sophocles and Euripides. As the great arena filled up ... thousands of lights illuminated a fantastic picture, and I allowed my mind to dwell upon the past.... Suddenly I awakened to the sounds of the opera's prelude and, some time later, with the splendid voice of the basso Chaliapin who was a superb interpreter and an inimitable actor."[119] Cavalieri was very pleased with her own performance of the dual roles of Marguerite and Hélène, describing them as "one of the most important successes of my artistic career."[120]

After spending the remainder of the summer resting, Cavalieri traveled to Genoa in October for one of her increasingly infrequent Italian appearances. Her first performance at the Theatre Politeama was of *Thaïs*, the first time that she had tackled this role since her performances in Milan two years earlier, and reintroduced now perhaps in preparation for the Russian premiere, which would take place in St. Petersburg in the following spring. The second work in which she performed in Genoa was something of a curiosity: the world premiere of *Mademoiselle de Belle Isle*, by the Greek composer Spiro Samara.[121] Based on a story by Alexandre Dumas père, with an Italian text by Galli, this four-act opera, now virtually forgotten, provided an appropriate vehicle for Cavalieri. In February of the following year, when she traveled to Monte Carlo for three further performances of *Mefistofele* with Chaliapin, two further performances of Samara's opera were also given, with largely the same cast as had sung it in Genoa.[122]

Gunsbourg's highly successful production of *Mefistofele* was restaged with substantially the same cast as at Orange and was conducted by Jehin, but the magic of that first staging could not be recaptured: "It was lacking that something that in Orange we all felt inside of us and between us... This ambience invading and pervading us won the day and triumphed with us."[123] Cavalieri's first performances in Monte Carlo, however, on February 6 and 11, 1906, were reserved for Samara's opera. *Le Journal de Monte Carlo* noted that "M. Raoul Gunsbourg staged the opera with his usual skill and this performance might be considered like a new creation.... The interpretation was excellent from all perspectives. The role of the Chevalier d'Aubigny was a debut here for M. Bassi, whose ravishing voice of pure timbre gains on the listeners throughout the performance.... They celebrated the re-appearance of Mlle Lina Cavalieri.... She sang her role with remarkable art and exquisite grace. The pathetic accents that she succeeded in finding showed her qualities as an impressive actress. She was hailed by everybody."[124]

Although the lion's share of the artistic praise for *Mefistofele* was quite predictably reserved for Chaliapin, the critics gave honorable mention to Cavalieri's recreation of her dual roles: "In the scenes where she incarnates Marguerite, the young artiste showed a remarkable plasticity: very natural and delicate in the scene of the meeting in the garden and tragic in the prison scene. As Hélène she succeeded in giving the attitude of a goddess to her performance and the most ardent lyrical accent to her singing. Her success fell in with the triumphal success of M. Chaliapin and of the excellent tenor de Marchi."[125]

In January 1906, the Russian newspapers were filled once again with news of Cavalieri's imminent return to St. Petersburg. Although the political situation remained worryingly unstable and several prominent artists declined to appear in the city, the impresario Ughetti was able to promise an Italian opera season featuring many established favorites, Arnoldson, Boronat, Anselmi, Figner, Battistini, Navarini, and, as a particular highlight, Cavalieri as Massenet's *Thaïs*, in a production imported specially from Milan.

Cavalieri gave her first performance for this Maly Theatre season on March 11, appearing in another Massenet role, as Manon. Although the critical response was generally very favorable, at least one observer continued to voice the now familiar reservations: "We heard Cavalieri one year ago and we cannot say that she has made considerable progress since that time.... Mme Cavalieri does not step above the level of the amateur. Gifted dilettante sing so, but not professional singers."[126] Such comments, however, now appeared to represent the minority judgment. Yuri Beliaev, who continued to be one of the singer's staunchest supporters, contributed a particularly poetic essay on her performance to *The New Time*:

> The role played by this remarkable actress is like a picture. The design is so beautiful that it forces us to forget some of the discord with the Abbe Prevost's heroine. If his Manon could be so chastely beautiful, so graceful and tender ... in the first place, Mme Cavalieri maintains aloofness from all vulgarity and that is why she threw the realism away and created a poetic image of Manon.... She invented her own poses, patterning herself after Watteau's coquettish temptresses.... She is intimate with the audience; her tender mezza voce interprets so delicately and naturally the stylish sentimentalism of the epoch.... She sings surely and was at ease in her role. She is ingenious and inventive in the use of her voice.... Now she is definitely a formed artiste who has fathomed the mystery of her art; she has advanced, before the audience's very eyes, into a beautiful and rare flower, a real adornment of the stage."[127]

Ossovski, writing in *The Word*, compared Cavalieri as Thaïs to the work of a quattrocento artist, firmly suggesting that this was the role that she was born to play: "There is a fascinating, child-like angularity and suddenness of gesture.... She expresses her feelings with tender, sincere lyricism and timidity. Her beautiful eyes are dreamy, as if this crystal-pure creature here on the earth is still dreaming of her beautiful native land.... That far country would appear before the eyes of Manon when des Grieux attracts the attention of the dying heroine to the first star in the sky."[128]

A scheduled performance of *La Traviata* was canceled on March 13 due to Cavalieri's indisposition. She also withdrew from a prominent public engagement on March 25, but for a somewhat different reason. All of the most beautiful actresses and singers were invited to staff the stalls for the Academy of Fine Arts' Artists' ball. Not only Lina, but also her namesake, Maria Cavalieri, had been invited. On learning this, Lina withdrew, unwilling to share a public platform with her unwanted imitator. The delayed performance of *La Traviata* finally took place on March 25 and found Cavalieri partnered with Nikolai Figner, now somewhat past his prime, his vocal shortcomings concealed largely by his highly developed technique, as Alfredo, and Battistini, whose singing drew much admiration from audiences and critics alike. The highest praises, however, were reserved for Cavalieri's Violetta: "Violetta is dead.... For the last time a delicate, slender figure swept up to a mirage of illusory happiness and crumpled under the blow of pitiless destiny.... Lina Cavalieri is especially affecting and inspirational in parts where beauty blends with suffering and sorrow blends with beauty, where possible and near happiness is cruelly ruined by fate.... The audience leaving the theatre on Sunday, took along the image of wondrous beauty.... The critic felt disarmed. Lina Cavalieri is created for adoration, beauty shines in her features, it sounds in her voice, and it flutters with any of her movements. Talent and beauty are blended to a fascinating harmony by Cavalieri."[129]

The much anticipated Russian premiere of *Thaïs* finally took place on March 27, a charity gala arranged by the Ladies' Society for the St. Petersburg Asylum for the endowment of a school for the daughters of Russian officers founded in memory of General Kondratenko, who had distinguished himself at Port Arthur in the Russo-Japanese War. Battistini sang the role of Athanael, in a version especially arranged for him by the composer. Sonzogno's spectacular Teatro Lirico production was imported from Milan, with new costumes created by Kaffi of the Imperial Theatre. Cavalieri's costumes and jewelry were designed by Doucet. Ticket prices were raised accordingly; a front-row seat now costing 25 rubles. The capacity audience at the Maly Theatre that night witnessed an unusual incident that was described in *The New Time*: "We advise the producer not to use such a large bust of Eros. Mme. Cavalieri handled the bust like a yearling baby, pressing it to her breast and singing. It was not graceful and it was far too heavy for her. Mr. Battistini took it from her hands and broke it. A fragment then fell down into the orchestra pit. It was most unpleasant. The statuette of Eros should be small.... The busts are mostly made of marble, and even Mr. Battistini, who can lift Mme Cavalieri with one hand, could not hold a marble bust for such a long time."[130] In fact, Battistini slammed the bust down on the stage floor with such force that it broke in two, the body flying over the footlights into the orchestra pit, where it hit one of the musicians on the head.

The Petersburg Newspaper thought little of Massenet's work but was greatly impressed by the appearance of its eponymous heroine: "In the first act her appearance was very spectacular. She was draped with a blue shawl that she then discarded, remaining in an absolutely transparent décolleté costume the colour of rose dégradé. There was a very beautiful and stylish gold parure on her head and an Egyptian gold belt decorated with diamonds and emeralds around her slender waist."[131] The critic of *The New Time* was also captivated by Cavalieri's Thaïs but unmoved by the opera: "No woman of 30 has such childishly pure eyes. They told many legends of Cavalieri's eccentric costumes in *Thaïs* in Paris. They talked of an unclothed nudity.

They waited for a scandal, but an impression of pure poetry was conveyed.... It is my belief that only Cavalieri's beauty is able to animate Massenet's stillborn offspring.... As much as the novel is interesting, the libretto isn't. Its seven acts lack movement and are dull (the audience were bored). The opera is also insignificant."[132] Even though this same critic recognized faults in Cavalieri's vocal technique, he also stated that she was so involved in her performance that she carried the audience with her and "shone out, like a real diamond."[133]

In spite of its weaknesses the opera met with such a level of public success that, when Anselmi was forced to withdraw from planned performances of *Manon* due to ill health, *Thaïs* was immediately substituted. The music critic of *The Exchange Gazette* noted: It was a real delight to hear a rare artist like Battistini and Mme Cavalieri as Thaïs. This part should be accounted as the best in her repertoire."[134] The final performance of *Thaïs* was given as a benefit for Cavalieri. The music critic of *The New Time* recorded the same total immersion in her role, which extended beyond the end of the performance and into the curtain call:

> It is difficult to find another such perfect performer of the role of Thaïs who, like Cavalieri, meets so completely the fantasy of the librettist and composer. It is something simple and moving, tender and touching to the heart. It is difficult not to hear and admire her when she transforms into a pure and beautiful child, into an angel full of sublimated love and unattainable happiness. Cavalieri is an inspirational artiste.... At the end of the performance there was a storm of applause, many floral tributes and gifts. It seems, however, that she was not interested in gifts. She stood bending gracefully before the audience, catching flowers thrown from boxes and stalls and throwing them at the orchestra pit. The whole audience stood, men and women, for several minutes... It seemed that it was not applause, but a continuation of the opera. It seemed that the audience partook of the destiny of the heroine that she had performed so perfectly, rather than that of the actress and singer herself.[135]

Eleven days after her final appearance as *Thaïs* in St. Petersburg, Cavalieri made her Moscow opera debut under the management of Sergei Zimine, in her now-familiar repertoire of *Manon, La Traviata, La Bohème* and *Faust*. This was in fact the fourth time that she had planned to sing in Moscow, but on all three previous occasions her plans had been thwarted. On the first occasion she had canceled due to illness; the second visit fell through when the management withdrew at the last minute; and the third planned appearance had been canceled due to political unrest in the city.

There was a great deal of interest in her forthcoming guest appearances at the Solodovnikov Theatre, and tickets sold out very quickly in spite of increased prices. Her fee was said to be 1,700 rubles per night. *The Moscow Leaflet* suggested several reasons to its readers for this anticipation: "Moscow is very interested to see and hear her. It is not because Lina Cavalieri is a great world celebrity. It is not known if she really is a great singer, it is Petersburg that shouts about that. But Petersburg is well known as a city easily fascinated, which creates sensational successes for artists who are not at all deserving of praise. The Muscovites are in seeing Lina Cavalieri now, in the full bloom of her glory as an opera singer, because they saw her at the very beginning of her career on the stage of Aumont's café-chantant, singing Italian folk songs. She was a very pretty woman then and she had a pretty little voice. We will see what time has made of Lina—we will see, if she actually arrives."[136]

Cavalieri arrived in Moscow on April 12, accompanied by Battistini and the tenor Aristodemo Giorgini. The impresario Zimine recalled Cavalieri's first rehearsal: "At the rehearsal the musicians of the orchestra looked more at her than at their sheet music. The conductor of the opera, Ippolitov-Ivanov, curbing his temper, was forced to ask her not to feel uneasy because all of the musicians gave her the eye, in admiration, because during the performance everything would be OK."[137] In spite of the fact that Cavalieri's transformation from café chanteuse to opera diva seems to have been almost completely accepted by St. Petersburg audiences by this time, the Moscow press did not take to the reinvented Cavalieri as readily as their Petersburg colleagues. Most of the critics seemed unable or unwilling to forget or forgive her origins as a cabaret performer, the guise in which they had first experienced her performing talents at the Aumont Theatre in 1897. The highly critical reception given to her opening performance by *The Muscovite* was representative of the majority response: "In spite of too high a price, she attracts a full house. But it is undoubted that if she had begun her career directly on the operatic stage she would never have become a celebrity. Mme. Cavalieri as an opera singer is mediocre, or even worse. He little voice has neither particular beauty of timbre or warmth of emphasis. Her voice is not at all deep or resonant in the middle register. As an actress she is even less interesting. Her poses are not beautiful, her gestures are angular…. She was coldly received, especially in the first two acts."[138] Although elsewhere her appearance seemed to draw the accustomed admiration, it was considered that "her performing leaves much to be desired in the musical aspect."[139]

Her second appearance, with Battistini in *La Traviata*, was evidently more successful. The stars received a standing ovation and many flowers at the final curtain call. *The Daily News* acknowledged that Cavalieri had made great efforts to inhabit her role: "She is able not only to prove a great draw, but also to touch the heart…. She is not a first class artiste but she is an extremely charming actress."[140]

Zimine seemed far less concerned about the reservations of the critics, perhaps understandably, since his enterprise was proving highly profitable: "They sang in *La Traviata* and the box office receipts were then unheard-of—10,000 roubles a performance! During each performance the most celebrated artists, such as Surikov, Korovin and Serov, went backstage to stargaze at close range and to make sketches of Lina Cavalieri. And what went on after the performance! The audience stood up, applauding, next to the orchestra pit…. Cavalieri won the audience's love and all of her succeeding appearances … went on with increasing success. *La Traviata* was even repeated at the audience's insistence."[141]

The St. Petersburg cultural magazine *The Theatre and Art* suggested that Zimine may have underestimated his good fortune. They estimated that box office receipts were actually 12,000 roubles a night and that in a week of Cavalieri guest appearances the management had made a profit of more than 70,000 roubles. So successful were Cavalieri's appearances that a rival impresario took the opportunity of exploiting the singer's name and engaged Maria Cavalieri, promoted both incorrectly and inappropriately on this occasion as Lina's sister, to appear at the same theater for a Sunday evening concert. Cavalieri's engagement was also extended to include a performance of *Faust* as a benefit for the orchestra and chorus and a repeat performance of *La Traviata*, in which she was once again accompanied by Giorgini. After this farewell, performed to an enthusiastic capacity audience, it was announced that the singer would now embark on a short Russian tour before returning to Moscow in three weeks' time.

In spite of the critical reservations of reviewers, a situation to which Cavalieri must, by now, have become painfully accustomed, it seems that she had scored yet another popular triumph in Moscow. Journalist Ilya Schneider, who was then writing for the Moscow magazine *The Footlights*, recorded his impressions of Cavalieri in his memoirs:

> If you bought a box of chocolates in Abricosov's confectionery you got a piece of candied pineapple or a small chocolate *Mignon* in the silver foil as an obligatory supplement. In the box of chocolates you found also a bar of chocolate covered with gold leaf and with a little portrait pasted on it. There were portraits of Lina Cavalieri or of Feodor Chaliapin. In any tobacco shop that was also a stationer's there were a lot of postcards with images of *the most beautiful woman of the world*, the Italian Lina Cavalieri. There were portraits of other beauties of the time: a French beauty Cléo de Mérode, a Spanish dancer Guerrero, a homonym of Lina Cavalieri—Maria Cavalieri and a *chansonette* singer Otero. But nobody was as popular as Lina Cavalieri. When her name appeared on the Zimine Opera playbills all Moscow stampeded into the theatre to see Lina Cavalieri live. The management ordered me to interview the famous beauty. It was absolutely impossible to find her at the Hotel Metropol where she stayed. Nobody was admitted to the rehearsals. I decided to interview her at the first performance, but between acts the corridor near Cavalieri's dressing room was so overfull with admirers and with curious people that it was absolutely impossible to push through the crowd. I intended to edge to her dressing room after the performance, when the audience would call Cavalieri on the stage and she would bow before the curtain. But I was not alone in wanting to be the first person into her dressing room. The corridor was crowded with her admirers and even the door was open because the room was filling up with the crowd. It went without saying that the interview was impossible, but I decided to wait for Lina Cavalieri's departure. I wanted to examine the world's beauty closely. At last the door was closed, the belle changed her clothes and the crowd filled her dressing room again. I could not enter, and nothing remained for me but to be kept waiting. At last the worshippers were forced out of the dressing room door like some forcemeat from the mincer. They rolled themselves into a lifelike ball and moved down the corridor. In the center of the *skein* a dark fur was showing. Some French-Italian hum was wafted to my ears. I was almost bringing up the rear, but then, down in the vestibule, suddenly I was in luck (I made a strike). The *tangle* was moving among the large crowd streaming out through a range of open doors. It was cool outside. Not having achieved the doors the *knot* eddied in a swirl. I was borne leftward like during the storm rolling on the ship, then I was carried back to the *ball*, in which center gently whirled Lina Cavalieri and I found myself alongside her.... In this moment we were driven outside into the street and I felt something soft underfoot. I don't know how I was able to swing the fur but it was in my hands! They pushed me and I was flung back so that I found myself near the open door of a carriage. I saw Lina Cavalieri inside; suddenly she anxiously passed her hand across her shoulders. "Madam!"—I cried with strained voice shaking the fur. Lina Cavalieri moved forward and she extended both hands to me. "Oh, merci!" she said, taking her fur, and suddenly she smiled and tapped

with her little hand on the free seat at her side in the carriage, inviting me to occupy it. All the rest passed in one or two seconds.... Then I saw that the carriage was without horses: instead there were a lot of people. Scared by this fantastic picture I shot out from the soft carriage seat as from a springboard and shut the door. The students (about twenty persons) grasped at the carriage shaft, slewed round recklessly in a complete circle to the shouting and applauding of the public and careered with the carriage down the Bolshaya Dmitrovka Street to the Okhotny Riad."[142]

When Cavalieri left Moscow for Kiev on April 27, on the first leg of her tour, the crowd showered her with flowers and carried her, shoulder high, to her railway car. She was scheduled to sing five performances in Kiev and three in Kharkov. The Kharkov newspaper, *South Country*, announced the forthcoming visit, stating that, in Kiev, Cavalieri would compete with Chaliapin at the city's two opera theaters, and ticket prices would remain the same for both artists' performances. In the first two days of booking for Chaliapin's appearances, the box office receipts had exceeded 10,000 rubles. The Kiev season was to include many distinguished guest performers as well as Cavalieri: Vialtseva, who would appear in *Carmen, Mignon* and *Samson and Dalila*, Figner, Battistini and Regina Pinkert. *Life Echoes* announced that Cavalieri would be the highest paid of all of these artists: "1,600 roubles, Vialtseva and Battistini—1,000 roubles, M. Figner—600 roubles."[143]

The increase in ticket prices in Kiev caused a significant public controversy. Apparently the city duma (council) had given special permission for the opera theater to increase the prices of the tickets for Cavalieri's and Vialtseva's performances to the premium level usually reserved for famous artists such as Chaliapin and Sobinov: "Now the committee has placed the pockets of the citizens in the service of two café-chantant singers.... The city of Kiev has built the theatre, going into debt, not for such performers at double prices at the expense of artistic and democratic opera for its citizens. It is an inexcusable error on the part of the theatre committee."[144]

The competition between the City Theatre and its rival, the Solovtsov Theatre, intensified. The main interest at the City Theatre seemed to be in the guest appearances of Vialtseva and Cavalieri, although the former had thus far failed to raise much enthusiasm from her audiences. Sammarco, who had also been contracted to appear at the City Theatre, withdrew from the engagement, preferring to accept a highly lucrative contract in America, leaving Cavalieri as the principal attraction. The primary advantage for Valentinov's season at the Solovtsov was the arrival of Chaliapin, who joined a company that already included Titta Ruffo. It was announced that Chaliapin would sing three performances, and the response was extraordinary: More than 1,000 people queued overnight for tickets, and 10,000 rubles was earned at the box office in a single day.

Cavalieri's opening night was well received: "[She] has a soft and attractive voice quite suitable for such roles as *Traviata*. The singer's coloratura gives evidence of good training. In general the performance was deliberate.... Mme. Cavalieri was a success and much encored."[145] The well-known and respected critic Chechott wrote of this same performance, noting that the audience's response was reserved at first: "The victory was achieved after the opera's epilogue.... Mme Cavalieri showed a

Cavalieri as Mimi in Puccini's *La Bohème*.

not very strong, but very pleasant, warm and beautiful voice.... The actress's mastery of delicate nuances was demonstrated in the excellent mezza-voce of the cantilena in the duet with Germont (Mr. Bocharov)."[146] Yanovsky, writing in *Echoes of Life*, though impressed with the singer's beauty, remained unmoved by the quality of her singing: "Just ordinary, decent at most.... Everything is nice and pretty. Just nice and pretty."[147]

Cavalieri's second appearance as Mimi scored a great success with the audience; she took seven encores at the end of the first half, although the critics tended to praise her acting rather than her singing of the role, reserving special praise for her playing of Mimi's death scene. After being forced to cancel a second *Traviata* due to ill health, Cavalieri's next appearance was in *Faust*. Chechott, writing in *Kiev Dawn*, went to some pains to suggest to his readers that they should not judge Cavalieri too quickly simply on her appearance and her reputation. The possession of such beauty, he stated sensibly, did not automatically preclude genuine talent, and he found much to admire in Cavalieri's performance as Gretchen, although perhaps not realized as Goethe had originally intended: "She was the personification of the Romance race, but not of the German one. Nevertheless we should praise her for her attempt at making a compromise: she didn't wear the famous blonde wig that was immortalised in the music pamphlet by Mussorgsky, as Patti had done.... Cavalieri proved that she had an excellent technique, in a wealth of byplay during the church scene, the scene of Valentine's death and the prison scene."[148]

Regardless of the quality of her performances, however, and the evident development of her acting technique, the public in Kiev, as elsewhere, continued to be as interested in Cavalieri the fashionable personality as they were in Cavalieri the opera star. Wherever she went, crowds quickly gathered. One such incident was reported by the local press. A large crowd virtually blocked one of the city squares waiting for a sight of the star, and there were fears for her safety and personal security. Murmurs were heard in the crowd that since Cavalieri and Chaliapin were receiving the same very generous fees for their performances, perhaps she should give a performance for the working population in much the same way that Chaliapin had sung a concert in the circus at far lower ticket prices than were charged at the opera house. As they waited, the crowd grew larger and more restless. At this point it seems that the police officers on duty started to become uneasy and attempted to forcibly disperse the crowd, using mounted officers. What had begun as a harmless, if overenthusiastic, gathering to wish Cavalieri farewell at the end of her short stay in Kiev developed into a potentially dangerous and highly unpleasant situation.

The box office for Cavalieri's debut performances in Kharkov, announced as *Manon Lescaut* and *La Traviata*, had opened on April 15 while the singer had still been performing in Moscow. In fact, the first opera was to be Massenet's *Manon*, being staged for the first time in the city. The local press reported a great deal of interest on the first day of booking: The cheaper seats sold out very quickly, but there was less demand for the more expensive ones. By the end of the first day, 3,500 rubles had been taken in advanced bookings. If the performances sold out, Cavalieri would be paid 2,000 rubles for each night of her engagement. *South Country* noted the great financial success of the Moscow season, stating that Zimine had incurred significant financial losses in the previous season and that this reversal of fortunes was largely due to the presence of Cavalieri; already the decision had been made to add a second performance of *Traviata* to her brief guest season. In Kiev, Cavalieri had faced strong competition from the presence of Vialtseva and Pinkert, but, in spite of this, it was estimated that Valentinov and Iakovlev had earned more than 34,000 rubles over the course of fourteen performances.

The company arrived in Kharkov on May 10 and was joined by Cavalieri on the following day. The public reaction to her appearances in the city once again raised some important questions about the real nature of her celebrity as an operatic performer. The performance of *Manon* on May 11 was treated to a long and detailed review in *Kharkov Life*: The critic appeared to be less than impressed by the production or its star, clearly indicating that the cosmopolitan society audiences in both St. Petersburg and Moscow were obviously more easily pleased than the far more level-headed operagoers in regional cities, allowing themselves to be duped by appearance rather than actual ability:

> The day before yesterday, the performance featuring Mme Cavalieri took place at the opera theatre. But it could not be called *an opera* with the best will in the world. It is really impossible to describe as an opera (in a rough and ready rehearsal fashion) the running through of two solo vocal numbers, diluted with two duets and with one or two ensembles. To this extent, Massenet's really very melodic and fine opera *Manon* was perverted. The fact is that Mme Cavalieri had to appear and the public had to see her.... In the first act, Mme Cavalieri appears, wearing a very simple dress without diamonds ... and sings in her lyric soprano voice, not large in size or strength. True, she sings very finely, displaying perfect Italian training and proficiency. The public listens and is surprised as to what the secret of her celebrity is and rewards Mme Cavalieri with very frugal applause after the first act. In the second act, in which Manon and Des Grieux bill and coo, the public is again puzzled, for the small arioso sung by Mme Cavalieri, and repeated by her in spite of the very frugal appreciation of the audience, provides no key to the answer. The third act began. Manon-Cavalieri appeared smartly dressed and glittering with jewels: her hair was decorated with diamonds.... She had a wonderful diamond necklace as well. Now the really spectacular Mme Cavalieri excited great admiration and the public understood what the great draw of the performance was. Just before the end of the first scene of this act, the crowd made a move towards the stage. All gangways were soon filled with representatives of the fair sex, and anyone who could not get near the stage climbed up onto the seats ... and hundreds of opera glasses were

riveted to Cavalieri's overpowering beauty. The spectacle was really touching: Mme Cavalieri looked at the audience, blew kisses and smiled; the public looked at Mme Cavalieri and also smiled, occasionally applauding and shouting "bravo Cavalieri!" The sight was the same at the end of the fourth act and the last act. However, I did not wait for the end of the last act."[149]

The critic suggested that Cavalieri was lacking in vocal power and, although possessing some fine qualities, certainly could never be classed as a singer of the first rank. His brief comments on the following night's performance of *La Traviata*, however, suggested a far better rehearsed production, with a better ensemble, but the large house was accredited to the fact that ticket prices were relatively low.

The incident provoked by Cavalieri's appearance was described in other newspapers in far more colorful detail. One observer noted that the crowd rushed at the barrier to the orchestra pit as soon as the curtain fell, pushing chairs over and treading on numerous feet in the process. Hundreds of peaked caps were thrown onto the stage, which Cavalieri attempted to throw back to their owners. At one point in the evening a crowd of over 200 young men and women without tickets burst into the auditorium, and the police were called to clear the foyer so that the audience could exit safely at the end of the opera. For most of the evening the theater appeared to be in a state of siege, and the police on duty seemed unable to control the volatile crowd. *The Day Before* carried the following announcement on the day after this riotous performance: "Wishing to give the public the possibility of seeing Lina Cavalieri's final performance the management could reduce ticket prices."[150] Evidently, the spectacle of Cavalieri and her diamonds was to be far more important in Kharkov than the nature of her performance skills, and ticket prices were reduced by a third. A perceptive observer writing in *The Day Before*, after describing what he judged to be a fairly lackluster performance, reached the final conclusion, "Who is guilty in this unmusical and commercial concoction that fills the art and music markets more and more, helped by advertising? Businessmen striving for profits certainly, and the public, willingly falling for the bait."[151]

Not for the first time, nor indeed the last in her career, Cavalieri was being exploited by opera managements for entirely unoperatic reasons: They are grasping the opportunity of making swift and substantial profits by relying on the singer's notoriety and glamorous stage persona entirely at the expense of the quality of the actual production. They provoked the crowds into extreme reactions and then exploited this situation by encouraging them to return with the expectation either of a repeat performance or one even more sensational. It is hard to know for certain Cavalieri's personal feelings about this exploitation. Because she was an intelligent woman and by now an experienced performer, aware of the power of her beauty and personality and equally of the machinations undertaken by the impresarios who employed her, it is hard to avoid the conclusion that her complicity with this strategy may well be indicative of her agreement with it.

Commenting on the audiences' unruly behavior, the critic of *The Kharkov Gazette* noted that this kind of reaction might be expected in the music hall, but certainly not the opera house, where a greater degree of civility and consideration for others was expected, adding "Unfortunately, everyone understands freedom in their own way."[152] Other observers recognized an all too easily understandable facet of human nature in the aggressive response of the Kharkov audiences: "The Kharkov citizens wince or swear, but everybody runs to see her even from a distance. During two evenings the diva aroused ... what do you think, amusement or delight?— Oh, no, more than anything—curiosity with a touch of slavish servility before a famous name.... Everyone is a slight pagan in their soul. Everyone has their idols before which they are ready to bend down."[153] The writer, however, went on to compare the situation with Hans Anderson's famous tale of "The Emperor's New Clothes," suggesting that in their desperation to witness something special the audience was being entirely duped by exploitative impresarios and that the modest success that Cavalieri's performances in Kharkov really deserved were grossly inflated by the impassioned reaction of the audience.

Immediately following the second performance of *La Traviata*, Cavalieri returned to Moscow. An engagement in Odessa that had previously been announced did not materialize, although no explanation was offered for the cancellation. Her final appearances in Russia this season were in two concert programs conducted by E. L. Gurevich at Moscow's Sokolniki. For the first of these, on May 18, she was joined by the violinist Avierino. In spite of fine late spring weather, however, the first concert failed to attract the capacity audience that might have been anticipated, perhaps due in part to the competition offered by Chaliapin's first Moscow performance of Gounod's *Faust* at the Aquarium Theatre. The program was not particularly successful, and the acoustics of the pavilion in which the concert was staged proved to be less than sympathetic, mainly due to the noise of the promenading audience drowning out the sound of the performers. The symphony orchestra of 60 players, promised in the advertising, actually consisted of not more than 45, and rather unconventionally, the evening also included the performance of a short, but entirely unmemorable, play by Gilet. It seemed obvious that the management had based their expectations of success entirely on the appearance of Cavalieri, and one observer noted that "as we now know, Mme Cavalieri is a singer of little interest, and the entire concert possessed the air of 'business,' its aim was a show of beauty in order to get good box office returns."[154] The concert appeared merely to be an excuse for a further display of glamor, and Cavalieri's performance was described as "amateurish."[155]

A second concert under Gurevich on May 23 seems to have produced even less encouraging results. After some mediocre orchestral items, Cavalieri came on stage, to be greeted by the now customary rush to get a closer look at the star: The noise created by members of the audience climbing over barriers, pushing obstructing chairs aside and swearing oaths in the process, completely drowned out the music— an unfortunate repetition of the events that had so distressed the musical press in Kharkov. *The Moscow Gazette* commented perceptively: "One cannot base the success of a musical enterprise on expectations that have nothing to do with music."[156]

After this rather ignominious farewell appearance, Cavalieri swiftly returned to her Paris home, taking time only to politely but firmly refuse the offer of further performances in St. Petersburg. She was not to return to Russia for almost a year, although by November 1906, announcements were already appearing in the Moscow and St. Petersburg newspapers promising Cavalieri's participation in forthcoming seasons in both cities beginning in March 1907. Perhaps the singer had wisely decided to take time away from her clamoring Russian public and review her career. Recent events suggested that she had simply become a beautiful and dazzling curiosity of the opera stage: prime material for unscrupulous opera managers who were prepared to exploit her celebrity to sell tickets at hugely inflated prices to a public whose enthusiasm had been manipulated by endless column inches of newspaper reports of her glamor and notoriety. Could Cavalieri ever really hope to consolidate the promise of a truly serious international opera career under such circumstances? The answer to this question lay in the New World, rather than the Old, in one of the most testing of all arenas, the Metropolitan Opera House in New York.

THE OPERA STAR II

New York and Beyond

Cavalieri first came to the United States in December 1906, when Heinrich Confide gave her a contract to sing at the Metropolitan Opera for a fee in excess of $1,000 a performance, far higher than that being paid to Geraldine Farrar, one of the most popular, homegrown stars ever to sing with the company.[1] The advance publicity for Cavalieri's debut was considerable. A transcription of a New York press report is lavish in its praise of Cavalieri: "The wonderful Conried has scored another triumph in obtaining for the Metropolitan Opera House Europe's greatest beauty, La Cavalieri, who is said to possess a voice of unusual charm, to have the histrionic ability of a Calvé and to dance like Fanny Ellsler ... but, alas and alack, New York is not to see and hear the wonderful artist until next season. La Cavalieri's best role is Mimi in Puccini's *La Bohème*, followed at close range by *Carmen*, and it is said that there are few artists who can excel her in these two parts."[2]

When Cavalieri arrived in the United States aboard the liner *Savoie* in September 1906, she was faced with a major reputation to live up to. Mary Jane Matz provided a vivid portrait of the Metropolitan's new star: "She was five feet six inches tall, with raven hair, an ivory skin and a face of a perfection that caused people to stop on the street. She had 'the longest eyelashes in the world,' the most beautiful figure, the finest clothes, the most daring décolletage."[3]

Cavalieri was contracted to sing no more than twenty-eight performances during the season: For this she would be paid an agreed total of 120,000 French francs in six installments of 20,000 francs each, which included an advance installment paid one month before she left Paris. In the final reckoning she actually sang fifteen opera performances, four Sunday concerts and two outside engagements under the aegis of the Metropolitan Opera. The details of her contract, preserved in the pay books of the company, provide valuable evidence of the favorable terms under which she was employed, indicating that the Met was very eager to secure her services. Return passage to the United States was provided in a deluxe cabin, "if cost above $400—artist to pay the difference."[4] "For each perf. above 28 during season 5,000 [francs], but only 4,200 [francs] deducted for missed perf. in case of illness etc. To sing an average of nine times per month, never three times in succession, and not more than three times per week. Four days indisposition per month allowed, if Co. notified three weeks in advance.... Not more than four public or private concerts.

Not more than one third of total number of appearances to be matinees."[5] Additionally, as was common practice at this time, Cavalieri was expected to provide her own costumes. In an interesting footnote to the main provisions of the contract, a footnote was added which stipulated the company's right to renew Cavalieri's contract for the four successive seasons: for 1907–1908 at 6,000 francs per performance, for 1908–1909 at 7,000 francs per performance and for 1909–1910 and 1910–1911 at 8,000 francs. The Metropolitan management obviously intended to protect its investment in this new star. The records confirm that by the end of the season Cavalieri had received a total of $24,064, which included a highly generous fee of $1,024 for taking part in a private musical evening given by Mrs. Pulitzer, under the management of the Met.

Cavalieri's Metropolitan debut, on December 5, 1906, was as Giordano's *Fedora*, a role which she had sung in Florence, Milan, Genoa and Paris. In this first Met production of the work, she was once again partnered with Caruso and Scotti, as she had been in the French capital eighteen months earlier. In some quarters, the premiere was accounted a triumph, and for the first time in the memory of most of those who attended, an entire scene was repeated during the performance to satisfy the audience's response.

In her autobiography, Cavalieri recalled not only her nervousness at facing the American public for the first time, but also the creation of another on-stage sensation that was to fix her firmly in the memories of all of those who witnessed this debut, and many who did not: "I was literally trembling…. The first act was over. The audience considered it favourably while I was worried about the success of the opera. When the curtain opened on the second act … I understood that a great part of my future was at stake. Caruso ended his aria and was much applauded. Our duet began…. Everybody was watching very attentively…. And as Caruso at the end of the love duet sang "Fedora, io t'amo," I was so caught with my part that I fell into his arms, and while the curtain was falling, I passionately kissed his precious lips. For the first time in America, an actress had given a real kiss on the stage. It was a triumph, but someone said it was a scandal, and this increased the success!"[6]

Sylvester Rawlings, the critic of *The New York Evening World*, witnessed the sensation from the opposite side of the footlights: "Simultaneously, the two ran towards each other, and hungrily kissed each other for a long time. Probably it was a matter of seconds but it seemed never-ending minutes had passed before the curtain fell. Subsequently the audience started to applaud. The singers were called many times to thank the public. Flowers were being thrown to them. Then, when everything seemed over, something strange happened. The curtain opened once again and the end of the scene was repeated in the full light of the theatre."[7]

Very early in her stage career, as we have seen, Cavalieri had learned and understood the value of publicity. There were to be many such events in her professional life, many of which appeared to be entirely spontaneous, and many more, carefully planned and equally carefully executed for maximum effect. The result of the incident with Caruso, as Cavalieri later recalled, "My first entrance in the most important theatre overseas was a triumph and Americans started to call me 'Lina, the kissing prima donna.'"[8]

W. J. Henderson noted her great beauty but was not overimpressed by her singing: "Her voice is a light lyric soprano, very pretty in quality but not rich or vibrant."[9] The critic of *The New York Telegraph* expressed similar reservations: "She is tall, serpentine, gracile, agile and sinuous. Her personality does not exactly dominate, nor is her temperament markedly expressive … yet her acting in the suicide scene … was viewed with a power and sensed with a poetry very rarely noticeable on the operatic stage. It must be confessed however that Mlle. Cavalieri has much to learn as a singer. She must, above all things, rid herself of a distressing vibrato."[10]

In spite of all critical reservations, Cavalieri's career in New York was safely launched and in spectacular fashion. The Sunday following her stage debut saw Cavalieri make a concert debut, in which she shared the stage of the Metropolitan with Jacoby, Scotti and Dippel, in a program which included an aria from Boito's *Mephistophele*. Whatever her vocal shortcomings, Cavalieri succeeded in carving a niche for herself with the Metropolitan Company, against formidable opposition. Her rivals within the company included not only Geraldine Farrar, who debuted in the same season, but also such distinguished names as Emma Eames, Olive Fremstadt, Johanna Gadski and Marcella Sembrich.

Perhaps the most prestigious roles she secured with the company were partnering Caruso in the first Metropolitan performances of *Manon Lescaut* and *Adriana Lecouvreur*. Cavalieri suggested that the sensation caused by her *Fedora* kiss secured her the role of Puccini's Manon, in preference to Geraldine Farrar, who was also under consideration to play the role. Her great beauty ensured her an enthusiastic public response. The critics also welcomed the new star, but with certain reservations, expressed in a review of *Fedora*, by Algernon St. Brennon, in *The New York Daily Telegraph*: "She has fire, rapidity of varied movement, impulse, emotion—a dash of originality and an eagerness to do something…. She lets her features play and change. About her singing one cannot speak so surely and so eulogistically. Sometimes her high notes are wrong, sometimes her low notes, sometimes her medium notes. She is at least impartial. It almost seems as if half a dozen teachers had worked at her voice and all of them contributed something good and something bad. The voice is good, sometimes ringing, but it has been sorely mutilated. She makes a rare and somewhat enticing figure upon the stage. There is nothing quite like her, with her Madonna face and serpentine, sinuous figure."[11] St. Brennon's insightful observation, particularly when viewed in conjunction with the comments of some of the more acutely critical Russian reviewers noted earlier, indicates that Cavalieri the singer was severely hampered by an incomplete technique, probably the result of too little training rather than a confusion of methodology. The warning signs had been recognized by the Russian critics, and without a satisfactory technique upon which Cavalieri could rely, it is hardly surprising that her voice was showing noticeable signs of wear even as early as this.

Puccini, who attended the premiere of *Manon Lescaut* in New York, on January 18 evidently did not share such reservations. On the following day he wrote to Tito Ricordi: "Extraordinary ovations—I've never seen anything like it…. Cavalieri was magnificent. I was really struck by her temperament, especially in the moments of spiritual exaltation and of emotion. Her voice sways the audience as I would not have believed possible, especially in her high notes."[12] Puccini was received on the opening night with rapturous applause. He had managed to enter the theater unnoticed by delaying his arrival in the director's box until after the house lights had already been dimmed for the beginning of the first act. When the lights were raised again at the end of the act, however, the composer was immediately recognized and greeted by a fanfare from the orchestra: "The audience cheered and waved handkerchiefs. There was an even greater demonstration after the second act, when he appeared before the curtain with Mme. Cavalieri, Mr. Caruso and Mr. Scotti. He was then given no fewer than eight curtain calls, in the course of which many floral offerings reached him."[13]

Cavalieri's performance in the title role was once again greeted with some reservations, mostly with respect to her singing. *Musical America* recorded: "As Manon, Mme. Cavalieri presented a picture of striking beauty and acted with convincing intensity of emotion. Her voice was less satisfactory. Occasionally she produced a clear, rich note, but on the whole her singing was uneven and colourless though better than in the role of Fedora. It was the forceful, human appeal of her acting that made her Manon an achievement worthy of high rank in the annals of operatic portrayals."[14] The critic of *The New York Globe* was also not entirely convinced by her performance: "There was a good dramatic intention in her acting, but no real histrionic skill."[15]

Even though Conried and his directors may, in the face of such comments, have harbored some doubts about the advisability of hiring their new soprano, Cavalieri was considered an important enough star to be invited to take part in yet another historic Met occasion. Two days after the premiere of the Puccini work, she sang a single aria from Boito's *Mefistofele*, as part of the gala performance that culminated in the U.S. premiere of Richard Strauss's *Salome*. The concert, which comprised the first half of the evening, included appearances from many of the Metropolitan's most important artists—Caruso, Farrar, Scotti, Homer, Kirkby-Lunn, Boninsegna, Stracciari, Sembrich and Journet. Cavalieri's inclusion on such a bill is a strong indication of her value to the Met at this time. Once again, Cavalieri was in the most exalted company.

On January 25 she appeared with Caruso again, this time in *Tosca*, and followed this two days later with a further concert appearance, singing arias from Massenet's *Cherubin* and from Puccini's *La Bohème*. The concert acted as a useful preview of her fourth principal Met role of the season, when on January 28 she sang Mimi, opposite the Rodolfo of Andreas Dippel. This was the role that had been promised to be her finest, and *The New York Herald* was far more impressed by her interpretation of this Puccini heroine: "among the best pieces of work she has done ... full of spontaneous vivacity and an arch gaiety.... On the vocal side it was fully as enjoyable as the prima donna's other roles."[16]

After the short run of performances in New York, Cavalieri appeared with the company on tour. On January 31 she repeated her Mimi at the Philadelphia Academy of Music; on February 5 Philadelphia heard her again, this time in *Pagliacci*, partnered with Scotti; and on February 21, *Manon Lescaut* was given in Philadelphia, with the same cast as at the premiere. On February 17 she was featured in another concert at the Met, singing an aria from *Manon* and joining Josephine Jacoby in a duet from *Mefistofele*; then appeared twice more with Caruso, in *Manon Lescaut* and *La Bohème*.

The popular press also began to show a considerable interest in the singer. One article claimed to reveal which stars had taken out insurance policies to protect their key attributes: It was claimed that Otero was insured against the loss of her fingernails for $16,000, Paderewski had insured his hands for $50,000, and the violinist Jan Kubelik, his, for $100,000. Cavalieri was included in this august company: She was said to have insured herself for $50,000 against the loss of her voice, even if the misfortune was a temporary one.

Carefully spaced performances and an engagement long enough to afford her the opportunity of becoming familiar and comfortable with her fellow artists began to pay dividends in New York. By early March 1907, when Cavalieri was saying a temporary farewell to American audiences, prior to a return to Europe, it seemed that her reading of Manon had matured considerably. Of her last Met performance on March 2 the critic of *The New York Telegraph* wrote, "[It] must be regarded, from a histrionic point of view, as a most powerful one.... Mlle. Cavalieri is, in some respects, the strongest actress at the Metropolitan Opera House.... Her singing is indeed faulty and ill regulated, but ... as an actress she has passion, approach and appeal."[17]

By the time that Cavalieri left New York in mid-March to return to St. Petersburg, she had succeeded in establishing the foundations of a promising career with one of the world's most important companies. Ironically, it was to be anything but music that was to fatally undermine her relationship with the company. Such clouds were very far away, however, as Cavalieri returned to the ever enthusiastic St. Petersburg audiences for a season at the Conservatoire Theatre, which promised *La Traviata*, *Manon* and *Thaïs*, coupled with the possibility of a new role, Tamara in *The Demon*.[18] Her imminent arrival fuelled the now-familiar speculation as to whether she had managed to retain her beauty since her last appearance in the capital. One journalist even speculated that since Cavalieri had not agreed to sit for any new portraits recently, she must almost certainly have lost her good looks.

Cavalieri's first appearance in the new season was advertised as *Manon*, but, at the last minute, Anselmi, her Des Grieux, was taken unexpectedly ill, and *Thaïs* was substituted. Apparently, the subscribers were quite happy with this change of program, delighted to get the opportunity of seeing the singer in what was fast becoming a signature role and one that would become very central to the development of her career. The Italian soprano Gemma Bellincioni was seen in the audience, carefully observing Cavalieri's performance, perhaps in preparation for her own assumption of the role in Rome later that year. The obsession with Cavalieri's appearance over considerations of her acting or singing was reflected in the reviews of her first performance: "First and foremost, how did the famous beauty look yesterday? She seemed to have lost weight and been tired as though she had not had time to rest after her long journey."[19] After suggesting that her voice improved from a very poor start as the performance progressed, the critic, Koptiayev, concluded, "What more do you want, she is a beauty!" The critics in general were not very impressed with

Massenet's opera: One described it as a kind of pseudo–Wagner diluted with sugar water. Elsewhere although Cavalieri was criticized for her nasally produced French pronunciation, she was considered by many to be highly effective in the title role of Thaïs. *The Petersburg Newspaper* was alone in praising Massenet's work, describing it as both colorful and poetic.

The Massenet work was followed on April 1 by *La Bohème*, in which Cavalieri was once again partnered with Anselmi. By this time, Puccini's opera was very familiar to Petersburg audiences through many homegrown and imported productions. In spite of this overfamiliarity, the production was very well received: It was noted that a pure-blooded Italian cast was exactly what was needed in this music.

Cavalieri's Mimi was described as "the very poetry, full of delight and charm; there is a grace and dignity in each of her gestures.... The inscrutable talent ... beyond doubt, hypnotises and attracts everyone."[20] Laying aside any remaining reservations that might have been expressed concerning Thaïs, *The Petersburg Leaflet* described the singer as "a wonderful interpreter of this role vocally and histrionically."[21]

Cavalieri continued her social life, now moving in distinguished circles. The actress Kshessinskaya, who invited Cavalieri to visit her home, remembered her as a "startling, beautiful and charming woman."[22] The singer apparently showed a great deal of interest in Kshessinskaya's five-year-old son, Vova. The child had many toy monkeys, and when Cavalieri went to visit his room he seemed so impressed by her that he announced that she would be the general of his monkey regiment—an unusual accolade for an opera star, but one which seemed to please Cavalieri greatly.

The St. Petersburg season ended with a benefit performance for Cavalieri of *La Traviata*, in which Anselmi and Battistini partnered with her again. The performance was a success, and a highly appreciative audience packed the Conserva-

Above and opposite: **Cavalieri in the title role of Massenet's *Thaïs*, the role for which she became most famous. (1907, Reutlinger Studio, Paris, from the collections of the author and Svetlana Vlasova).**

toire Theatre. Many encores were demanded, and the audience showered the stage with flowers at the final curtain calls. The season had been a great success, certainly in financial terms; once again, every one of Cavalieri's performances was played to a full house. Some observers noted that Cavalieri appeared to be making little headway with the improvement of her voice in spite of the fact that it was widely thought that she was having lessons with Jean de Reszke at this time. A certain nasal quality, attributed by at least one critic to her poor French pronunciation, seems to have crept into her vocal sound, although it is unclear if this was the result of some new training regime.

Cavalieri returned to her Paris home and, after a short break, appeared at the Paris Grand Opera in seven performances of *Thaïs*. This was her third appearance in the French capital, each of the previous occasions being important gala productions in which she shared the stage with Caruso, and much was expected of her when she took the stage for her first performance on June 17. There had been rumors which had appeared in September that Cavalieri had planned to hire the Teatro Argentino in Rome for a short season, apparently to appear in a new opera, *Amore*, especially written for her by an unknown composer. If any such plans ever existed, evidently they were sacrificed to this far more important career development.

Thaïs had first been staged at the Opera thirteen years earlier when the role had been played by the American soprano Sybil Sanderson. The production was still fresh in the minds of all that had witnessed it, and it was therefore quite natural that Cavalieri's reading of the role would be compared to this performance. In the estimation of the critic Edmond Stoullig at least, Cavalieri, accompanied by Delmas as Athanael, in the role that he had originally created at the premiere, was quite the equal of her notable predecessor:

> Whatever hard and persistent work there has been, it is not sufficient to make an artiste like Mlle Cavalieri if she does not possess her rare gifts from nature. Her talents depend, of course, on her personality, but also on her Italian breeding: they manifest themselves

in her vocal ease and in the natural charm of her musical interpretation. Her grace is perfect, her gestures and her attitudes are harmonious and spontaneous. Mlle Sanderson gave to this role the tone of majesty that was dictated rather by her sublime beauty than by the intelligence of her personage. Mlle Cavalieri, who is not less beautiful than Mlle Sanderson, carries off a grace more bewitching and vivacious and who, being abhorrent of excess, seems to be proper to the character of the heroine. Her delicate fineness, her noble appearance and melancholic expression of her face create, to the very best, the converted Thaïs at the end of the opera.[23]

Once again, Cavalieri had succeeded in winning over the Parisian audience and in a role that was to become a milestone in her career.

While Cavalieri was still in Paris at the end of October, the *New York Times* announced that she would shortly be returning to New York for a five-month engagement at the Met, where she would open the season with Feodor Chaliapin and give her first performances as *Carmen*. Interviewed by an American journalist on the day before she set sail for New York aboard the liner the *Kronprinzessin Luise*, Cavalieri said that she was returning to America because of her particular love of the Americans themselves: "I have had many tempting offers from all over Europe. I was so delighted with the reception that New York gave me last year that I could not resist Mr. Conried's offer to take me over again."[24] She further claimed that Confide had specifically offered her the role of Carmen, which she had been eager to play for some time, that she had been studying the role and that she was keen to let New York audiences be the first to see her in it: "I hope to create a real sensation. I haven't appeared at the Opera in Paris this season because I wished to retain my entire strength for my appearance in New York, which I shall consider the crowning point in my career."[25] Press reports also claimed that Cavalieri would be taking with her the most extensive wardrobe ever brought to America by an opera star and that her Paris home was so full of luggage for the voyage that it had been almost impossible to open the front door.

As it turned out Cavalieri neither sang *Carmen* at the Metropolitan or shared its stage with Chaliapin. Her reappearance in New York, however, was to be in an equally high-profile event. Her new contract with the company guaranteed her thirty performances during the season at a fee of $1,000 per performance: She was also guaranteed not less than one performance each week, with no more than five Sunday concert appearances, granted an advance payment of $5,000 and given permission to appear in public concerts outside of the Metropolitan's management, providing that she notify them in advance. Additional to the clauses familiar from her previous contract, the new agreement stated: "In case of inability in replacing another artist on same day's notice, said missed performance not to count against her.... No rehearsal on performance day."[26]

Even with a relatively short track record in America, such now was Cavalieri's international celebrity that she was invited to open the 1907–1908 Metropolitan Opera season by adding Cilea's *Adriana Lecouvreur* to her repertoire. This would be the first American performance of the work, partnered again with Caruso, repeating the role which he had created for the world premiere five years earlier, and by Antonio Scotti. This was Conried's fifth season as director of the Met, and now firmly in competition with Oscar Hammerstein's Manhattan Opera, he chose an unusual novelty to engage the public's interest. *Adrianna Lecouvreur* was based on the familiar play by Scribe and Legottye, with a score by Francesco Cilea, described by *Musical America* as "a member of the younger Italian school of composers."[27] The opera itself was not received with any great enthusiasm. *Musical America* reported, "It is seldom that a first night Metropolitan audience forgets itself so far as to show any excess of enthusiasm over the musical bill of fare, whatever it be; its members are primarily interested in themselves and one another, and this lack of responsiveness makes the singers' task all the more difficult. Strange as it may seem, the spirit of apathy was more pronounced this year than ever before.... This was probably due to the weak impression made by the opera itself."[28] Even Caruso, considered to be the greatest attraction of the evening, received less than unqualified praise: "It cannot be said that his voice showed all of the luscious beauty and mellow richness characteristic of it in the past."[29]

Cavalieri's performance in the title role met with an equally mixed response: "Mme. Cavalieri was, as frequently noted of her performances last season, more satisfying to the eye than to the ear. She was at all times picturesque, if not as imposing as the stickler for accurate portrayals could have desired."[30] Such reservations were now becoming the regular response to Cavalieri's performances at the Met. Another critic described the debutante as "more potent as an actress than as a singer."[31] Others, however, were still prepared to overlook such evident vocal shortcomings and supported the suggestion that Cavalieri's operatic career was on a distinctly upward curve, stating that the singer "distinguished herself beyond anything that she has ever done here ... far beyond the expectation of those who heard her last season."[32]

As her New York career developed, Cavalieri was invited to take part in many private and semiprivate concerts, usually at the request of wealthy patrons and frequently to benefit charitable causes. She was invited to appear in pageants, often making a guest appearance in a tableau vivant, which were very popular at this time. She was often to be seen on the streets on Manhattan in an open carriage in the company of some of the most influential society figures. Mrs. Jacob Astor took the singer under her wing and ensured that she was received in all the best houses and invited to all of the really important social gatherings. Some of these appearances were reviewed, and these give us a brief portrait of the singer's musical activities off the opera stage. One such was a recital with the pianist Ernest Schelling, at the Congress Hotel in Chicago, given shortly after the *Adrianna* premiere, in December 1907. The concert was arranged by Mrs. Maude Ballington Booth in aid of prison charities. *Musical America* recorded that "the audiences are confined to the most exclusive circles, furnishing a big subscription, to keep strictly within the 'Four Hundred' limit."[33] The article also stated that a sum of $12,000 had been reserved to pay fees for the six concerts planned in the series; therefore it is safe to assume that Cavalieri was in receipt of a substantial fee for her services. However, it is impossible to avoid the conclusion that the majority of the audience attended to see Cavalieri rather than to hear her sing; the report of the performance supports this conjecture: "Heinrich Conried's beauteous singer manifested little charm beyond the mere pul-

Cavalieri as Marguerite in Gounod's *Faust*.

chritude of physical embodiment to interest a musical audience. Her first selection, an aria from Boito's *Mefistofele*, found her off key most of the time and otherwise not brilliant: the same faults and weakness were less observable, however, in the gavotte of Massenet's *Manon*, Leoncavallo's *Mattinata* and Tosti's *Penso*. Her final offering was a group of old Italian songs that were so simple she sang them unaffectedly so that they pleased as she gracefully waved her farewell."[34]

Throughout the winter of 1907 and 1908, Cavalieri continued to appear at the Metropolitan and also with the company on tour in Philadelphia, Boston and Baltimore. She sang again in *Fedora*, partnered with Caruso, and in further performances of *Manon Lescaut*, *La Bohème* (with Bonci), *Adriana* and *Pagliacci*. Whatever her singing may have lacked at this time, she continued to intrigue audiences and to draw some favorable critical comment. Of her appearances in *Manon Lescaut* on tour in Boston and Baltimore in April, "Olin Downes judiciously paid tribute to her talent in *The Boston Post* ... pronouncing her an instant success."[35] The Baltimore performance marked the end of her short guest contract with the Metropolitan, and she returned immediately to Europe. Carlo Guidi had announced his spring season of Italian opera at St. Petersburg's Maly Theatre six months earlier. He promised not only established favorites, but also new singers including Rosina Storchio. Cavalieri would share the star billing with Boronat, Arnoldson, Sobinov, Battistini and Anselmi. Guidi had also wanted to engage the tenor Eduard Garbin, with whom Cavalieri would shortly appear in London, but the singer had declined, not wishing to appear in the same season with such a prominent tenor as Anselmi, who had already secured all of the best roles for himself. Sobinov had been engaged specifically to sing with Cavalieri in five performances of *Manon*, *La Traviata* and *Faust*.

Leonid Sobinov as Faust in Gounod's opera.

They first appeared together on April 27 in *Manon*, and although Cavalieri was well received in the role, Sobinov was considered by some to be a poor substitute for her usual partner, Anselmi: "His open sound, which in Italy is called *tenoro russo*, has, for us, a particular charm when he sings in the Russian language, but he loses much in Italian (or rather in Italian-Muscovite pronunciation…. He sang with great skill although with his accustomed coolness."[36]

Sobinov's situation may not have been assisted by the fact that Cavalieri had arrived in the Russian capital the day before her first scheduled performance, and consequently there had been no time for any proper rehearsals. *The New Time* noted: "Mme Cavalieri has had much success in singing since last year, her voice has developed."[37] So great was the interest in seeing Cavalieri again that the St. Petersburg newspapers almost completely ignored a performance of *Boris Godunov* at the Mariinski Theatre which had been staged to raise funds for the new Pushkin memorial. Cavalieri was singing at the Maly to a full house, and the Mariinski was virtually empty.

Sobinov, in an interview published in *The Exchange Journal*, claimed that he had been watching Cavalieri's career ever since she had first appeared at the Aquarium Theatre and that he had planned for a long time to sing with the soprano. Their second performance of *Manon* on April 29 was altogether more successful, and both stars were highly commended for their interpretations. On May 1, Guidi staged

Cavalieri as Santuzza in Mascagni's *Cavalleria Rusticana* (from the collection of Svetlana Vlasova).

Thaïs especially for his star soprano: It had been two years since the St. Petersburg audiences had seen her in this role, and, once again, although the opera was very coolly received in most quarters, and Nani was considered no match for predecessor Battistini, Cavalieri was welcomed in the title role. On May 3, Cavalieri appeared in her third role of the season, Violetta, about which one critic observed that the star's overall assumption of the role was far more important than any specific shortcomings: "One can sing it better, but it is impossible to imagine an actress and a singer who could perform more harmoniously than Cavalieri so fascinating a creature as Violetta."[38] For once, it was not Cavalieri's appearance that seemed to interest the observers so much as that of her costar, Sobinov: "Sobinov's new costumes are original but not beautiful. His large velvet trousers make him look fatter and not at all elegant."[39]

Traviata was given again on May 9 as a benefit performance for Cavalieri, and the season closed with a performance of Gounod's *Faust* with Cavalieri and Sobinov, the last occasion on which he performed the title role. This final performance met with a tremendous reception: There were seemingly endless calls for encores,

Opposite: **Cavalieri in the title role of Giordano's *Fedora* (photographs by Dupont, New York and Reutlinger, Parris, 1905, from the collections of the author and Svetlana Vlasova).** *Bottom right*: **An artist's impression of Caruso and Cavalieri in Giordano's *Fedora*.**

bouquets and baskets of flowers too many to count and a special presentation to Sobinov of a portrait painted of him especially to mark the occasion, as Des Grieux in *Manon*. Guidi must have been delighted with the final results of his latest enterprise, to which Cavalieri had contributed greatly: All twenty of the subscription performances were sold out, and the remaining twenty performances all attracted very large audiences.

Throughout Cavalieri's stay in St. Petersburg, the newspapers continued to publish stories about her private life, some of which may have had basis in fact while others were patently fictional. One rumor, picked up from the Italian press at this time was that, during her early career as a cabaret singer in Rome, Cavalieri had married a humble barber and that she had a fifteen-year-old son from this marriage. It was also suggested that Cavalieri declined to have anything to do with her child, refusing to help him in any way. There are certainly some elements of truth in this story. Cavalieri did have a son about whom very little ever appears to have been publicly recorded. He was old enough to serve as a soldier with the Italian army in World War I, and although little is known of his parentage, it seems quite possible that Cavalieri may have entered into an early marriage, which, later in her career, she may have found more expedient to forget.[40] The same sources also appear to be responsible for another unsubstantiated rumor that circulated at this time that Cavalieri was fond of whiskey, a habit that she may have acquired in the United States, and drank it with great enthusiasm.

After the conclusion of her performances for Guidi, she certainly remained in the Russian capital, at leisure, for some time. *The Petersburg Newspaper* reported that she had attended a popular restaurant on the outskirts of the city, famous for the performance of popular gypsy music. Apparently, Cavalieri captivated her fellow diners by giving an impromptu performance of some of the Neapolitan songs for which she had been famous during her time at the Aquarium. Cavalieri also continued to improve her grasp of the Russian language, under the tutelage of the daughter of a Russian general. She said that she wanted to master the language in order to sing the gypsy romances that she enjoyed so much. Earlier in her career, at the Aquarium, she had caused much unintended laughter among the audience with her inaccurate rendering of these songs.

The Cavalieri style was widely admired and copied at this time among young society women, particularly her hairstyles. It seems that the secrets of Cavalieri's coiffeur were revealed by one of her closest friends at this time. Ironically, this friend may have been Catherine, wife of Cavalieri's former lover, Prince Alexander Bariatinsky. Serge Oblenski, Catherine's second husband, suggested in his memoirs that after Alexander's marriage, Cavalieri made a sudden reappearance in his life, much to the anxiety of his new bride. Catherine, however, was a clever woman and decided to befriend the singer rather than become her rival. Oblenski suggests that Catherine learned and copied Cavalieri's method of arranging her hair. Bariatinsky was often seen in Paris in the company of his new wife and his former lover. They often attended opera and theater performances together: "Once, as they prepared to go out together, Catherine admired the emeralds that Cavalieri was wearing. The singer gave her a startled look. After a moment, she took off the collaret and placed it around

Catherine's throat. 'I really have no right to them,' she said. 'They are yours.' They were the Bariatinsky family jewels that he had given her."[41]

Coincidentally, it was only a few days after the end of Cavalieri's season at the Maly Theatre that the papers reported extensively on Bariatinsky's bankruptcy. The case had been precipitated by the imperial jeweler, Fabergé from whom Bariatinsky had commissioned a pearl necklace several years previously, at an estimated value of 180,000 rubles. Although he had paid a cash deposit for the necklace and taken the item, he had failed to make any further payments. A writ was finally served on Bariatinsky in Biarritz, and the case came before the Petersburg district court. At this time it was revealed that the prince also owed substantial sums to other debtors, including the furrier Lelianov. Bariatinsky did not attempt to defend the case, and the newspapers revealed that although he received an allowance of 24,000 rubles a year, the law did not allow this money to be sequestered by the courts as it was given to him as a freewill offering by his parents. The reports did not speculate as to whether the necklace in question was one of the many such gifts that the prince had given to Cavalieri. However, it was said that Bariatinsky, who was educated with the children of Tsar Alexander II, "used this friendship in the days of his passion … having borrowed 100,000 roubles from the Tsar [Nicholas II]."[42]

A week after her final performance at the Maly, Cavalieri appeared at the Bolshoi Theatre in Warsaw at the invitation of the directors of the philharmonic society. It was announced that she would be seen in *Manon*, *La Traviata* and *La Bohème*. The opening performance was delayed for a day as the singer was suffering from a slight illness. Her first appearance as Manon was coolly received. It would seem that the audience had high expectations of the star, based on her reputation and the high price being asked for tickets. It was noted, however, that the singer, well supported by a strong cast of local singers, was obviously unwell and therefore unable to perform to the best of her abilities. The performance of *La Traviata*, which followed two days later, was received with far greater enthusiasm. *The Warsaw Diary* commented that the role of Violetta seemed to suit Cavalieri far better than Manon and that the singer "is without a rival in the opera world. Her beauty extinguished all others. She performed perfectly the effecting parting scene with Alfredo in the second act, and she provoked a merited storm of applause."[43]

La Bohème was revived especially for Cavalieri's final appearance on May 26. Although not seen for some time at the theater, the production was considered to be particularly fine. The perceptive critic of *The Warsaw Diary* noted that the evening was a great personal success for Cavalieri, made the more so by the fact that the audience was not merely applauding her physical appearance but rather delighting in the quality of her performance. Describing the singer as a "talented and amiable artiste,"[44] the critic described the "good and pleasant impression" that she made on Warsaw audiences on this visit, commended the quality of the supporting cast and suggested that much of the evening's success was due to adequate rehearsal time.[45]

At the conclusion of her short Warsaw engagement, Cavalieri returned to Paris, which had now become established as her permanent home. She had formed a friendship with the actress Elise Baletta, a member of the French theater company in St. Petersburg and mistress of the Grand Duke Alexis. Baletta had encouraged Cavalieri to enroll her son in a French school, as she had done with her own son, and the two women had become firm friends, often visiting each other's Paris homes.

The newspapers continued to run stories about the increasing number of fake relatives now making use of the Cavalieri name. Recently, it emerged, the genuine Cavalieri had received a barrage of telegrams enquiring about her health. Apparently one of the several impostors had circulated a rumor about her own death as a publicity stunt, and numerous friends and acquaintances of the genuine Cavalieri had read the rumors and assumed that it was she who had died. *The Petersburg Newspaper* published a story that it claimed had originated with the soprano herself: "She received the visiting card of an unknown lady who wanted to see her. 'I don't know this lady. Ask her what she wants...' said Lina. When the lady heard the answer, she said 'Oh, sorry! I am at fault! I didn't want to see the genuine Cavalieri. I wanted the counterfeit one.'"[46]

Around this time *The Petersburg Newspaper* published a strange story which it claimed had originated from Italian sources. The story concerned the death of a Signor Bendinelli, a poor barber, resident in Rome, who, the newspaper claimed, had been married to Cavalieri: "She had married him many years ago when she sang and danced in a local café-chantant, Marguerita.... Her son from this marriage, Luigi, is now 22 years old ... and he is working as a billposter. Cavalieri sent him money for her husband's funeral and asked her son 'to be more economical and discreet.' Cavalieri's mother is a very old woman, living in Rome now, who sells newspapers on the via Nazionale."[47] It is certainly possible that Cavalieri had entered an early marriage while still in Italy and borne a child as a result: There are numerous references to a son, but it appears that the child was much younger and living in his mother's Paris home. Cavalieri was 34 years old when this story was published. If her son were actually a 22-year old Italian laborer, she would have been only 12 years old when he was born. Although this is possible, it seems unlikely that she would have entered into a marriage at this age. There were frequent references to Cavalieri's son later in her career, including his service with the Italian army in World War I, but there appear to be no further references to a marriage with Signor Bendinelli.

In response to Cavalieri's growing international reputation, the major Russian impresarios began to compete for the singer's services. Guidi announced that Cavalieri would appear in his autumn season, while in Moscow, Sergei Zimine issued a statement that she would sing for him again in the following spring. The Moscow engagement was subsequently canceled, however, when the management insisted that she include *Carmen* in her repertoire, and the singer refused.

Cavalieri was to return to St. Petersburg in March 1909, but before that she had two very important contracts to fulfill: January 1909 would witness a high-profile return to New York to make her debut with Hammerstein's Manhattan Opera Company, the Met's principal rival. In the summer of 1908, however, Cavalieri faced the challenge of conquering another of the world's greatest opera houses, London's Covent Garden.

On June 18, 1908, Cavalieri made her operatic debut in London, at Covent Garden, in Puccini's *Manon Lescaut*. She gave a total of six performances in the house:

two further of *Manon Lescaut*, on June 24 and July 3; one of *Fedora*, on July 7; and two of *Tosca*, on July 18 and 28, one of which was given in front of an audience which included Queen Alexandra and the Princess Victoria. Her performances in London were met with a mixed reception, with critics generally of the now familiar opinion that her acting was far superior to her singing. Harold Rosenthal later summed up the achievements of this first London operatic venture: "Her vocal gifts were accomplished but she was never accepted in London as a great singer. There was never any question concerning her capabilities as an actress and as Manon Lescaut, Fedora (specially revived for her) and Tosca, she was greatly admired."[48] Rosenthal also emphasized the great advantage of singing with an artist of the caliber of Antonio Scotti, with whom Cavalier appeared in all three productions, but equally noted that in both Fedora and Tosca she was "handicapped by a poor tenor— Edoardo Garbin."[49]

As one might expect, however, her debut did generate media interest. In early May the *London Musical Courier* ran a nine-page article under the title "Opera at Covent Garden," in which they previewed the highlights of the forthcoming season. This included five pages of photographs of the leading singers, described as "The galaxy of talent ... many of the most brilliant stars in the operatic firmament."[50] Cavalieri was described as "Roman by birth and inheriting musical talent and no little ambition.... According to the concerns of opinion in the press, she possesses a beautiful voice and a magnetic personality."[51]

Later that month, *The Tatler* ran a short article that repeated the by now well-known story of a rise from poverty to riches. This article, however, departed from the established version by attributing the advice given to Cavalieri to make the transition from variety to opera to Colonel Mapelson,[52] the famous opera impresario, "who told her that she had a great fortune in her voice. Acting on his advice she went back to Italy and studied singing for three years."[53] As Mapelson had been dead for seven years it would have been impossible to corroborate such a story, although it is highly possible that he would have attended some of Cavalieri's early performances in London or Paris. The comment on the extent and location of the singer's initial operatic training was certainly exaggerated.

The Tatler followed this with an article purportedly written by Cavalieri herself, "How I Became a Singer."[54] This was one of many similar autobiographical articles that appeared in the magazine at this time, carrying the names of distinguished performers including Alessandro Bonci and Emma Calvé, although these were very probably largely the work of ghost writers or editors. Although in this article she did not name "the great impresario who heard me sing and gave me so much encouragement,"[55] she did make two further inaccurate claims: "For three years I studied with the great tenor, M. Jean de Reszke, and various other teachers all over the Continent.... My first appearance as an operatic singer was as Fedora in Paris, where I was fortunate enough to meet with immediate success."[56] The contribution of Mariani Masi, the only important teacher with whom there is any evidence that Cavalieri studied, and the early, unhappy experiences in Naples and Lisbon, appear to have been forgotten. Perhaps more revealing of Cavalieri herself was her closing statement in the article: "I confess that a nervous tremor passed through me at first

when as Manon Lescaut at Covent Garden I sang before one of the largest and most brilliant audiences that the world perhaps could assemble and one which I knew would be impartial in its criticisms; but the first bursts of applause reassured me and told me that the zenith of my ambition had been attained, that my dream had been realised, that I had won its favor."[57]

The serious press, who devoted some considerable attention to reviewing her actual performances, showed very little interest in her arrival. In many ways, however, the new star was upstaged in London by the presence of many far more established continental visitors: Yvette Guilbert was concluding a highly successful run at the Palace Theatre, and Sarah Bernhardt was completing the last few dates of her latest tour. On June 24, the day of Cavalieri's second performance of *Manon Lescaut*, Dame Nellie Melba gave a charity matinee at Covent Garden in aid of the London Hospital. The event marked her twentieth year of performing in the house, and it was attended by King Edward VII and Queen Alexandra. The program opened with the first act of *Madame Butterfly* with Emmy Destinn and ended with Melba in the first act of *La Traviata*. Against such competition, it is not entirely surprising that Cavalieri's presence in London received relatively little publicity.

For her debut in *Manon Lescaut* Cavalieri was partnered with Giovanni Zenatello and Antonio Scotti in a performance conducted by Panizza. *The Times* devoted a lengthy review to her performance, reluctantly conceding that the former cabaret singer had, at least, some ability on the operatic stage: "The debut of Mme. Cavalieri in Puccini's charming opera had been expected with much curiosity, for the fame of her beauty has been known, through photographs at least…. It was of course expected that a music hall artist would be but a poor singer, but everyone was surprised to find that her voice, though not in its full freshness, was quite effective in grand opera and of remarkably agreeable quality…. She sings excellently in tune, and phrases well and musically…. As an actress she showed remarkable power, but strangely enough her faults were those of the amateur, and the little awkwardnesses … gave her performance an unconventional charm."[58] The reviewer praised the quality of the revival, and both Zenatello and Scotti were highly commended for their performances.

With an equal reluctance, *The Daily Telegraph* critic noted that "a brilliant and crowded audience … welcomed her very warmly"[59] and commented on the naturalness of Cavalieri's singing, qualifying this by adding, "To a pleasant if not very powerful voice, Mlle. Cavalieri adds a very attractive personality, well adapted to this particular part…. The voice is easily produced, and the impression is created … that singing … is the most natural means of expressing a mood…. There is a feeling also of superficiality … that the interpretation is acquired by hard work rather than the outcome of spontaneous inspiration."[60] The reviewer was compelled to add, however, that the performance was greeted with "cheer after cheer"[61] and that Cavalieri had certainly proved herself to be an "undoubtedly accomplished actress and singer."[62]

Opposite: **Cavalieri as Puccini's Manon Lescaut (from the collections of the author and Svetlana Vlasova).**

Royal Opera Covent Garden

Proprietors, THE GRAND OPERA SYNDICATE, LTD.

General Manager   ...   Mr. NEIL FORSYTH

Musical Director   ...   Mr. PERCY PITT

THIS EVENING'S PERFORMANCE

Tuesday, July 7th, at 8.45

GIORDANO'S Opera

FEDORA

(IN ITALIAN)

Fédora ...	Mlle. CAVALIERI
Olga	Mme. LEJEUNE
Loris Ipanow ...	Signor GARBIN
De Siriex	Signor SCOTTI
Dimitri ... Piccolo Savoyardo }	Mme. SEVERINA
Désiré	Signor ZUCCHI
Rouvel	Signor GORONI
Cirillo	Signor MARCOUX
Borow	M. CRABBÉ
Lorek	Signor NAVARRINI
Gretch	Signor GIANOLI
Boleslao Lazinski ...	Signor LIERCHAR

Nicola, Signor SAMPIERI   Marka, Mme. EGENER

Sergio, Signor PINI   Basilio, Signor BOCCALINO

Michele, Signor ZANNINI   Ivan, Signor MARZOLI

Conductor   ..   Signor PANIZZA

Stage Manager   ...   .   M. ALMANZ

Royal Opera Covent Garden, program for *Fedora*.

On July 7, Cavalieri sang her first London performance of *Fedora*, in which she was joined by Garbin and Scotti. Of this performance, Arthur Notcutt recorded, "Supposedly opera has been resumed expressly for Cavalieri, as everybody considers it as a minor form of art. Cavalieri was particularly successful as protagonist, especially because of her acting."[63] The opera however was not well received by the critics.[64] The review in *The Musical News* was typical of the response to Giordano's work: "The music is unsatisfying and unequal in its attempts to exemplify and assist the action of the play."[65] The critical response to Cavalieri's performance was, by contrast, almost entirely favorable, suggesting strongly that, in Sardou's Fedora, a role originally written for Bernhardt, the singer had found a character far more suited to her talents.

The Times review recorded: "Last night Miss Cavalieri more than confirmed the impression made at her first appearance here: the part of Fedora not only allows her to display wonderful costumes and dazzling jewels, but gives scope for her dramatic powers, which are now seen to be very considerable. Sincerity was in every scene; and to get sincerity into the very machine-made scenes of Sardou is no easy task, more especially when they are not aided by music of any sort of distinction or individuality. For neither M. Cavalieri's great natural gifts nor the remarkable vocal skill she has acquired can disguise the shortcomings of Giordano's opera. She sang with more confidence and vigour than last week, and her success was quite unequivocal."[66]

Other critics observed a significant improvement in Cavalieri's singing but were far more reticent on the matter of her acting skills. *The Musical News* noted that "her singing showed a remarkable improvement as compared with her first appearance.... Having become more accustomed to the house, she sang the dramatic music with much beauty of tone, and her phrasing was, at all times ... consistently good ... her acting, as such, was rather disappointing. It lacked conviction because she never appeared to lose her own identity in the character and thus failed to an extent to really grip the attention of her hearers."[67] Similar reservations were expressed in *The Daily Telegraph*: "As Fedora, Miss Cavalieri sang much more powerfully than when she first appeared as Manon and moves gracefully. Yet, with all her pleasant voice and attractive bearing, her Fedora is dramatically not very convincing. The emotion expressed in the moment of tenderness when she sang "Oh grandi occhi," or when seducing Loris's secret from him, or when she sacrifices herself to save Loris, seemed not very deep and always self-conscious."[68]

By the time that London had the opportunity to witness Cavalieri in a third role, one of the greatest dramatic roles in the operatic repertory, Puccini's Tosca, a clear critical assessment of her abilities as both actor and singer appeared to have been reached. *The Daily Graphic* stated that Cavalieri "sang better than on any previous occasion and acted with uncommon power and conviction. Her performance of the great scene with Scarpia roused the audience to genuine enthusiasm."[69] The critic of *The Times*, who had supported the singer so enthusiastically as Fedora, now gave the following, more balanced, judgement: "It is as an actress primarily that Mlle. Cavalieri commands the attention of her audience, and, though she sang her songs with sufficient charm to preserve the character, her voice must often have been inadequate to the impassioned declamation had it been her only, or even her chief means of expression. She acted the part strenuously and fully, using gestures that would have seemed extravagant if they had been less spontaneous. At the end of the second act, for instance, there was none of the subtle suggestions of horror and fear which Mlle. Cavalieri gives so finely. Everything was acted out to the uttermost and the realism was insisted upon."[70]

The full-blooded nature of Sardou's drama, in this role also created for Bernhardt, Cavalieri evidently found the right vehicle for her powers of dramatic expression. She and Antonio Scotti received a tremendous ovation at the end of the second act. So great was the audience's enthusiasm that the conductor, Campanini, was called on to the stage to join his singers in acknowledging the applause. Although it could not be said that Cavalieri had scored a triumph to equal the impact she had had on St. Petersburg audiences, it is certainly true that she left London having established very respectable operatic credentials, and recognition of a growing ability, both musically and histrionically. In their review of the Covent Garden season, among the distinguished company of Tetrazzini, Melba, McCormack and Zenatello, *The Musical News* noted that "another successful appearance was that of Signora Cavalieri, a beautiful Roman singer."[71]

For the remainder of the summer and into the autumn of 1908, Cavalieri was at leisure, dividing her time between her Paris home and traveling in Europe. In November she took part in an automobile competition in Rome organized for the benefit of local charities. She won first prize for stylish design, having transformed her car into an enormous basket of narcissi. A reporter covering the event asked if these were her favorite flowers: "Oh yes, they are! I adore them! The narcissi were companions of my first serious success on the opera stage. When I performed *La Traviata* there were three baskets of narcissi all presented to me at once. Those flowers are indispensable in my home."[72]

Cavalieri returned to New York at the end of 1908, having accepted a contract with the Metropolitan's great rival, Oscar Hammerstein's Manhattan Opera Company. Her short stay with the company caused one of the great operatic sensations of the decade, which became known as the Prima Donna War.[73] The resultant rivalry between Cavalieri and Hammerstein's established star soprano, the redoubtable Mary Garden, over who should sing Massenet's *Thaïs* with the company sparked a long and colorful feud between the two singers.

The growing media interest in the lives and activities of opera stars at this time is very well illustrated by the story. Oscar Hammerstein, who well understood the value of a media story to stimulate public interest and subsequent ticket sales, could hardly be viewed as a totally innocent party in what was a brief but memorable controversy. Such rivalries as these titillated the salons, fueled society gossip, and provided ideal copy from the earliest origins of sensational journalism.

To those who possess them, good reputations are precious acquisitions, earned through effort and maintained at cost. The greater the struggle to achieve premiere status in your chosen profession, the more acute the knowledge of the value of that status. The greater the star, the greater the need to maintain the stellar advantage. Perhaps the heightened emotions and evident glamor of the operatic stage provide an ideal backdrop to such tales of rivalry, sometimes appearing to emulate the ripe and red-blooded drama of the very plots that provide the protagonists with their popular stage personas. The battle which broke out in the operatic community of Manhattan and which was reported, blow by blow in the *New York Times*, involved two of the world's most glamorous operatic stars, and to the victor would go the seemingly modest prize of two performances of Massenet's opera *Thaïs* at Hammerstein's Manhattan Opera House.

Mary Garden had become more closely associated with the title role of *Thaïs* than any other soprano.[74] She made her debut in the role at Aix-les-Bains in August 1901, and was to perform it on over 140 subsequent occasions. In company with Charpentier's *Louise* and—arguably her most historically significant creation - Debussy's Melisande, *Thaïs* can be counted as one of Garden's signature roles. The original creator of the role, Sybil Sanderson, had a summer home at Aix and accompanied Garden to the theater on the night of her debut. In her published autobiography, Garden recalled how Sanderson suddenly decided that Thaïs could not possibly appear unless bedecked with pearls and promptly solved the problem by providing several priceless strings of her own, which Garden wore for her performance, much to the consternation of the theater management.

Thaïs was to be only the first of many performances of Massenet's operatic heroines, which were to become a central feature of Garden's career.[75] Massenet had first heard Garden sing at a rehearsal of Debussy's *Pelleas et Mélisande* shortly before the work's premiere in Paris and was moved to congratulate her after her performance as Manon at the Opéra Comique in October 1902. Garden recorded her first recollection of meeting Massenet during the preparations for *Cherubin*. She was not impressed: "I'm afraid I never cared for Massenet.... [He] was the yes-man *par excellence*. Everything was 'All right, fine, perfect.' He was always gushing. He could say the most marvellous things to someone.... And the moment the door closed behind that someone he would turn to the others in the room and say something quite the contrary. Then he would write endless letters dripping with the most sickening kind of sentiment.... He hadn't the character I liked in a man."[76]

Evidently, the plain-speaking Aberdonian element in Garden's character made her question the sincerity of such fulsome praise. Always apparently aware of her own worth, she was perhaps less in need of hearing her own good opinions confirmed. Although unimpressed by Massenet's character, Garden was apparently impressed by his music. Massenet's operas had already provided her with many opportunities to excel, when in October 1907, she sailed for New York to make her debut there for Oscar Hammerstein's Manhattan Opera. The work chosen for this most important occasion was *Thaïs*. The day before the scheduled debut, Garden succumbed to a serious cold and was unwisely prevailed upon to sing. The performance, on November 25, 1907, was greeted with mixed reaction from the press. Afflicted with a probable case of bronchitis, Garden's vocal shortcomings became the main focus of the New York critics' responses. *The Globe* reported that "her singing was a hindrance rather than an aid ... and sounded somewhat worn.... The high notes were forced and shrill.... There was no true legato. The phrasing was often a blur.... In the final scene the redeemed Thaïs shrieked like a lost soul." In Garden's own recollection "the papers just pulled me to pieces.... The avalanche of abusive criticism that followed my New York debut in *Thaïs* would have made any other singer pack her trunk and go back to where she had come from. Not me."[77]

Hammerstein sensibly arranged for his new star to have a few days convalescence in Atlantic City. He had signed a five-year contract with Garden and, after such a disappointing beginning to their association, may have seriously questioned the advisability of such an undertaking. On her return to the house at the end of November, matters improved greatly. Reviewing a December performance of *Thaïs*, the *New York Times* critic stated: "Miss Garden's portrayal of the title role is remarkable for plastic grace and pictorial beauty, while it is dramatically satisfying. She is an actress of unusual skill. As a singer Miss Garden improves on acquaintance."[78]

In the succeeding months, Garden recreated her Melisande for the New York premiere of Debussy's opera and also gave American audiences their first chance to experience her acclaimed interpretation of Charpentier's *Louise*. Repeating *Thaïs* for the second night of the Manhattan season in November 1908, Garden would find herself described by the *New York Times* as one of Hammerstein's "most popular artistes."[79] "Miss Garden returns with all the potent force of her personality undiminished," the *Times* critic stated, commenting that the role of Thaïs "is one in which her individuality can most characteristically express itself ... brilliant, lithe, intensely alive and active and wonderfully versatile." [80]

Although Garden's vocal attributes in the role remained the subject of some critical uneasiness, there was no doubt that to a New York audience at this time Garden *was* Thaïs. On the crest of this wave of success, it was announced that Garden's next assumption on the New York opera stage would be Richard Strauss's *Salome* and that she would perform the notorious Dance of the Seven Veils herself, rather than allow a dancer to substitute. At such a moment, when the New York opera-going public was eager to see just how Garden would present such a potentially scandalous characterization, it seems inconceivable that Oscar Hammerstein would take any action that might disrupt the highly propitious omens for yet another company triumph. Yet that appears to be exactly what he did.

On January 19, 1909, the following brief, but highly inflammable announcement appeared in the *New York Times*. Under the headline "Lina Cavalieri for the Manhattan" it relayed the following simple statement: "Oscar Hammerstein has engaged Lina Cavalieri, the Italian soprano who appeared last season at the Metropolitan, for a series of four performances at the Manhattan Opera House. Miss Cavalieri will probably make her first appearance next week as Mimi in *La Bohème*. It is understood that she will also appear in the title role in *Thaïs*."[81] Garden claimed in her published autobiography that she discovered the news written on a billboard outside the theater, on her way to a rehearsal for the forthcoming production of *Salome*: "There, staring at me in large letters, were the words: FRIDAY NIGHT, THAÏS, WITH LINA CAVALIERI."[82]

Garden's immediate and passionate indignation would appear to be based upon a number of factors. She had established her position with Hammerstein's company as the leading lady for the French repertory, and was therefore reluctant to relinquish it to any newcomer, even for only two performances. *Thaïs* had not been an automatic success in New York. Garden recorded that "After the second performance ... Hammerstein told me that there was not enough money in the box office to pay the gas bill."[83] Garden attributed her central contribution to the subsequent change in fortunes for Massenet's opera. She wrote; "Through my efforts, and those of Maurice Renaud, *Thaïs* had become an immense success.... I was amazed to read that Lina Cavalieri was billed to sing 'my opera.'"[84]

At the time of this controversy, Garden and Cavalieri were already known to each other, both professionally and personally. In February 1905, they had appeared together at Monte Carlo, in the premiere of Massenet's *Cherubin*, Garden excelling in the title role, Cavalieri creating the role of L'Ensoleillad, in a cast that also included Maurice Renaud and Marguerite Carre. As we have already established, Cavalieri was not an untried or untested performer of the role of Thaïs. She created it for the first Milan production of the opera in October 1903, at the Teatro Lirico, which prompted Massenet to recall in his memoirs: "Her beauty, her admirable plasticity, the warmth and colour of her voice, her passionate outbursts simply gripped the public, which praised her to the skies."[85] In his extensive and scholarly study of Massenet, Demar Irvine expresses the opinion that "Without the talent and beauty that Lina Cavalieri brought to the title-role in 1907, *Thaïs* would perhaps be as little known today as *Le Mage* or *Ariane*."[86] In some perverse way, therefore, Garden might be said to owe part of her success to the singer who now appeared to be her principal rival.

By this stage in her career, Cavalieri certainly possessed the same degree of fascination prompted by sensationalism, or at least the suggestion of it, that attracted audiences to Mary Garden. Cavalieri also had the added attraction of mystery, actively endeavoring always to cloud the facts about her past life, which only served to make her an even more alluring subject of public interest. The matter of Cavalieri's vocal limitations had become a constant subject for critical discussion, but the evidence strongly suggested that, in common with Mary Garden, she had developed into a highly accomplished stage performer who knew exactly how to create an effect, both on stage and off. Hammerstein, the consummate publicist, saw the engagement of Cavalieri as having two main purposes: First, he could effectively capitalize on her celebrity and notoriety, which would ensure good ticket sales, and, second—and perhaps more importantly—it was a very effective way of hitting out at his competitor, the Metropolitan Opera, who had recently dispensed with the diva's services, and, as we shall shortly discover, under highly delicate circumstances.

The established rivalry between the Metropolitan and Hammerstein's Manhattan Opera was about to reach a climax. The 1909–1910 season was to be the last for the Manhattan Company. The many successes that Hammerstein had secured, mostly at the Metropolitan's expense, caused the senior company to view their competitor not simply as an irritation, but as a serious economic threat. It was decided to buy out Hammerstein, and, subsequently, he was paid a sum in excess of a million dollars to cease his operatic production activities in New York.

Hammerstein's contract with Cavalieri called initially for only four appearances, confirming perhaps that he saw his newly acquired star more in terms of a tactical move against his rivals than as a significant artistic addition to his company.

Since his company already had the services of Mary Garden, what need did they have of a second prima donna with very similar qualities, other than as part of an elaborate point-scoring exercise? It might reasonably be supposed that his seemingly uncharacteristic and what might be viewed as undiplomatic action of offering his new star the role so jealously guarded by his existing star was intended as nothing more than another publicity stunt. If that was the case, the plan, which on superficial examination, might seem to have backfired spectacularly, was in fact a considerable success.

According to Garden, Oscar Hammerstein had asked her permission for Cavalieri to sing *Thaïs*, which Garden claimed in a newspaper interview and later in her autobiography that she absolutely refused to grant. Under the headline "Mary Garden will have no new Thaïs," the *New York Times* printed a statement by Garden: "I told Mr. Hammerstein that if he allowed Miss Cavalieri to sing in any of my French roles he would have to take the consequences. He knows what those consequences are.... I have no objection to Miss Cavalieri singing in the company. I shall be delighted to have her so long as she confines herself to Italian operas, but I will not allow those French operas which I have brought to this country to be taken from me. I have worked too hard and earnestly in them."[87] When a *Times* journalist later read this statement to Hammerstein, the impresario expressed himself disinterested in the singer's comments. He claimed that Garden was currently overworked in her preparations for Strauss's *Salome*, which she had been rehearsing for the past month. He explained that the company had scheduled several performances of both *Salome* and *Pelleas et Mélisande* in New York and Philadelphia and that if Miss Garden was to maintain the physical stamina needed to complete these performances, it was considered expedient to substitute Cavalieri for some dates. Her first appearance as *Thaïs* was confirmed as being on January 30. Furthermore, Hammerstein announced that Maurice Renaud, Garden's usual costar in this opera, would appear in his accustomed role of Athanael, opposite Cavalieri.

Garden's darkly veiled threats, noted above, of "consequences" should Hammerstein persist with his plans, materialized in the *New York Times* the following morning. Garden had tendered her resignation. The text of her brief letter to Hammerstein was reprinted in full: "My Dear Mr. Hammerstein: On Monday afternoon, when you told me that you were to engage Mme. Cavalieri to sing *Thaïs*, I said to you that the day this announcement was advertised in the newspapers I would leave the Manhattan Opera House. This morning the published announcement appeared, and accordingly I hereby send you my resignation. Mary Garden."[88]

If Hammerstein had fabricated this friction simply in the hope of generating harmless publicity for his company, it seemed that his plan had badly misfired. Whatever he had hoped to gain from employing a rival star, the imminent departure of his established leading lady, who had contributed so much to both the artistic and financial success of the Manhattan Company, would surely not have been his aim. Thus he acted quickly in an attempt to resolve the situation, and the *New York Times* published his statement in answer to Garden's letter: "Miss Garden has ever been loyal and faithful to me. Our relations are of the most friendly character. If the occurrence has caused her anguish I deem it my duty to remove the cause."[89]

To further appease his disgruntled star, Hammerstein canceled Cavalieri's appearance in *Thaïs*, adding the announcement that Miss Garden would sing her accustomed role and would also appear in the scheduled premiere of *Salome* as advertised. Whether or not Garden had actually agreed to this settlement is not known. At the time of Hammerstein's statement she was said to be out of New York and therefore unable to comment. Superficially, it would seem that Hammerstein had recognized his defeat and capitulated quickly to prevent any further disruption. But the *Times* article suggests a much more manipulative character in operation. Hammerstein, after stating conciliatorially, that he had only "the kindest feelings toward Miss Garden," claimed that his engagement of Cavalieri had simply been an attempt to lighten Garden's work load.[90] "The fact that I engaged Miss Cavalieri for only six performances is ample proof that I did not mean to cast the slightest slur upon Miss Garden."[91] The next paragraph of his interview is, however, far more revealing of the character of this man who had forged a career for himself as one of the most enterprising impresarios of his era. He stated: "Even should Miss Garden persist in her present course I have laid plans whereby all crises may be met. Mlle. Labia and Miss Cavalieri are both rehearsing *Salome* and can sing the part if necessary, and I have even thought of cabling Mme Aino Ackté, who has made a great success in the opera in Europe. Mlle. Espinasse can sing *Louise*, so you see, not one woman, not even Miss Garden, is absolutely necessary to me."[92] This appeared to be a thinly veiled threat, and Hammerstein's plan now seemed clear. Although he was prepared to give way to Garden over the matter of *Thaïs*, he was not prepared to pay ransom to any "one woman." If Garden did not accept his concession, he would not only replace her not only as Thaïs but also as Louise and recast the forthcoming prestigious Strauss premiere.

On closer examination, it is relatively easy to dismiss Hammerstein's threats as empty gestures. It is hard to believe that he would seriously consider the comparatively light-voiced Cavalieri as possible casting for Salome. She is not recorded as having sung this or any other Strauss role during her career, and there is no indication that she had attended any rehearsals in New York. On the contrary, her brother had issued a statement that she was suffering from "a nervous attack that confined her to her bed."[93] It seems equally unlikely that Ackté would have been either willing or able to substitute in an entirely new production on less than a week's notice, even if it had been physically possible for her to travel from Europe to New York in the time available.

However implausible Hammerstein's contingency plan might seem under close examination, he possessed one "trump card," and he was perfectly prepared to make it publicly known. If threats of replacement would not impress the need upon Garden to comply with his requirements, perhaps legal constraints would. He added, almost as a postscript to his statement, "Of course Miss Garden has no right to resign from my company. I have a four-year contract with her, and if she breaks it I can hold her for damages even if I cannot compel her to sing."[94] This was clearly a serious threat of reprisal. The prospect of such a sensational event as that of New York's leading independent impresario suing his leading lady for breach of contract may have sent quite a ripple of expectation through the city's opera-going public, to say nothing of the anticipation it must have raised among the city's newspaper proprietors. Such stories made excellent headlines.

Garden's response was both speedy and unequivocal. She stated that she had consulted with her legal advisor, Samuel Untermyer, and responded with the following counterattack: "I can see no occasion for further discussion of the unpleasant subject-matter of our controversy.... You have violated both the letter and the spirit of our understanding.... I am advised that your action constitutes a distinct breach of my rights, entitling me to hold you for such damages as I may sustain. I shall say nothing at this time of my great disappointment at your extraordinary attitude or of the injustice you have sought to do me.... That you must settle with your own conscience. Whenever you are prepared to respect the rights that you agreed to accord me, and not sooner, I am ready to do my part ... but as I understand your attitude our contract relations have now been severed and I shall not again appear at the opera house until I receive proper assurances that you withdraw from your present attitude.[95]

Evidently, Garden chose a different interpretation of her contract and one that protected the exclusivity of her repertoire, and on this point, her lawyer was in agreement. An inevitable stalemate appears to have set in, with the threats of each party countered by the other. At this uncomfortable juncture the third and up to this time silent party joined the fray. From the relative security of her sickbed, Cavalieri issued a statement through her brother to say that she had been contracted by Hammerstein to sing four roles, and she was quite happy to comply with the terms of her contract. Thus far, Cavalieri had appeared purely compliant in this altercation, so that it might almost seem that she had unwittingly and innocently become a pawn in a burgeoning power struggle. However, further examination of her statement in the *Times* indicates that she was not to be an entirely passive adversary; her brother added, "She intends to appear in *Thaïs* ... whatever Miss Garden may say. Miss Garden's interpretation of the part is very fine, but it is not the only possible interpretation. My sister has another one that might also be interesting, and as she appeared in the part in Paris even before Miss Garden did, it is absurd for Miss Garden to object."[96]

Cavalieri's public bravado, however, was not matched by her private actions. the *New York Times* of January 22 published the text of a letter Cavalieri had sent the previous day to her new employer: "In view of the unexpected developments resulting from my brief engagement by you, I hasten to assure you that in no circumstances would I for one moment cause you the slightest embarrassment or give pain to a fellow artist. I beg therefore to ask you to omit *Thaïs* from the list of operas which you have asked me to sing.... Believe me very sincerely yours, Lina Cavalieri."[97] This letter provided Hammerstein with the perfect instrument with which to extricate himself from an awkward position without appearing to relinquish the privilege of management. With great good sense, he chose to use it, sending a copy of the letter to Garden that same night. In a cover letter he stated his "consent to you having the roles you created and will create in the repertoire of my operas exclusive during the existence of the contract between us."[98] Within a few hours, Garden's sister delivered a reply, the formal tones of which clearly indicate the guidance of a legal hand: "I hereby accept the modifications of our existing agreement set forth in your letter.... It is of course understood that *Salome* as well as any operas hereafter produced by you in any opera house or theatre under your management or in which you produce for the first time in this country, and in which I take part, are included in our present arrangement.... You are not to produce or permit the production of any such operas ... unless I sing and play the roles in such operas created by me. You are not to substitute any one in any role without my express consent."[99] In the acceptance of this letter, Hammerstein effectively ceded a substantial degree of casting control to Garden. He would make no substitution, and *Salome* was secured.

In a telephone interview given from her New York home Garden informed the readers of the *New York Times* that she and Hammerstein had restored their friendship. She confirmed that she would sing *Thaïs* the following night and that Cavalieri would perform her Italian roles as planned. She claimed that she had never objected to Cavalieri appearing in these roles and that she was very glad that the problem had been resolved. Miss Cavalieri, safely ensconced in the Savoy Hotel, claimed a continuing incapacity and declined to give an interview. The *New York Times* of January 23 published the following brief statement: "Lina Cavalieri, whose withdrawal from *Thaïs* yesterday served to heal the breach between Mr. Hammerstein and Miss Garden, will make her debut at the Manhattan Opera House in *Tosca* on Monday night. *Pelleas et Mélisande* was to have been the opera, but was withdrawn to give Miss Garden time for further rehearsals of *Salome*."[100] As Garden had said, everything had turned out well for everyone concerned.

Superficially, the greatest victory appears to have gone to Mary Garden, her supremacy reinstated, her repertoire assured for the foreseeable future, and all confirmed in the public forum of the nation's leading serious daily newspaper. Yet, although Hammerstein had been impelled to admit defeat and make several important concessions to his resident star, these were little more than her exclusive contract might already have provided for. She was a great draw and immensely popular and successful with New York audiences at this time, and the free publicity generated by this controversy would only serve to sell even more tickets.

It is worth asking why all parties in the dispute readily and regularly handed all of their correspondence to the press and happily furnished the *Times* with every apparent detail of their conflict. Without copy there could be no story, and who was better placed to supply the copy than the protagonists themselves? Due in greater part to her conciliatory offer of withdrawal, Lina Cavalieri emerged, quietly, as the most sympathetic and ethical party in the dispute. She could however afford to appear magnanimous. Giving up the prospect of two performances of *Thaïs* had very little significant effect on her American career, the foundations of which were already securely established. On the contrary, her willingness to sacrifice her Manhattan debut to preserve the feelings of a fellow artist might only serve to underline her characterization as the unfortunate third party drawn unknowingly into a contractual disagreement between star and producer.

Although Cavalieri subsequently appeared with the Manhattan company only in her delayed debut as *Tosca*, followed by *La Bohème*, she was to be amply rewarded

Top left: Cavalieri as Massenet's Thaïs (1907) (photograph by Reutlinger Studio, Paris). *Right*: Cavalieri as Salome in Massenet's *Herodiade* (from the collection of Svetlana Vlasova). Bottom: Cavalieri as Giulietta in Offenbach's *The Tale of Hoffman* (photograph by Davis and Eickmeier, New York, 1911).

for her peacemaking. Hammerstein contracted her for some thirty performances in New York and Philadelphia in the 1909–1910 season, and she was later accorded the privilege of opening the new season on November 9 as Salome in the American premiere of Massenet's *Herodiade*, presumably with the consent, or at least acquiescence, of Garden. The production featured Dalmores as John the Baptist, Renaud as Herod and Gerville-Reache as Herodias and marked the New York debut of the conductor Henriques de la Fuente.

TO-NIGHT, at 8 o'clock

HERODIADE

OPERA IN FOUR ACTS *(In French)*

Music by JULES MASSENET.

SALOME	Mlle. LINA CAVALIERI
HERODIAS	Mlle. D'ALVAREZ
HEROD	M. MAURICE RENAUD
A PROPHET	M. JEAN AUBER
VITELLIUS	M. ENZO BOZZANO
PHANUEL	M. HENRY WELDON
HIGH PRIEST	M. P. VERHEYDEN
A SLAVE	Mlle. DELVA
A VOICE	M. LEROUX

Stage Director, JACQUES COINI

Musical Conductor - Signor LUIGI CHERUBINI   Ballet Mistress - PAULINE VERHOEVEN

SYNOPSIS OF SCENERY.

Act I.   **A Court within the Palace of Herod**   Act III.—Scene I.   Home of Phanuel the Chaldean
Act II.—Scene I.   Herod's Chamber   Scene II.   Interior of the Temple. Before the Sanctuary
       Scene II.   Public Square in Jerusalem   Act IV.—Scene I.   A Dungeon.
                                                 Scene II.   Grand Hall in Herod's Palace

Correct Librettos for sale in the Lobby.   Photographs by ETIENNE, BERT, DESGRANGES, FÉLIX, SERENI, BUYLE and Mr. S. LEO.
The Weber has been chosen by the Management as the only Piano to be used in this Opera House.   Costumes designed by LANZILOTTI.   Wigs by CLARKSON.

Extract from the Rules made by the Lord Chamberlain. 1.—The name of the actual and responsible Manager of the Theatre must be printed on every playbill. 2.—The public can leave the Theatre at the end of the performance by all exit and entrance doors, which must open outwards. 3.—Where there is a fireproof screen to the proscenium opening it must be lowered at least once during every performance, to ensure its being in proper working order. 4.—Smoking is not permitted in the Auditorium. 5.—All gangways, passages and staircases must be kept free from chairs or any other obstructions, whether permanent or temporary.

London Opera House, program for Massenet's *Herodiade*.

Why Garden should change her mind so radically within the space of ten months is open to speculation. Could this have been a reciprocal gesture for Cavalieri's earlier capitulation? Garden was strongly established in the role of Thaïs, and would brook no rival interpretation, whereas Massenet's version of the Salome story had not previously been seen in New York, and the only possible comparison with Garden could be with Strauss's heroine, a very different characterization, a role to which Garden had already established her claim at the sensational Manhattan premiere on January 28, 1909.

In any event, Garden was very well represented in the company's early season performances. She sang Massenet's *Sapho* and *Le Jongleur de Notre-Dame* on tour in Philadelphia and then returned to New York for further performances of *Thaïs* and *Salome*. Her career continued with the Manhattan Opera until the company's demise in 1910, from which time she began to forge the connections with Chicago that were to dominate her work for so many of her later years on the operatic stage. Her creation of the starring role of Fanny in Massenet's *Sapho* for Hammerstein in November 1909 was not well received. The *Times* critic was moved to say that "for whatever reason, whether the part is unsympathetic to her or not, she has not given so unsympathetic a performance in New York before."[101] Her appearance in the title role of *Griselidis* in January of the following year brought forward Garden's "remarkable versatility and skill as an operatic actress ... an indefinable grace, an aloofness, an exquisite delicacy of touch that are fascinating ... a truly poetic imagination."[102]

Reutlinger Studio photograph, 1910.

This Manhattan production of *Herodiade* would mark Cavalieri's farewell to the opera stages of New York. A planned revival in the role scheduled for February 12, 1910, did not materialize. Cavalieri was taken ill at short notice, and the role of Salome was played by Mariette Mazarin, who earned herself the gratitude of Hammerstein by appearing as Strauss's Electra at the matinée and as Massenet's wayward heroine that same evening. Hammerstein was quoted in the *Times* as acknowledging "the most extraordinary tour de force of which I have ever been a witness."[103]

The short-lived but spectacular controversy revealed fascinating insights into the lives, careers and personalities of those involved and tells us much of the ability of the media, even in the first decade of the twentieth century, to recognize a story of public interest, establish a platform for that story to be told, and support it through to a satisfying conclusion. A good show-business story has always made good copy, and good copy sells not only newspapers, but also opera tickets.

Perhaps the most revealing comment of all on the events of January 1909 is to be found in the unpublished manuscript of Mary Garden's first autobiography. After describing how she won her battle with Hammerstein, she added, almost casually, "Now all New York was interested in our quarrel, and when I sang *Thaïs*, the house was sold out in 24 hours. I loved all this, and Hammerstein did too."[104] In the summer of 1911, Garden sang a series of performances as Strauss's Salome at the Paris Opera. Cavalieri was then in residence in her home at Ave. de Messine and hosted what Michael Turnbull has described as "an anti-Garden reception" on the night of Garden's first performance.[105] "In the most prominent place in the room was hung a painting of a giraffe. Fierce electric lights beat upon its long neck and some mischievous anti-Gardenite uttered the phrase, 'The American Thaïs.' The uproarious fun which followed this could not be halted for a long time. Then Cavalieri herself, clothed in white and wearing her $30,000 rope of pearls and with emeralds as big as hazelnuts in her ears, stood next to her cream and gold piano and sang snatches from Thaïs. Mary's counter-attack consisted, it was rumoured, in telling her friends that Lina Cavalieri ate a raw onion before retiring, so as to give her skin its creamy white colour."[106]

Having resolved the conflict over the casting of *Thaïs*, Cavalieri made her somewhat belated debut at the Manhattan Opera House on Thirty-fourth Street on January 25, 1909, as Puccini's Tosca. The first night's audience was much smaller than might have been anticipated under the circumstances, but the soprano received a very enthusiastic welcome occasioning a number of curtain calls. The *New York Times* noted that perhaps the audience's warm response was attributable rather to recognition of Cavalieri's personality and her honorable settlement of the *Thaïs* controversy than directly to appreciation of her singing. In reference to her previous tenure at the Met, the *Times* critic stated that "Her singing and her acting have undergone no change since then, though it may be that they are shown to a little better advantage in the smaller frame of the Manhattan. Her voice has little beauty of quality or expressive dramatic potency. Its lower tones are of small power or value, and the higher are often strident. She knows little of the finer art of singing, and her phrasing and delivery are crude. She sang effectively certain passages ... when they lay within her best range, and called for a powerful output of tone."[107]

The critic, in a surprisingly detailed assessment for this period, was moved additionally to remark on Cavalieri's acting of the role, with certain specific reservations: "She is, as she has always been on the operatic stage, fair to look upon, lithe, sinuous, and, till she is moved to the expression of strong passion or emotion, graceful. Such passion she denotes vehemently, but with a small range of gesture, frequently angular. Subtlety and suggestive power are not included in her dramatic equipment. There was a certain kind of main strength in her acting in the scene of the conflict and murder in the second act that made an impression on the audience."[108]

Musical America also emphasized the great enthusiasm with which the audience greeted Cavalieri: "The applause which greeted Cavalieri throughout the evening was tremendous, and the curtain calls with which the audience ... awarded her efforts should have delighted the prima donna."[109] The critic, however, noted similar shortcomings in Cavalieri's singing, suggesting that her voice was too small to fill the theater and that she did not entirely warrant the enthusiasm with which she was received. Her acting, however, apparently affected the audience deeply. An unintentionally humorous incident was also noted in the first act. "As Cavalieri sang a top note she rushed up a flight of steps which suddenly collapsed, and the singer, with a frightened look, landed on the stage—on her feet. It took some seconds, during which she continued singing, to extricate herself from the debris, while Zenatello giggled fortissimo."[110]

During the winter season, Cavalieri also made the pages of the *New York Times* for another reason. The paper announced that the singer was to move into business by opening a perfume shop on fashionable Fifth Avenue. Rather ungallantly, the paper suggested that one principal reason for this change was that her "beauty [was] waning and her voice lacking its old-time power."[111] In August 1908, however, the *New York Times* had announced that Cavalieri had been contracted by J. Saunders

Gordon to undertake an extensive concert tour of the United States and Mexico in the autumn. A further reason was said to be the collapse of this tour; Cavalieri apparently explained that "the funds which had been promised did not materialise, and that although she had no intention of quitting the stage, nevertheless, as she was alone, with no one to back her, she would for the present go in business for herself."[112] Elsewhere, it was suggested that Cavalieri had opened the business for her brother's benefit: "She is an affectionate sister, and she wanted her brother to get on in his own career and make money as she did."[113] The salon was guaranteed an extensive and exclusive clientele. It was set up "to see cosmetics made in her own laboratory, based on the secrets of Catherine de Medici, whose art Lina had discovered in an ancient volume in Messina. On the day of the shop's opening Lina ... received customers in a Pacquin gown covered with a Worth apron. A pink hair ribbon held her own black curls in place as she politely conversed with the first customer, Emma Calvé."[114]

Cavalieri sang relatively few performances with the Manhattan Company in her first season: She followed her house debut with two performances at the Philadelphia Opera House with the company on tour: *Faust* with Florencio Constantino, and a second *Tosca*, again with Zenatello, and with Maurice Renaud as Scarpia. A further *Faust* in Philadelphia and two performances of *La Bohème* in Manhattan, once again with Constantino, composed her entire season.

Her first Mimi with the company, delivered at a matinee on February 6 was generally well received, the critic of *Music America* noting that "The splendid acoustics came gallantly to the rescue of Cavalieri ... and her singing would have pleased even Puccini."[115] Of this same performance, the critic of *Variety* noted, "The one and only woman I have seen in grand opera who appears human is Mme. Cavalieri."[116] It was the passion of her physical realization of character that caught the imagination of critics and public alike, and increasingly, it seemed, Cavalieri was supplementing her limited vocal powers, with ever more colorful acting. The bass Andres de Segurola, who had become a close friend, remembered the impact she had on the audience in a characteristically sensational appearance as Tosca: "The appearance of the soprano on stage was greeted with an outburst of applause. She looked radiant in her Empire costume. Diamonds and pearls were the jewels on her person.... When [she] entered Baron Scarpia's room in the second act of the opera, wearing a long cape of snow-white Caucasian ermine, artistically wrapped around her body from neck to feet, Lina/Tosca remained for a few moments, motionless against the frame of the door. And in a graceful motion she artfully let the cloak slip onto a nearby chair, and the three thousand persons in the audience saw that vision of glowing white satin and luscious flesh, topped by the deep green emeralds of her tiara, necklace and brooch ... a wave of exclamations and gasps roared through the house from the parquet to the roof, completely over-riding the orchestra."[117]

Rodolfo Celletti also noted Cavalieri's ability to use her physical acting and sensational stage presence to supplement any vocal shortcomings: "She especially liked some operas such as *Fedora, Tosca* and *Adriana*, that were strictly lyrical, but that attracted her as they allowed her to show her 'physique du role,' sumptuous hair styles and beautiful jewels. Despite her humble origins, she looked and behaved like a lady, and only a few prima donna were able to wear the mantle of Fedora with her grace. The grace and elegance of her performance on stage greatly helped her.... When she was also sensual and coquettish, as in Thaïs ... the effect was remarkable. Another factor ... was the expressive nature of her physique, particularly her big luminous eyes that at times were more expressive than her voice. As a performer, however, she was not capable of extraordinary performances."[118]

At the end of February 1909 Cavalieri sailed to Europe aboard the liner *La Provence* to fulfil engagements in St. Petersburg. She made a stopover in Paris, where she caused much speculation with rumors that she was about to wed an American millionaire. The *New York Times* reported that, while in the French capital, "she left a resplendent trail in the Rue de la Paix buying new gowns and new Thaïs costumes."[119] In the interview contained in this report, Cavalieri told of her future plans: "it is true that Oscar Hammerstein has engaged me for five more seasons, and I shall sing many new parts—just what won't be decided until Mr. Hammerstein comes to Paris—but many new ones, that is certain. I love Mr. Hammerstein and I'm in my proper place at the Manhattan Opera House. It is the only place for me to sing in New York. It is a theatre where the audience is thoroughly *en rapport* with the stage."[120]

In January 1909, the Russian press had announced a charity performance for victims of the earthquakes in Sicily. It had been intended to stage Gounod's *Faust* at the Maryinsky, with Chaliapin as Mephistopheles, Sobinov as Faust, Battistini as Valentine and Cavalieri as Marguerite. Unfortunately this performance did not take place. Presumably it was impossible to assemble the cast; Cavalieri at least was still in New York at this time. The Italian opera season would be the fifteenth under the direction of Carlo Guidi and would run from mid-February for two months, with a company to include Sembrich, Arnoldson, Boronat, Anselmi and Battistini. Cavalieri would be seen in *Thaïs*, *Manon*, *La Traviata*, *La Bohème* and *Tosca*, and Mathilda Kshessinskaya would perform the role of the dumb girl in an opera called *Fenella* [*The Dumb Girl of Portici*].

Cavalieri made her first appearance at the Conservatoire Theatre as Thaïs on March 7. Once again, the critics did not respond to the music with any great enthusiasm, and *The Exchange Journal* published the following assessment of the leading role: "It seemed impossible for Cavalieri to be yet more beautiful, but it is so.... Her voice is the same as before. Some high notes are even voiceless, but the next sound suddenly strikes home by its brilliance. She was accorded a rousing welcome.... It seemed that the greatest success happened during the entr'actes when Cavalieri took numerous curtain calls. Her face had lost the preoccupied expression and she was smiling joyfully and amiably."[121] All seats for this performance had been sold, and the audience had come for the express purpose of seeing Cavalieri again. Evidently, they were not disappointed: "Mme Cavalieri interprets the Thaïs character very well. This first meeting of the queen of love with Athanael, her love scenes with him, her deploration [*sic*], her decision to seclude herself from society and her death ... all is very beautifully performed. She encored her duet with Mr Battistini in the third act. As a result there were many flowers and a remarkable success."[122] Battistini's performance was singled out for special acknowledgement, described as "incomparable

... beyond all praise."[123] Cavalieri's second appearance, as Violetta, with Battistini and Pintucci, brought about a very favorable comparison with Olympia Boronat, who had recently been heard in the role in St. Petersburg. The critic of *The Petersburg Leaflet* considered that Cavalieri's acting of the role was stronger than Boronat's and that her singing was equally successful.

On March 12, the Maly Theatre celebrated the fiftieth anniversary of their director, Alexis Suvorin, equally distinguished as a writer, dramatist, publisher and theater entrepreneur. The celebration, held on the stage of the Maly, included scenes from two of Surovin's most successful plays. Kshessinskaya and Pavlova both danced, and Cavalieri performed some popular Neapolitan songs and romances and presented the welcoming address. The evening ended with a tableau vivant: "Lina Cavalieri, with a flaming torch, represented the genius of universal art and knowledge holding the torch of learning, progress and liberty. She was like a symbol of talent and energy illuminating the way for others. The picture provoked a storm of applause and the show ended at midnight."[124] At the end of the performance, the celebrations moved on to the Medved restaurant, where more than 500 guests, including Cavalieri and Kshessinskaya, enjoyed a lavish feast.

In early March, there was a ten-day break in the season, during which Cavalieri's presence was noted at a number of important social occasions. Perhaps the most significant of these was a benefit concert held at the French embassy, attended by all of the leading members of St. Petersburg society, at which Cavalieri joined a group of performers which included the ballerina Karsarvina and the singer Rosalia Lambrecht and performed Neapolitan songs accompanied by the guitarist Amici. Prior to the actual performance, Cavalieri sold glasses of champagne for charity in the foyer and was mobbed by an enthusiastic crowd of eager young male admirers. She was generally considered to be the most sensational success of the evening. During this "dark" period, the company began rehearsals for a new production of *Tosca*, with Cavalieri in the title role, joined by Nani as Scarpia and Silvano Isalberti making his St. Petersburg debut as Cavaradossi.

When performances resumed, Cavalieri appeared in her now familiar guise as Massenet's *Manon*, partnered with Fernando Carpi, making his debut with the company. The soprano was certainly the center of interest in this production: "The talented actress executed her part successfully and they cheered her loudly demanding endless encores."[125] *The Speech* recorded: "Her plasticity is amazing, some dramatic moments are perfect and the scene with des Grieux in the convent is breathtaking. Her few vocal faults pale beside her wonderful artistry."[126] On March 31, all members of the company took part in a gala concert to celebrate the fifteenth anniversary season of their employer, Carlo Guidi. Guidi had staged his first St. Petersburg season at the Aquarium in 1894 and two years later had moved to the Conservatoire. In partnership with Antonio Ughetti and Nikolai Kuznetsov, Guidi had enjoyed a remarkable run of success, introducing many important works and performers, including Caruso, to the St. Petersburg audience. The three leading prima donnas of his company, Boronat, Lipkovskaya and Cavalieri, all took part in the concert, and Cavalieri read a specially composed jubilee testimonial. The new production of *Tosca* opened on April 1, and although Nani was said to be in poor voice, the debutant

Isalberti was very well received. Cavalieri's Tosca was described as "absolutely one of her best roles," and a capacity audience, fuelled with news of her success in the part at the Metropolitan, flocked to hear her sing it in St. Petersburg for the first time.[127] The critic of *The Speech* considered that she was quite equal to the challenge: "Her dramatic talent captivates with its lucidity.... Her expression is so strong that sometimes it appeared to hamper her singing.... Her power of expression is exceptional."[128] Even though certain vocal weaknesses were noted, the critic stated that "the essential Cavalieri is in creating the dramatic character."[129]

On the following day, the benefit performance for Cavalieri which had been scheduled, was canceled, as the singer was experiencing throat problems. She did however make an appearance at a charity concert in aid of the poor, held at the residence of Drachevski, governor of St. Petersburg, which was attended by many prominent society figures and members of the diplomatic corps.

Her engagement completed, Cavalieri prepared to return to Paris, while the press speculated over the next development in her career. *The Theatre Review* suggested that she had recently signed a three year contract to sing exclusively in America; while *The Footlights and Life* published a story that a Moscow millionaire and patron of the arts was planning an international celebrity season which would feature Cavalieri along with many other important singers, including Caruso and Ruffo. During the summer she sang a handful of performances of *Thaïs* at the Paris Opera but otherwise spent her time attending numerous society events, including the opening of the Chatelet theater season and several charity concerts. In May, a rumor was

29 - PARIS   *L'Opéra*   L'H. — Paris.

The Paris Opera

spread that Cavalieri was about to marry a wealthy Italian industrialist, but there appears to have been no truth in the story. There was also press speculation on her health and general lifestyle. One newspaper reported that during her winter season in St. Petersburg she had always slept with the window open and never caught a cold. *The Petersburg Newspaper* began publishing Cavalieri's tips for health and beauty and reminded its readers that her postcard photographs were still the best and fastest selling of all subjects then available.

As prominent as ever in the public's eye and interest, Lina Cavalieri arrived back in New York aboard the liner *Kronprinz Wilhelm* on October 26, 1909, complaining to a correspondent from the *New York Times* that the crossing had made her so ill that she had been unable to leave her cabin for the entire voyage. Fashionably dressed, as always, in a sealskin coat and matching hat, she told the *New York Times* reporter: "I am very glad to get back to New York, and hope to satisfy my ambition this winter by singing the role of Carmen, which I have been studying.... I am going to sing Salome in *Herodiade* by Massenet for the first time in this country. In the first act I dress as a Hebrew maiden and in the second as a dancer."[130] Of her recent performances in Paris, she was quick to relate her great success: "I sang Thaïs five times. It was only scheduled for two performances, but the demand for seats was so great that the Directors decided to give three more performances."[131] The *New York Times* stated that Cavalieri would also sing Strauss's *Feuersnot* and Offenbach's *La Belle Hélène*, and in an interview with a reporter from *The New York Sun* she confirmed that she would be adding these new roles to her repertoire at the Manhattan.

The day following the publication of this interview, Oscar Hammerstein announced his plans for the new Manhattan season. His leading lady, Mary Garden, would appear in two Massenet operas, a revival of the highly successful *Thaïs* and the New York premiere of *Sapho*, while Cavalieri would open the season on November 8 with the American premiere of another work by that French composer, *Herodiade*. Additionally, Hammerstein announced that Tetrazzini would return to the Manhattan in Verdi's *La Traviata*, singing opposite the Irish tenor John McCormack, who would make his American debut as Alfredo. Other highlights were to include the American debut of Mariette Mazarin in *Aïda*, Tetrazzini and McCormack paired again in *Lucia* and *Daughter of the Regiment*, and Cavalieri as Nedda in *Pagliacci*, accompanied by Zenatello and Sammarco.

The opening of the Manhattan Opera season gave New York the opportunity of witnessing Cavalieri in a highly colorful role, Salome in Massenet's *Herodiade*. This new assumption was greeted with a mixed reception: Some were full of praise, "dramatic force, and splendid vocal accomplishment"[132]; others expressed largely the same doubts that had accompanied virtually all of her performances in New York: "lean and lissom in form and uncommonly attractive.... Her singing, while much better than last year, still inclines to explosiveness and to undue sforzando endings

Cavalieri in the title role of Massenet's *Thaïs*, the role for which she became most famous. (1909, Paris, photograph by A Bert, from the collections of the author and Svetlana Vlasova).

of every phrase."[133] The opening night was a major social occasion and drew a glittering New York audience, in spite of heavy rain which caused such congestion outside of the theater that the start of the performance was delayed. Mary Garden occupied an upper box, resplendent in a pure white chiffon gown and carrying an extravagant fan of osprey feathers, presumably intending to assess any new threat from her possible rival. *Musical America*, evaluating what they described as a "brilliant performance,"[134] proceeded to describe the work on offer as "no educational opera—it was the real thing; a gorgeous entertainment for luxurious and frivolous society, or a serious presentation of an art work, according as one chose to view it."[135]

Although Cavalieri's role was recognized as being absolutely central to the opera, her ability to do justice to such a role was, once again, brought into question: "As an oriental princess she presented an attractive figure to the eye, slender, with a mass of red hair. Her Salome was girlish both dramatically and vocally. Her tones were clear and sweet. Only on a few occasions did she make the effort to produce a note worthy of carrying power. Instead of producing her greatest effects with 'Il est doux' in the first act, as is customary in this opera, Mlle. Cavalieri was much more effective vocally in several later scenes."[136] The *New York Times* review was even more precise and included an unflattering comparison: "Miss Cavalieri, who sang the part of Salome, has gained something in the beauty and quality of her voice since she sang here last, and perhaps even something in her skill in vocalization. In both respects there was evidence of an intelligent effort at improvement. She has still much to learn as to acting, her bodily contortions expressive of Salome's trials, griefs, longings, supplications were not only excessive but also awkward. There was indeed room to suspect that she was trying to model her impersonation on the Salome of Miss Garden—an attempt that the total differences in the two characters foredoomed to failure, if nothing else did."[137]

Her *Carmen*, with Zenatello and Dufranne, which followed the Massenet performances on November 25, was generally well received, though many observers felt that her interpretation lacked real fire and that the part actually lay far too low for her voice. *Musical America* suggested that it was unlikely to become among her best roles, "but, nevertheless her performance of it possesses many superficial attractions at least. It is not a subtly seductive and heartlessly wicked Carmen that she suggests, but a beautiful romping girl out for a lark."[138] The suggestion was clear that her performance lacked the prerequisite passion: "There was more of naughtiness than devilry in it; too much of the lady and too little of the animal."[139] The critic proceeded to praise her appearance in the role and gave special mention to her dancing, particularly in the second act. The problem, however, remained in the singing: "She did not sing so well as she does in *Herodiade*. Much of the music ... is too low for her voice, and she was not in her best voice, even in the upper register."[140]

This was the first time that Cavalieri had undertaken performing the whole of Bizet's heroine on stage, having avoided it on several previous occasions, and, in view of the fact that she had already refused to sing it for Zimine in Moscow, it seems likely that she had already decided that this was too taxing a role. However, every prima donna of the period seemed eager to undertake the role, and she performed

it on five further occasions during this New York season and included it in the repertoire for her next St. Petersburg engagement.

On Christmas night, she performed the role of Giulietta in Offenbach's *The Tales of Hoffmann*. *Musical America* stated that her performance was a marked improvement over previous incumbents of the role, "both in the matter of voice and action. She sang the Barcarolle with taste and feeling.... She was extremely hand-some and sang better than she has many times before."[141] The *New York Times* agreed and provided a sympathetic assessment of her appearance: "Miss Cavalieri made a very beautiful picture as Giulietta, the Italian courtesan, and wore more jewels than she has ever been blazoned with on local stages before. There was a gasp of aston-ishment from the audience when the rising curtain disclosed her. She was a distinct improvement over her predecessors in this part, both vocally and dramatically. She did some of the best singing which she has given to this public since her recent and evidently sincere attempt to learn more about the artistic side of voice produc-tion."[142]

Just as it seemed as though Lina Cavalieri was becoming truly reestablished as a significant figure in the operatic life of New York—*Musical America* noted that she was among the busiest of Hammerstein's stars and that "She sang to immense audi-ences on each occasion"—an extraordinary event occurred which, while causing a fracture in her musical career, nevertheless boosted her salability as a celebrity almost beyond price: her engagement to Robert Winthrop Chanler, a painter of murals, who was, far more significantly, also the grandson of John Jacob Astor, one of the wealthiest men in America.[143] The death of Prince Bariatinsky had been announced early in March, and, even though Cavalieri no longer had any claims upon him, per-haps this final parting gave her the freedom she needed to enter into the Chanler engagement.

The Chanler family was certainly unlike the majority of their more celebrated relatives. In his history of the Astor family, Harvey O'Connor wrote the following description: "Whether writing sonnets in an insane asylum, circling Kilimanjaro, running guns to the Cuban rebels, sponsoring Bahaism, or painting with aluminium and gold leaf, this family ... showed the only touch of genius in the Astorian strain since the Founder."[144] John Winthrop Chanler, a young lawyer and aspiring politi-cian from a South Carolina family, had married Margaret Astor Ward in 1861. Chan-ler later rose to be a Democratic party congressman and died in 1877, leaving a fortune estimated at $3 million. The marriage had produced eight children, the sev-enth of whom, Robert Winthrop Chanler, was born in 1872. The Chanler children indulged in an extraordinary range of pursuits and unconventional lifestyles. The eldest son, John Armstrong Chanler, educated at Columbia and trained as a lawyer, caused a sensation among polite society when, at the age of twenty-six, he married the young Virginia novelist Amelie Rives, author of the notorious and daringly explicit romantic novel *The Quick and the Dead*. Prior to his marriage, John Arm-strong had lived with cowboys in New Mexico and accompanied General Crook on his expedition to the Apache nation; now he faced an even more daunting prospect, that of becoming the spouse of a celebrated and notorious author. This role did not appeal to him, and the couple parted two years later and was subsequently divorced.

John Armstrong settled in Virginia, but his behavior became ever more erratic, and his already volatile personality appeared to be becoming ever more violent in nature. He became obsessed with Buddhism and seemed to believe that he possessed unusual psychic powers. After a series of heated arguments, many involving other members of the Chanler family, John Armstrong was judged insane and sent to Bloomingdale Asylum as a private patient. In 1900 he absented himself from the institution, later presenting himself as a voluntary patient in Philadelphia and obtaining certification from the courts which confirmed his sanity. He returned to live in Virginia, where he removed himself even further from the mainstream of his family by abandoning their name and adopting the name Chaloner. In 1909 he shot dead one John Gillard but avoided arrest on the grounds of justifiable homicide as he claimed that he had been protecting the drunken Gillard's wife from her husband's fierce temper at the time.

The second Chanler sibling, Winthrop Astor, educated at Eton and Harvard, also caused a major stir in the Astor clan by marrying a Catholic, Margaret Terry, in 1886. His younger brother, William Astor, who was four years his junior, joined Winthrop in a gun-running expedition to Cuba during the Spanish-American War, in which Winthrop was wounded and later created a colonel in the Cuban army in recognition of his bravery. Colonel Winthrop Astor Chanler then took to a life of hunting in Europe, while William Astor undertook an extensive expedition to explore Kilimanjaro and later staged and led the most ambitious expedition yet to explore that region of Africa. After a short period in Congress, which evidently he did not enjoy, William Astor surprised his family again by marrying an actress, Minnie Ashley, leading lady of a number of highly successful musical comedies and a divorcée. The fifth Chanler sibling, Lewis Stuyvesant, became involved in the Fenian movement in Ireland before returning to a political career in America. He was elected to the office of lieutenant governor in 1906, but on failing to win the governorship in 1908 he retired from politics and dabbled for a time in the law. Influenced by the pacifist beliefs of his wife, Julia, Lewis became a prominent supporter of the Bahai movement and a promoter of world peace and international union.

Against such extraordinarily colorful competition, John Winthrop Chanler's seventh child and youngest son, Robert Winthrop might not have been expected to shine. His early artistic leanings led him to study in Paris, where he met and married his first wife, Julia Chamberlain. His talents were recognized by his sister-in-law, Amelie Rives, who recommended a career as a painter. Bob Chanler was divorced in 1901, bought an estate near the family home at Rokeby and became involved in local politics, being elected sheriff of Dutchess County. He became a prominent local figure and a respected member of the community, but the security of a New York state society lifestyle could not hold him for long, and he returned to the glamor of Paris, where he was to meet Cavalieri and enter into the notoriously brief marriage.

In 1909, Cavalieri had been named in a divorce suit involving a member of the Vanderbilt family, and the prospect of her marrying into the Astor family caused many raised eyebrows and considerable consternation among the powerful and wealthy families who dominated the great Four Hundred of New York society. This was subsequently to seriously affect the further progress of Cavalieri's New York stage career: Although it seems obvious that the Chanler affair prevented the Metropolitan Opera from featuring Cavalieri again in their New York season, presumably for fear of offending their many wealthy patrons who had business and family connections with the Astors, they were quite happy to consider engaging her services for touring productions. Prior to the Chanler scandal, Cavalieri's exotic persona and colorful reputation were acting as an obvious bonus to the publicity-hungry opera managers, not only in New York, but also throughout the opera-going world. As Quaintance Eaton wrote: "Her beauty still stirs the senses even from ageing photographs. As a living presence, she dominated the early century, trailing Russian princes in her wake."[145]

In order perhaps to find a little breathing space, Cavalieri absented herself from this controversy and on May 3 arrived in St. Petersburg from Paris to fulfil a short engagement with Guidi's company at the Conservatoire Theatre. On the day of her arrival, *The Exchange Gazette* published an interview with the singer. Apparently, a week earlier she had sent a telegram to Guidi saying that she would not be able to make the trip because of her impending marriage. She did however arrive and in the middle of an unaccustomed heat wave: "Oh yes, I am getting married.... My intended husband is Robert W. Chanler, a fabulously rich man and relative of the billionaire Astors. He is 37 years old, he likes art very much, and he is a good painter himself. Before our betrothal he insisted on including in the marriage settlement his obligation to pay to me 100,000 [*sic*] annually, even in the case of a divorce."[146] She went on to assure the interviewer that she would not abandon her stage career as a result of her marriage but that she would avoid engagements during the summer so that they could have this time together. She also talked of a three-month contract to sing in Buenos Aires, although it appears that this engagement did not materialize.

НОВЫЙ СПУТНИКЪ ЖИЗНИ ЛИНЫ КАВАЛЬЕРИ.

Лина Кавальери и ея второй мужъ Чандлеръ, котораго она выдаетъ за американскаго милліонера.

A newspaper photograph showing the newlywed Cavalieri and Robert Winthrop Chanler.

On this visit, Cavalieri sang only four performances. "Next week … I will take my farewell of the Petersburg audience and for a long time…. I do not know when my husband will let me come to Russia again."[147] This constraint appears to have been true; *The Theatre Review* reported that Cavalieri had been offered an engagement in Moscow to follow her St. Petersburg visit, but she had declined on the basis that she did not have enough time. Following her first performance as Thaïs, Koptiayev, in *The Exchange Gazette*, commented on her seemingly ageless appearance: "For a beautiful woman, Cavalieri sings too well. Or, on the contrary, for a good singer she is too beautiful … she is so many years older than she looks. And Cavalieri looks twenty-ish … Even younger."[148] The critic of *The Petersburg Leaflet* noted the large and appreciative audience that greeted the singer's return and suggested that she made great efforts to ensure a good performance: "As to her singing and her dramatic playing, they lost some of their former shortcomings…. As before, her middle register is distinguished by weakness of sonority. Of course, Mme Cavalieri is far from being a first-class singer, but she is able to give a good account of herself … [and] undoubtedly represents an artist of the first water. It is evident that she works hard constantly and conscientiously…. She is not resting on her laurels."[149]

The second performance of *Thaïs* on May 6 was canceled as Cavalieri was reported to be suffering from suspected appendicitis, a condition which would later be the cause of further professional difficulties. At about seven o'clock she had complained of severe pain in her right side, and a doctor had been called. The doctor diagnosed an attack of appendicitis and suggested than an operation might be necessary. It was impossible for Cavalieri to appear, and the management decided to substitute with a performance of *The Demon* and sent for Mme. Finzi-Magrini, who was singing the role of Tamara. The singer, however, had gone out for the evening, and a search across the city failed to locate her. Eventually the performance, which had been sold out, had to be abandoned completely, and tickets were refunded. Matters had improved considerably by the following day, and Cavalieri was able to appear, for the first time in St. Petersburg, in *Carmen*. Perhaps mindful of the critical response that greeted her in this role in New York only three months earlier, Cavalieri had agreed to a single performance only of the Bizet opera. The Petersburg press reacted in a very similar fashion to their American counterparts. Her performance was described as exaggerated, and it was suggested that she did not really understand the character or have the vocal resources in her lower register to perform the music. The *Petersburg Newspaper* went so far as to suggest that Cavalieri had feigned her illness on the previous day in order to conserve her energy to tackle the far more demanding role of Carmen. The critic concluded that if this was indeed the case, she had wasted her efforts, as she was entirely unsuited to the role: "Mme Cavalieri has some nice high notes but her middle register sounds not nearly so good. And this vocal part is for a real mezzo-soprano with a strong voice."[150] The *Exchange Gazette* noted exactly the same shortcomings, reaching the conclusion that "as a tragic Carmen, she is powerless."[151] The reviewer for *The New Time* added, philosophically, "Every artist has his limits and it is outside the confines of every possibility to transcend them."[152] A final performance of *Thaïs* on May 11 concluded this brief engagement, and Cavalieri left St. Petersburg, returning to her Paris home via a short stay in London. While there she suffered further health problems, probably occasioned by the condition of her appendix. In May it had been announced that Cavalieri would sing the title role in the French premiere of Pucini's *Manon Lescaut*, with Caruso again as Des Grieux and Pasquale Amato as Lescaut, in a production to be conducted by Toscanini. In deference to Massenet's version of the Manon story, the Puccini work had had to wait seventeen years for a Parisian hearing.[153] Now the Metropolitan, on tour at the Chatelet theater, would provide audiences with the delightful spectacle of reprising Cavalieri in the role. The month-long visit by the company was also to include Destinn in *Aïda*, Scotti as Falstaff, and Slezak and Alda in *Otello*. But Paris, though captivated by the prospect of this delayed introduction to Puccini's work, was deprived of hearing Cavalieri in this, one of her most significant roles. "Shortly after the company arrived, Cavalieri became ill—it was rumoured that all was not well with her appendix but that she preferred to avoid an operation than scar her beautiful skin."[154] It was suggested in some quarters that Cavalieri was feigning illness in order to buy time in which to settle matters with her insistent suitor, Robert Chanler. This seems unlikely, since the Puccini premiere was a highly important event and might reasonably be seen as keeping her options open for further engagements at the Met. The question of her health was finally resolved in July, however, when she underwent an operation at her Paris home in the Avenue de Messine to remove her appendix. This somewhat undermines the comment made by Alexander Smallens that "if she awoke with a wrinkle, she stayed in bed."[155] On the recommendation of Andres de Segurola, who was singing Ramfis and Ludovico with the company, the young Lucrezia Bori was brought in at short notice to replace the ailing Cavalieri and made such an impact in the role that two extra performances were added to the schedule, and she was immediately offered a contract to repeat her assumption of Manon in New York in 1912.

Chanler had pursued Cavalieri to Paris, and they were finally married there in a civil ceremony on June 18, 1910. The morning ceremony had been arranged quietly to deter would-be gatecrashers. The guests included a few close friends, Chanler's lawyer, Cavalieri's brother and her friend Edmond Risella, who both acted as witnesses. Only three journalists had been permitted to attend; however, news of the wedding had leaked out, and an English press photographer succeeded in taking a photo of the newlyweds as they left the mayor's office. News of the marriage created much interest, especially in St. Petersburg, where Cavalieri had always enjoyed her greatest popularity. One newspaper reported that Battistini, who had often partnered with Cavalieri in the Russian capital, was so shocked by the news that he had gone into complete seclusion in his castle outside of Madrid. Cavalieri's name had often been romantically linked with the great baritone, and many stories had suggested that they might themselves marry. The next development in the Chanler affair was to cause an even greater sensation however. Cavalieri shared a marital home for only a week with her new husband. Their legal marriage lasted barely three months, and in September they were separated.[156]

Cavalieri was to later claim that she and Chanler agreed to stay married for only one week, as a wager. Whatever Chanler might have hoped to gain from such an arrangement, the considerable financial inducements for Cavalieri were clear: "He gave me all he had as a present: Jewels, works of art, money. I did not want to buy a new house because I was sure our relationship would have lasted only a week, so he came to live in my house. According to his plans, we would have left for New York after a few days, where I would have seen the three mansions I had acquired and visited the ranch in the West, another present he had made me."[157]

In his history of the Astor family, Harvey O'Connor described a relationship in which he suggested that Cavalieri shamelessly exploited Chanler's infatuation: "For 'one week of joy and terror' he lived with Lina, who demanded he sign over his entire fortune to her.... When he asked for pocket money she told him to 'work for your living like other American husbands.' A friend lent him fare to escape to America, where to his relief he found that his trustees—his older brothers—refused to recognize his deed of gift to Lina."[158]

In September 1910, when the scandal of the broken marriage was at its height, the *New York Times* published the entire text of the prenuptial agreement that Chanler and Cavalieri has signed in Paris.

Published under the front-page headline, "Chanler gave up all to wed Cavalieri," the document lists all of the property signed over to Cavalieri, which included three farms with approximately 350 acres of land in Dutchess County and a lengthy list of New York properties on Ninth Avenue, Tenth Avenue, and West Fifty-Fifth Street. The agreement, dated May 31, 1910, was witnessed by Hanson Coxe, United States deputy consul general in Paris.[159]

Some reports suggested that Chanler had made a settlement of $20,000 on Cavalieri; others said $30,000 or even $50,000. When he returned to New York in September 1910, however, Chanler refused to discuss his broken marriage with the press, which only served to fuel further speculation, which was to last for many months. The Russian Prince Dolgorouki was named as Cavalieri's lover, and many press sources hinted that this was possibly the real cause of the separation. The matter of Cavalieri's personal and public morality also became a subject of some debate. So heated did the controversy become that, in November, Cavalieri announced that she would not return from her European retreat for at least a further six months. She canceled an engagement to sing with the Boston Opera and was reported in *Variety* as discussing a contract with Alfred Butt to appear for a month at the Palace Theatre in London.

In December, the *New York Times* published a short article in which Cavalieri was interviewed in Rome, complaining of "'exaggeration of the press and the malicious insinuations' of journalists in regard to her personal and private affairs."[160] Stating that she planned to spend the Christmas season in Rome with her son and that she hoped to be engaged to appear in the city as part of the forthcoming celebrations of the proclamation of Rome as capital of a united Italy, Cavalieri also stated that she hoped she would be "better able to explain by word of mouth how badly she has been treated and how she has been deceived."[161] Although separated, however, Chanler and Cavalieri remained legally married. Early in April 1911, Cavalieri gave an extensive interview to the American press in which she spoke at length of her feelings on divorce and upon whose head the blame should fall. Her account suggests a very different relationship from the one widely portrayed: "A divorce ... may be the outcome, but, although I have decided to have it in Paris, I don't quite know yet on what grounds—perhaps desertion, perhaps incompatibility of temperament; either would fit the case perfectly. I have never revealed it before, but the responsibility for all the actions for which I have been blamed here and in America rests entirely on my husband. It was actually by his specific order that I went to the opera with him, parading all my most valuable jewels, and on one occasion he went so far as to appeal to his marital authority to oblige me to give a dinner party at which the guests of honour were my former suitors—Constant, Say and Prince Dolgorouki. It was then his fixed idea to defy the opinion of the world, because he boasted that he had settled on me an amount of money equal to all my property."[162]

Furthermore, Cavalieri blamed her estranged husband for her own current financial difficulties. She stated that the Chanler family had demanded that she renounce the marriage settlement that had been agreed upon and that the psychological pressure of the breakup had caused a nervous breakdown which had caused her to cancel several engagements at a loss of $30,000. "Whatever I can realise from Mr. Chanler's property will go toward compensating me for that and refunding me the money I actually spent out of my own pocket for the wedding and so forth. Mr Chanler never contributed a cent toward the household expenses either."[163] Perhaps understandably, Cavalieri seemed very reluctant to relax her overwhelming legal claim on the Chanler estate. In September, Chanler's lawyer, Sidney Harris, traveled to Paris to make what was described as "a final offer of $70,000 cash in exchange for full renunciation of the marriage settlement on the part of Cavalieri and her consent to a divorce."[164] She also stated decisively that "There is absolutely no hope for them to make me back down.... I see no reason why I should bargain for a thing that is absolutely legally mine.... As for a divorce, I am in no hurry to get it, as I do not contemplate re-marrying. My first experience was unpleasant enough."[165] By December, however, Cavalieri's position had changed. The *New York Times* announced that she had agreed to annul the premarital agreement for a settlement of $80,000, which Chanler had raised by mortgaging most of his New York property. Furthermore, it was suggested that as the principal financial barrier had now been removed, the couple might be expected to conclude a divorce within three or four months. Significantly, although it might seem that Cavalieri's reluctance to settle this matter could be interpreted as pure greed on her part, the *New York Times* reminded its readers that, in fact, under the terms of the original agreement, Cavalieri would have been entitled to an annual payment of $20,000 generated from the income from certain trust estates of which Chanler was the beneficiary. She had now settled for very much less.[166]

The finale of this troubled story was reached earlier than had been expected. On January 3, 1912, Cavalieri was granted a divorce by the First Chamber of the Tribunal of the Seine in Paris. Cavalieri's lawyer, Albert Clemenceau, was present in court to hear the judgement, but Chanler was not represented. The presiding magistrate's judgement caused some amusement: "Considering that Mr Chanler replied to a formal demand for the restitution of conjugal rights by a positive refusal; considering that he formulated such refusal in the words 'that he had had enough of it, that he had built a new existence for himself, and that in case his wife succeeded in entering the door he would jump out of the window'; considering that he repeated such words several times, and that he finally consented to sign a receipt of the summons only on the express condition that he would never hear any more of his wife, the court grants a divorce in favour of the plaintiff."[167] Recalling these turbulent events thirty years later, Cavalieri recorded a far less complex version: "The divorce was a very simple operation. I gave him back everything, mansions, ranches and jewels ... even though he had said privately to his lawyer that as a reward for that week he would have left me everything."[168] Bob Chanler was disowned by most of his family and derided by New York society. Undeterred by this, he returned to painting, setting up a studio on East Nineteenth Street in New York City and building a clientele for his murals and painted screens and panels which included some of the richest and most influential collectors in New York. The French government commissioned a mural from him for the Luxembourg Palace.[169]

The events of this unhappy association were so widely and publicly reported that the Metropolitan Opera felt compelled to revoke Cavalieri's contract. The Chanler marriage also led to a widely reported story, believed to be true, which brought about the coining of a popular catch phrase in the United States. When the news broke that his supposedly sane brother had proceeded with the marriage and settled virtually his entire fortune on his new wife, John Armstrong Chaloner, still considered legally insane in several American states, sent his brother a telegram which simply read, "Who's looney now."[170]

In the wake of the controversy surrounding the Chanler affair and as the result of this final break with the Metropolitan, Cavalieri spent some time in Europe. In October 1910, she returned to Paris to sing the second act of *Fedora* with Fernando De Lucia, under the baton of the composer, Giordano, as part of a gala in honor of Victorien Sardou. It was also announced that she would make her debut at the Opéra Comique in an unlikely choice of role, Carmen. In view of her previous experiences in the part it seems hardly surprising that this engagement did not materialize. In November the Russian press confirmed that she had agreed to return to St. Petersburg in February, with a repertoire which included the favorite, *Thaïs*, and possibly some Russian roles including Tamara (*The Demon*) and Tatiana (*Eugene Onegin*).

In mid-January, Cavalieri arrived in St. Petersburg to join a now familiar roster of star singers, Arnoldson, Boronat, Battistini, for a short season at the Conservatoire Theatre. From the comfort of an expensive three-room suite at one of the city's exclusive hotels, Cavalieri gave an interview to the press, eager to hear her version of the recent Chanler scandal. Wearing a pretty black dress and matching bonnet, in spite of her recent distressing experiences, the singer was said to be looking positively rejuvenated: "Today I got up at 10 o'clock in the morning and went for an airing in the frost. I feel excellent ... and I am very glad to have succeeded in visiting the Hermitage, how many wonderful things are there! ... I adore painting but I do not like to pose for a portrait, it is so wearying to sit still for a long time."[171] She also addressed the topic in which all of her readers would be most interested: "I am divorcing.... It requires that we follow a lot of formalities before the matter can be completed. Broadly speaking, it is more difficult to divorce than to marry."[172] On the matter of the operas that she would sing in Russia, Cavalieri was less forthcoming. She said that Boito's *Mefistofele* was a possible contender if a suitable singer could be found for the title role and that she hoped to include Carmen once again.

Stage rehearsals for the new season began on January 25. The original plan that Cavalieri would open the season with *Thaïs* was abandoned due to the singer's poor health, and a performance of Verdi's *Ernani* with Battistini was substituted. On February 1, however, Cavalieri was able to take part in one of the most important social events of the season, a concert held at the Winter Palace. In addition to several members of the imperial family, the invited audience included a large proportion of the diplomatic corps, foreign ambassadors and the leading members of the Russian government. Cavalieri, who performed several Neapolitan songs to great acclaim, was joined by her colleagues from the Italian opera, Battistini and Pintucci. This was only the first of several high-profile engagements which Cavalieri attended during this visit: On February 3 she attended a charity reception at the French embassy and two weeks later took part in a jubilee concert in honor of the actor Constantin Varlamov of the Imperial Theatre, in which she shared the stage with Battistini and Vialtseva. She gave her first performance as *Thaïs* on February 3 to a capacity audience at the Conservatoire. The review in *The New Time* described her as "the most perfect incarnation of Massenet's heroine. It is hard to imagine a more becoming interpreter than this talented actress."[173] Even though the critic of *The Petersburg Leaflet* reminded his readers that Cavalieri's singing, as always, was not entirely above reproach, he noted the "ovations and demands for encores,"[174] which had become an established feature of virtually her every appearance in the city. Almost as a confirmation of this continuing popularity, the distinguished impresario Reznikov announced to the press that he had secured a contract with Cavalieri for the forthcoming season for a concert tour of twenty dates in principal Russian cities, comprising a repertoire of *Carmen* and *Thaïs*. The Moscow paper *The News of the Season* also claimed that Reznikov had secured the singer's services for a gala concert in Moscow, to include costumed extracts from some of the most popular roles in her repertoire. There is no evidence that any of these projected engagements ever took place. If the Russian public were to be deprived of additional opportunities to view their idol, then they would have to take full advantage of the opportunities that did exist. One such, now-familiar scene was described by *The Theatre Review*: "On Saturday ... it was impossible to push one's way through the crowd during the entr'actes. The dense crowd including old and young people, men and women, adolescents ... generals and ancients, secret councillors and collegiate registrars, people of all professions and ranks, all orders and degrees of men, filled both gangways in the stalls. Like hypnotics they all stare into space. What was there that had caught their attention? In the last large box, Lina Cavalieri was sitting.... She resembled a queen.... One interval succeeded another but the filing of all ranks of people before Cavalieri's box continued. I think if an extravagant impresario dreamt of announcing that wherever Cavalieri appeared there would be a charge of 5 roubles just for the right to see her, it would prove to be a great draw!"[175]

On February 11, Cavalieri ventured the role of Carmen once again. Although the critics acknowledged that the singer had obviously worked on both her acting and singing of the role, the same criticisms were leveled: the role did not appear to suit her temperament, and the part lay far too low for her vocally. Nevertheless, the packed audience responded warmly, and it was noted that the performance of *Tristan und Isolde* under Mottl being staged at the Mariinski that same night played to a comparatively small audience. The review in *The Speech* registered general disappointment in the production but noted that the audience responded to Cavalieri with their accustomed enthusiasm. He was forced to conclude, however, "Bizet's music merits to be treated with more respect."[176]

Cavalieri's engagement concluded on February 16 with a benefit performance for her of *Thaïs*. On the following evening, she joined her fellow artists for a jubilee concert in honor of Antonio Ughetti, marking his twenty-five years managing the Italian Opera Company in St. Petersburg. Ughetti, who had originally sung with the Imperial Italian Opera, enjoyed an evening which included Arnoldson in Tatiana's letter scene from *Eugene Onegin* and the first act of *Thaïs* with Cavalieri and Battistini. The stars of the Opera Company were joined by a ninety-five-piece orchestra and a guest appearance by the ballerina Mathilda Kshessinskaya. This gala officially marked the closing of the season.

On the following night Cavalieri appeared in yet another gala concert, this time a benefit for the St. Petersburg Academy of Arts. She performed some popular Neapolitan songs and was presented with a luxurious bouquet of carnations and mimosa. During the intermission, the students persuaded Cavalieri to sell glasses

Cavalieri with Titta Ruffo and Muratore, in a posed scene from Giordano's *Siberia* (Paris 1912, from the collection of Svetlana Vlassova).

of champagne in the foyer, which vastly increased the rate of sales. The press continued to report on Cavalieri's activities, both professional and personal: Her attendance at the newly opened American roller rink caused some interest, and she assisted with the preparations for a benefit performance by Kshessinskaya to mark the twentieth anniversary of her first performance at the Mariinski theater.

Cavalieri finally left St. Petersburg to return to Paris on March 11. Several further projected engagements in Russia failed to materialize. Once again, Reznikov had proposed Moscow appearances: two performances of *Thaïs* with Battistini in the great hall of the Conservatoire and further dates for the following season. Cavalieri, however, had a potentially far more significant engagement in mind. In May 1911, it was announced that she had signed a contract with Messager and Broussant to appear at the Paris Opera once again in another Giordano work, *Siberia*, in which she was to play the role of Stephana opposite the French tenor Lucien Muratore, with whom she would shortly form a significant relationship. The role had originally been offered to Cavalieri's great rival, Mary Garden, but Garden had decided that she did not want to return to Paris as early as the management of the opera had wished. Messager and Broussant decided to offer to role to Cavalieri instead, although they did not inform Garden of the identity of her replacement. On her return from Russia, Giordano spent several weeks in Paris coaching Cavalieri for the role. The Petersburg audience hoped that she would return to the city in June to take part in the celebrations of the silver jubilee of the Aquarium, where she had scored her first great successes. By this time, however, she was completely absorbed in *Siberia*.

The premiere took place at the Palais Garnier on June 9. *Musical America* reported a triumphal first night, but the reviews for Cavalieri's performance were not entirely encouraging. The Russian press took exception to a foreign opera company's attempting a Russian subject and Russian characters. The *Theatre Review* noted: "Judging from illustrations in the French press, the opera is furnished with beautiful costumes, although the military uniforms worn by some characters are taken from different epochs."[177] During her stay in Paris, Reznikov approached the singer again with offers of engagements in Russia: a tour of twelve provincial dates was suggested along with five performances of *Thaïs* and *La Traviata* in Moscow. Although the optimistic impresario was happy to release the details of his future plans to the press, ultimately they were to be disappointed.

Returning to Italy for the summer months, in July and August she sang Leoncavallo's *Zaza*, with Tito Schipa at the Quirino in Rome. This was a role much loved by her old Metropolitan Opera rival, Geraldine Farrar, and she played it to a largely admiring audience. In the middle of August a story was circulated that Cavalieri was to marry her long-established opera partner Battistini. The baritone was quick to deny the rumor, however. In the autumn, Cavalieri announced several ambitious plans for her future career. These included studying the title role in *Aïda*, ten performances in Boston for Henry Russell's company and a season in Mexico City in the spring of 1912. As with the thwarted plans with Reznikov, none of these schemes reached fruition.

Late in 1911, Cavalieri made a return visit to London to sing once again for

Top left: **St. Petersburg, 1912 (from the collection of Svetlana Vlasova.** *Right*: **Lina Cavalieri in St. Petersburg 1912 (photograph by Loren Studio, from the collection of Svetlana Vlasova).** *Bottom*: **Cavalieri as Massenet's Herodiade. (a Reutlinger Studio photograph, 1912, author's collection).**

Oscar Hammerstein at his newly opened London Opera House.[178] Although she had originally discussed the possibility of making her first appearance in Jean Nougues's opera *Quo Vadis?*, her actual debut, scheduled for December 15, was to be as Salome in Massenet's *Herodiade*, with Marguerite d'Alvarez, Maurice Renaud and Jean Auber. The London press speculated upon the choice of repertoire: "One wonders whether there will be any interference from the censor such as occurred a few years ago, on the ground of the Biblical character of the text, when the work was produced at Covent Garden."[179]

The opening of a new opera house in London created much interest in the press on both sides of the Atlantic. In September, The *London Musical Courier* ran a lengthy article on the opening that included many details about the new building. In the same issue, Columbia Records took a half-page advertisement using the slogan "Cavalieri to be prima donna of Oscar Hammerstein's new London Opera House."[180] The text of this early example of exploiting a news event for promotional purposes—and vice versa—claimed Cavalieri to be "the most beautiful living soprano," and that her newly recorded discs were "some of the most perfect records ever issued." The advertisement also appeared in the November issue of the same magazine. *Music* magazine also reviewed two of Cavalieri's records in their September issue: The twelve-inch, double-sided discs, issued in the Columbia Grand Opera series, were of the "Habañera" from Bizet's *Carmen* and "Mi chiamano Mimi" from Puccini's *La Bohème*. The reviewer considered the Bizet disc "full of melodious abandon…. It is one of the best things in the opera and is sung by Mme. Cavalieri in French, with that spontaneity of voice and effective colouring that the aria demands."[181] The comments on the Puccini aria were similarly encouraging and linked the release to the new opera season: "In Mi chiamano Mimi … the same delightful soprano reveals qualities which indicate her experience as an operatic singer. As Mr. Hammerstein will present her to us in the flesh at the opening of his new opera house in November, owners of these records will be able to compare the living voice with these records of her singing."[182]

In the following month's issue, *Music* magazine published an interview with Hammerstein himself, in which he described his new venue in detail: a theater that

Advertisement for Columbia Records, published to coincide with Cavalieri's appearance at Hammerstein's London Opera House, 1910.

boasted forty-five boxes and seated a total of 2,400 people. Hammerstein was eager to emphasize the populist nature of the London Opera House: "I rely, and will rely, solely, upon popular support.... If I give great productions I am positive English people will appreciate them.... What one has to do is to make the productions so inviting and attractive that even people who do not know anything about music will appreciate them."[183] He also made readers aware of the considerable financial investment that he had made in this new venture: "The scenery of a single act of *Quo Vadis?* has cost £2,000. Over 12,000 costumes have been made ... and I shall have invested over £300,000 in it before I am through."[184]

Hammerstein opened his new opera house, designed by the distinguished theater architect Bertie Crewe and built in the Kingsway, on November 13, 1911 with Nougues's *Quo Vadis?*, which had previously been heard only in Paris. *Musical America* reported on the event: "While it is impossible to prophesy so early as to the lasting success of the venture, there was not a moment's doubt as to the triumph Mr. Hammerstein achieved on this occasion."[185] A cast that included Maurice Renaud and Madame Olchanski was treated to a "tumult of applause" in response to a production that was "generally admitted to be one of the most gorgeously mounted operatic productions that ever graced the British stage."[186] The glittering first night audience included the prince and princess of Greece, the duke and duchess of Rutland, the duke and duchess of Manchester, Lady Cunard, the lord mayor of London and the American, French, German and Austrian ambassadors. Hammerstein's theater was also considered a great success, and *Musical America* added, "all London will flock to the new opera house."[187]

Hammerstein's achievement was also recorded in *The Daily Telegraph*: "Never in the whole history of opera has one man before built his own opera house, selected his own departmental superintendents, his own singers, his own repertory, his own scene painters, chorus, orchestra, every detail."[188] The task was achieved, however, largely against the odds: A few days before the opening night, the chorus singers went on strike, claiming that they had been overworked. Shortly after this difficulty was settled, the London county council informed Hammerstein that his new building did not conform to safety regulations and that if certain alterations were not made immediately, his public performance license would be withheld. The work was completed, and the license was finally granted only a few minutes before the opening performance began. Hammerstein followed his successful opening with productions of Rossini's *William Tell*, with the American tenor Orville Harrold, and Bellini's *Norma*, with Victoria Fer, his first major critical success coming with the debut of a nineteen-year-old American soprano, Felice Lyne, as Gilda in Verdi's *Rigoletto*, which caused a sensation, comparable to Luisa Tetrazzini's debut some years earlier.

By the time that Cavalieri made her London Opera House debut, Hammerstein's company had already enjoyed a five-week run, with steadily consolidating business at the box office. He had also succeeded in attracting a particularly notable audience: The premiere of *Herodiade* was attended by the king's sister, Princess Victoria. Earlier concerns for the censorship of the opera were settled when the Lord Chamberlain's office granted a license subject to the agreement that the name of

John the Baptist would be altered to "a prophet."[189] In this production, Hammerstein once again lived up to his promise of high production values. *Musical News* recorded that "The present production is on a scale of unequalled grandeur, several of the scenes being triumphs of colour and effect."[190] In his biography of Hammerstein, Vincent Shean noted that Cavalieri and her colleagues were "not particularly well received; even M. Renaud was thought 'too noble' for Herod.... His [Hammerstein's] admiration for Mme. Marguerite d'Alvarez was not particularly helpful, in that it led him to make her more important than Lina Cavalieri in the advertising for *Herodiade*. True, d'Alvarez was singing the title role, but the centre of the drama was Salome, and Cavalieri objected with vehemence."[191] She was probably also very aware that her name was one of the principal selling points for the production. The critic for *Musical America* was more encouraging: "Lina Cavalieri was the Salome.... Her voice showed considerable improvement ... and she was warmly welcomed.... The greatest honour of the performance, however, went to Maurice Renaud, who never in his life gave more remarkable proof of his great artistry."[192]

The London critics were mixed in their response, generally giving high praise to both the production and the performances of Renaud and Marguerite D'Alvarez, the Peruvian contralto who was making her London debut in the title role. Although much notice was given to Cavalieri's physical appearance in the role of Salome, many commentators were critical both of her singing and her portrayal of the character: "Lina Cavalieri ... made a picture of striking beauty and sang the music cleverly, though she hardly seemed to be in perfect voice."[193] "The Salome of Mlle. Lina Cavalieri was appropriately sentimental according to the mild and sugary story Massenet has set to music. Vocally she was not particularly distinguished."[194] "Miss Cavalieri's voice did not please me greatly and her reading of Salome seemed to err a trifle on the side of ingenuousness. She contrived, however, to capture the suffrages of the audience."[195] A further report that appeared in *The Daily Telegraph* under the encouraging headline "Herodiade Triumphant" described the opera as Massenet's masterpiece and judged the new production to be far better than the London premiere, seven years earlier, which had featured Calvé, Kirkby Lunn and Renaud. The critic noted that there had been "no finer performance, or one more elaborate and beautiful in its staging.... It drew a special significance from the fact that much curiosity was aroused by the details of the cast. Was not Miss Lina Cavalieri the Salome, for the first time here, and has not the whole wide world borne her in remembrance since last she appeared in London? True, she was inclined rather to maltreat her voice last night by unduly forcing it, but there still remained much of the old liquidity of tone and sinuousness of body in her performance."[196] *The Daily Graphic* noted that Massenet's opera was "a less sensational experience than Salome [but] a very gorgeous entertainment," adding that Cavalieri "looked very beautiful ... and sang with much effect."[197]

In spite of some critical reservations, Cavalieri's engagement with Hammerstein's London company was also part of a highly important development in the pattern of London opera production. One observer noted perceptively: "Mr. Hammerstein is doing things with a particularly lavish hand, and although he is perhaps inclined at times to pile on the colour, he also secures effects which are as restrained and artistic as anyone could desire. There was one scene in *Herodiade* which reminded me of Reinhardt.... Perhaps when Mr. Hammerstein has made his audience (and it is growing apace), with the showy things of operatic art, he will give us some of the modern music, and the classical for that matter, which really counts. To contrast Strauss's *Salome* with Massenet's *Herodiade* is to compare the great with the small, but audiences have to be educated and it is something that the London Opera House is becoming the centre of.... A new field seems to be exploited: may there be 'rare and refreshing fruit' for the impresario, and the art!"[198] The writer might have added that Hammerstein's particular talent for exploiting the value of publicity, which had borne such fruit in his New York ventures, was also in evidence here as part of this new development. The casting of such a notable figure as Cavalieri, regardless of any vocal shortcomings, was yet another publicity coup that assisted with ticket sales and press coverage alike.

The London Opera House closed from December 18 to 23, presented an evening concert on Christmas eve, and reopened with a further performance of *Quo Vadis?* for a Boxing Day matinee. That evening, Cavalieri gave her second performance with the company as Giulietta in what was described as a newly edited version of Offenbach's *The Tales of Hoffmann*. In front of a large and enthusiastic audience, she shared the three principal soprano roles with Felice Lyne and Victoria Fer, in a production that *The Times* described as "bringing to the lovely work the success it has never fully enjoyed in London."[199] *The Daily Graphic* prefaced its comments on the production itself by reminding readers that this was a particularly popular period for Offenbach, as *Orpheus in the Underworld* was also enjoying a successful run at His Majesty's Theatre. Describing the performance as a "very brilliant affair," the critic noted that Cavalieri, appearing "in marvellous diamonds and the sketchiest of gowns, was a very handsome and dramatic Giulietta."[200] In what was described as a "wholly delightful" performance, Cavalieri was also judged to be "an entrancing and gorgeously seductive Giulietta."[201] Once again, however, the principal honors lay elsewhere: "No one—not even a prima donna, be she the divine Miss Cavalieri, who sang Giulietta's role so well; Miss Felice Lyne, who was by far the most expert English-speaking doll (otherwise Olympia); or Miss Victoria Fer, who played Antonia capitally—can be scornful of the remarkable Copellius [*sic*] of Mr. Maurice Renaud, whose diction, histrionic ability and musical phrasing were alike of the most distinguished order."[202]

In any event, it was Cavalieri who quite literally stopped the show, drawing such a spontaneous round of applause for her singing of the "Barcarolle," that the action of the opera was temporarily suspended, much to the displeasure of some audience members who, in turn, began to hiss their disapproval of the cheering faction. One critic suggested that this incident was indicative of a regrettable slide in the general standard of behavior in opera audiences. Cavalieri, however, was certainly not without her admirers among the critics. *The Times* described her performance as "voluptuous as it should be, and she is the central point of a scene of magical beauty."[203] *Musical News* noted Cavalieri's "strong sensuousness. There was a fervour about her singing, and an allurement in her acting, distinctly suggestive of the passion of the scene."[204] Once again, many critics commented on the overall quality of the production itself: "excellent stage management ... charming and wholly humorous ... a very smooth performance."[205] *Musical News* added, "The staging and lighting were extremely picturesque, the Venetian scene in particular."[206]

Following on the considerable success of *Herodiade*, the opera was repeated on the following evening, replacing a scheduled performance of Gounod's *Faust*. On December 29, *Hoffmann* was repeated with the same cast, but for the matinée performance of *Herodiade* on the following afternoon, Isabeau Catalan and José Danse replaced both Cavalieri and Renaud. During the first week of January 1912, Cavalieri gave three further performances: once as Salome, and twice as Giulietta, making her final London appearance in the Offenbach opera on January 6. After this date, in the subsequent performances of *Herodiade*, Catalan took Cavalieri's role.

Less than a month after the conclusion of her short London season, Cavalieri returned to St. Petersburg for performances of *Tosca*, *Thaïs* and *Manon*. Original plans that she would also sing *Mignon*, and her first *Eugene Onegin*, with Sobinov as Lensky, were evidently abandoned. News reports of the singer's divorce from Bob Chanler had kept her name prominently in the press, and it had been suggested that she might set up a beauty shop in St. Petersburg, to rival the store that she had opened in New York. It was further suggested that such a move would provide her with an excuse to stay away from America for a time until the furor over her divorce settlement had died down.

The plan to open the season on January 20 with *Thaïs* had to be abandoned as Cavalieri's arrival in St. Petersburg had been delayed by two days. *The Petersburg Leaflet* noted: "They reported from Paris that Lina Cavalieri had fallen for one of the artists of the Grand Opera and that is why she adjourned her arrival in St. Petersburg until her new lover had the possibility of coming to Russia with her."[207] This seemingly sensationalist story actually contained more than a grain of truth. During her season in Paris the previous summer she had met and worked with Lucien Muratore, who played opposite her in *Siberia*. This had seen the beginnings of a new romance that was later to lead to marriage. Whether her new liaison could fairly be attributed as the cause of her current tardiness was, however, entirely speculative.

Cavalieri's late arrival was not to be the most difficult setback facing Guidi at the start of this new season. On January 19 a fire had destroyed a large part of the theater in the newly built People's House of Nicholas II, where the season had been scheduled to take place. Guidi had chosen to use the new theater because its far greater capacity would allow him to reduce ticket prices and, thereby, capitalize on the great popularity of his stars. At two in the morning, a night watchman in the new building raised the alarm: The fire destroyed the stage area and four floors above, including the scenery storage area and its entire contents. The theater had been equipped with the latest fire safety installation, and the new fire curtain had prevented even worse damage from occurring. Unfortunately, the water pressure in the fire hoses was insufficient to reach the worst of the flames, and the room in which the fire extinguishers were kept was found to be locked. As the night staff struggled to break down the door, a loud explosion racked the building, causing further damage. Guidi had no alternative but to transfer his productions to the great hall of the Conservatoire.

Edition
„Richard"
St. Pétersbourg.
190

M. BIELAVSKY.

СОБИНОВЪ

Leonid Sobinov as Alfredo in Verdi's *La Traviata.*

After these many problems, the season finally opened on January 25 with Wagner's *Tannhäuser* with Battistini and Arimondi. The performance of *Thaïs* had to be delayed three times: Although Cavalieri had not actually arrived in the city, the official reason given for the delay was that the scenery had been destroyed in the fire. So many changes had been made to the performance schedule and Cavalieri's appearances had been delayed so many times that one journalist likened the playbills to those used in remote provincial theaters or even the circus. When Cavalieri's first appearance finally took place, in *Thaïs* on February 3, the critical response was much as would be expected: Cavalieri was still as beautiful as ever, her voice still betrayed the usual shortcomings, yet she remained an object of intense attention and fascination. Her performance in *Tosca*, partnered with Garbin and Battistini two days later, was considered an improvement over her last reading of the role, two years earlier: "Her performance has become more musical, her phrasing more expressive.... Mme Cavalieri has worked hard on the part ... although we could dispute her interpretation."[208] Elsewhere, this less frequently staged work was warmly welcomed as a worthwhile addition to the repertoire, and Cavalieri's acting of the role was applauded even if it was considered far superior to her singing.

The succeeding performances of *Thaïs* and *Manon* met with a very similar response. The final Manon performance, however, presented the St. Petersburg audience with something of a novelty. Edoardo Garbin, who succeeded in stealing most of the vocal honors for the evening, had replaced Cavalieri's accustomed partner in this opera, Anselmi. On February 18 the management of the Italian Opera Company marked the end of the season with a gala concert at which all the leading artists were expected to perform an extract from their most celebrated role, on demand. Cavalieri, however, had already left the city to return to Paris. The gossip columns speculated that she would travel on to Nice, there to marry her new love, Muratore, and from there the couple would embark on an American tour. The more serious newspapers added that the singer was contracted to take part in the Russian season in Paris and would finally add Tatiana to her repertoire. The season was scheduled to begin in early May, and the singers would include Chaliapin, Smirnov, Ruffo and Caruso.

Cavalieri, however, had other events on her mind. In April 1912 her forthcoming marriage to Lucien Muratore was officially announced. A report in the *New York Times* gave Muratore's date of birth as 1878 and described him as a "tenor of the Paris Opera."[209] This began many months of speculation on the couple's actual marital status that may have been viewed as useful publicity for their professional engagements, although these too were proving highly speculative. In May 1912, *The New York Telegraph* announced Cavalieri's return to the United States in a concert tour of seventy cities, in which she would be accompanied by Muratore. The tour was to be under the management of Friedlander of San Francisco and was scheduled to begin in October and last for four months. The tour did not materialize. The following month, Henry Russell stated that he had secured the performing rights for the world premiere of Riccardo Zandonai's opera *Francesca da Rimini* and that he planned to stage it at his Boston Opera in February 1913. He said that the composer himself would supervise the production and that Cavalieri and Muratore would have the leading roles. This production did not materialize either, although Muratore did make his Boston debut later that year.[210] In June, when the newly settled couple were at leisure in Paris, they received a visit from the impresario Sergei Zimin. Apparently he had come to offer the couple a guest engagement in Moscow, but it appears that the offer was rejected.

The summer of 1912 must have held very little genuine society news, for in July, the papers carried an entirely spurious story that Cavalieri's new marriage was on the verge of dissolution. It was said that she had met a twenty-two-year-old Parisian from a wealthy family and had fallen in love with him. It was further suggested, however, that the young man's horrified family had called upon his uncle, the prefect of police in Paris, to assist in breaking up the affair: Muratore apparently had refused to grant his new wife a divorce. Further information continued to be published on the exploits of the Cavalieri imitators. A café in Nizhny Novgorod reputedly boasted an all-female cabaret that included a Spanish dancer called Oterita and a singer billed as Linda Cavalieri. One of the earliest of the Cavalieri clones, Maria Cavalieri had apparently been absent from the stage for some five years but now returned to sing in productions of *Pagliacci* and *Cavalleria Rusticana* at the Adriano Theatre in Rome. The *Theatre Review* suggested that both Maria and Lina Cavalieri would be singing in St. Petersburg in the coming season and that Lina would share the concert platform with her new husband. Both the Petersburg and Moscow press announced the forthcoming appearances in their cities of Milita Cavalieri, credited as a singer from La Scala Milan. This additional Cavalieri was supposed to appear in concert in the company of a singer called Sevastianov, formerly of the Imperial Theatre. There is no evidence that any such concerts ever took place or that Milita actually existed.

In the autumn, Reznikov announced an Italian season at the Conservatoire Theatre that would include Cavalieri, Anselmi and Didur. A rival impresario, Askarin, responded by publicizing a rival season at the theater of the People's House, with Maria Cavalieri as the primary attraction. Although Maria Cavalieri's appearance in *Tosca* did take place, Lina's did not. The Theatre Review announced that Lina would arrive in St. Petersburg at the end of December, but on the last day of

1912 (old calendar), the paper carried the following: "Yesterday, a message was received from Lina Cavalieri. She will not come to Petersburg this season because she goes on tour in America."[211] Even though Reznikov continued to deny rumors that his star would not appear, in fact Cavalieri was never to appear again before the Russian audiences who had done so much to help establish her operatic career, other than on a movie screen.

In January of 1913, The *New York Herald* carried the headline "Miss Lina Cavalieri to return and give series of recitals."[212] Cavalieri, accompanied by Muratore, under the management of Haensel and Jones, would give her first performance in Baltimore or Washington in March. Sixty recital dates were planned, including appearances in Boston and New York. Cavalieri and Muratore arrived in New York aboard the *Kaiser Willhelm II*, on February 13. The *New York Herald* announced that they would begin their tour in Boston and would appear in New York at the Hippodrome on March 9. The recitals were to consist of two contrasting programs: The first would include, uncharacteristically, a group of Schumann lieder, sung in French, the St. Sulpice scene from *Manon*, and a selection of Neapolitan songs; the second would comprise opera scenes, played in costume, from *Madame Butterfly*, *Romeo and Juliette* and *Cavalleria Rusticana*. In an interview given to Charles Henry Meltzer, Cavalieri confided, "I do not intend to abandon opera for concerts. I have just learned the music of *Aïda* and I am studying *Madame Butterfly*."[213]

An impression of this tour is provided in an unidentified press report from February 1913, under the headline "Jewels Bedeck Lina Cavalieri." This gave details of a debut concert at the Empire Theatre, at which she was accompanied by Lucien Muratore, with Edouard Touran at the piano. The published program included extracts from *Carmen*, *Cavalleria Rusticana* and *Manon*, Neapolitan songs and duets, and a selection of Provençale songs sung by Muratore. The critical response was most encouraging: "Her dramatic art is finished and her vocalisation is punctuated with superb quality, wide range and brilliant colouring."[214] The *Rochester Times* reported a concert at that city's Lyceum Theatre on the following night. The program consisted of extracts from *Werther* and Saint Saens' *Dejanine*, sung by Muratore, the "Habañera" from *Carmen* and Grieg's "Ich Liebe Dich," sung in French, both performed by Cavalieri. Duets by Schumann and Lully were followed by the St. Sulpice scene from *Manon*, Neapolitan songs by Cavalieri, Provençale songs by Muratore, and the final scene from *Carmen*.

An appearance scheduled at the Boston Opera House on February 24 was canceled. Very few tickets had been sold in advance for the concert, and Cavalieri withdrew on grounds of ill health. Concerts at the Hippodrome in Cleveland and the Majestic Theatre in Fort Wayne were followed by an appearance at the New York Hippodrome on March 9, at which the couple were accompanied by the Nathan Franko Orchestra, conducted by Tournon, and at which Cavalieri included the popular ballad "Last Night Was the End of the World," by Harry Von Tilzer. *Musical America* reported that the New York audience included several distinguished former colleagues from the Met, among them Frieda Hempel, Riccardo Martin and Andreas de Segurola.

Cavalieri's marriage to Muratore, which had continued to be a subject for speculation, was announced in several American newspapers as planned to take place in

Detroit on March 28. Neither singer was prepared to confirm these rumors. American reporters constantly trailed the pair attempting to extract a story. The *Theatre Review* carried an interview with Cavalieri in which she provided a very revealing picture of the press treatment of the celebrity, even as early as 1914:

> When we arrived in New York, of course, a whole battalion of reporters intruded on us. Their first question was—Are you really married? This curiosity seemed rather impertinent to us and we did not want to answer questions like this. But obviously the question interested some American newspapers, because, some months later when I came to Philadelphia and a reporter from the most influential local newspaper visited me, he asked the same question with a very severe and grim expression. He looked like a real inquisitor when he asked me if our marriage was held to be valid. I had no reason to be unkindly or ungracious to him and I answered, "Yes, we are officially married"—"Why did you not give the answer right off the bat to the reporters who visited you then?"... "Because the American papers would busy themselves with fabrications and spinning stories about our family life." One day later a fantastic story of our marriage appeared in this gentleman's newspaper. We allegedly tied the marriage knot on the Mediterranean coast in the South of France. The small chapel where we were married allegedly stood on a high rock and hung onto the rock like a swallow's nest. The seamen and fishermen allegedly sang and danced during our wedding.... Soon after, we found that the newspapers could publish still more amazing things. In Chicago a reporter visited me.... He asked me a lot about the South of France. A few days later he wrote the following downright nonsense in his newspaper: "When Lina Cavalieri painted a landscape in Provence in oils, she was attacked by a crazy cow who knocked her easel over. Lina Cavalieri quickly collected her paintbrushes and colours and incidentally daubed the cow with red paint. When the artist got over the shock, she saw her teacher in painting, the artist Reyer, standing near her. [He] promised to compensate her for her fear. He intends to paint her as a heroine and give her the features of Sigurde.'"[215]

The concert tour continued throughout March, seeing the couple perform in Philadelphia, Providence, New Haven, Hartford, Bridgeport, Pittsburgh, Youngstown (Ohio), Toledo, and Detroit and at the Orchestra Hall in Boston. Though, in most cities, Cavalieri's fame and glamor seemed to be all that was needed in order to secure and please an audience, her performances were not always so universally well received by the critics. Glenn Dillard Gunn reported that "Madame Cavalieri's voice is flat, colorless and uneven.... She reinforces her slight command of interpretative nuance with the meagre resources of a restricted repertory of stereotyped gestures.... The program was atrocious."[216]

It seems likely that Cavalieri's limited technique and somewhat fragile vocal reserves were not equal to sustaining the rigors of a busy and physically demanding touring schedule, and cancellations became more frequent. *Musical America* reported that a second visit to the Boston Opera for a performance of *Carmen*, planned for mid–March, was again canceled on health grounds. The final concert date appears to have been at the Shubert Theatre in Kansas City on April 3, after which Cavalieri sailed for Paris aboard the *Oceania*, accompanied by Muratore, amidst further speculation as to their marital status. Although it was not known at the time, the final concert of the tour was also to mark Cavalieri's farewell to the American opera stage.

Muratore and Cavalieri on tour; a press publicity photograph, 1913.

Even though her association with the Metropolitan Opera Company, indisputably the high point of her American operatic career, was now long over, her name remained associated with them throughout the next stage of her career, as a film actress. In May 1916, *Vanity Fair* published a short report: "At last, the Metropolitan Opera Company has gone into the movies. Cavalieri will be the first great feminine star, and Scotti will play opposite her in the earliest of the Metropolitan's films—i.e. the opera of *Tosca*. The Opera Company was driven into forming its own film concern because so many of its stars were going into the movies on their own account. The films will be sold to distributing companies, and will not be operated by the Metropolitan itself."[217] Although other press reports suggested that Cavalieri was to appear in a *Tosca* film, regrettably there is no evidence that any such films were ever made. Presumably the company decided to allow its great homegrown diva, Geraldine Farrar, to pursue her cinematic career away from the activities of the opera house, as she had already done with great success.

Although Cavalieri had now bid her operatic farewells to both St. Petersburg and New York, she had one further major performance to deliver. In June, she returned to the Paris Opera for a single performance of *Thaïs* opposite the Italian bass-baritone Vanni Marcoux. *Figaro* stated that the Paris audience had declared this to be the finest *Thaïs* ever to appear on a Parisian stage and particularly praised Cavalieri's graceful acting of the role. A projected appearance opposite Muratore in *Fedora* in Chicago in December 1913 was canceled due to a throat infection. In May

1914, the Paris Opera announced that Cavalieri would replace Mary Garden in performances of Giordano's *Siberia*. A dispute had arisen between Garden and the opera management over the date upon which was she was expected to arrive in Paris to rehearse. Messager and Braussant withdrew her contract, and Giordano himself was said to have personally coached Cavalieri for the role.

Cavalieri's doting Russian admirers continued to speculate about return visits that would never materialize, and to indulge in patently absurd rumors of the singer's private life and escapades: A sensational story appeared in the autumn of 1913 that the singer was about to enter a convent. The *Theatre Review* carried a quote from the singer: "I have dreamed all along of a peaceful life.... How many times I have forsaken this way of life, but on stage as Thaïs. Now I have decided to realise this."[218] Apparently, Muratore, understandably, prevented her from taking this course of action. As war in Europe loomed, Cavalieri's return to Russia became less and less likely. Hopes of guest appearances in Moscow and St. Petersburg in the autumn of 1914, which were hinted at in the Russian press, were dashed by the increasing chaos of the conflict to come. World War I finally put an end to the Belle Epoch, of which Cavalieri had been such a potent symbol. The singer recorded in her memoirs: "The war violently knocked the bottom out of my life. In a short time my husband left me to join the Transalpine Republic army, my two brothers and my son went off to the Italian army."[219] When Cavalieri herself joined the nursing service of the Sisters of Mercy, the press commented, "Is it not significant that artists from such different genres and outlooks, from Sarah Bernhardt to Felia Litvinne to Lina Cavalieri, and from Isadora Duncan to Ida Rubinstein, refused all the conveniences of their comfortable lives and devoted themselves to serve their fellow creatures and their country?"[220] The singer had far more than a merely academic interest in the progress of the war, and a sense of its true horror was brought home to her in the most inescapable manner when her son was seriously injured in fighting on the Italian front in the summer of 1916.

In common with the many conflicting stories that constantly appeared about Cavalieri's life and career, it has proved impossible to establish exactly when her operatic stage career finally reached its end. Some evidence exists of at least one performance of *Pagliacci* at the Grand Teatro Circo in San Sebastian in the summer of 1913. And although it has been accepted that the final appearance was as Violetta at the Teatro Carcano in Milan in 1916, the chronology of performances at the Politeama Greco in Lecce includes a note of two performances of *La Traviata* as late as April 1920. No definitive proof has been found that these performances actually took place. Even as late as 1923, the post–Revolutionary Russian press speculated on the diva's return, suggesting that she might come to Petrograd in March for performances of *Thaïs*, *La Traviata* and *La Bohème*.

We can be certain, however, that an announcement appeared that Cavalieri would sing with the Chicago Opera in the autumn season of 1916. On October 8 she arrived in New York on board the liner *Espagne*, whose passenger list also included Sarah Bernhardt. During October and November, she accompanied Muratore on tour with the Ellis Grand Opera Company, but purely as a companion and spectator. The Ellis Company comprised singers from both the Metropolitan and

the Chicago Opera and included Louise Homer and Geraldine Farrar, with whom Muratore appeared in *Carmen*. Cavalieri accompanied her husband on many of the tour dates, and, as Farrar recalled in her autobiography, her presence was not always helpful: "Cavalieri ... laboured incessantly, with commendable tenacity but doubtful wisdom, toward a re-establishment as prima donna.... She accompanied him back and front stage, a pleasant figure, but delivering artistic counsel to her artist-husband that was of little value and often collided with the views of the conductor and other artists. Both of them were indefatigable press agents for themselves, but as their front page 'scoops' were based on his appearance in Carmen, that vehicle served him well."[221]

In April 1917, Cavalieri made a rare stage appearance at the Hippodrome Theatre in New York City, in a grand patriotic gala in which she played France in a tableau representing the allied nations. This proved to be one of her last major public appearances. From this time onward her main association with the world of opera would be through her husband, Lucien Muratore.

After Mary Garden took over the direction of the Chicago Opera, Cavalieri signed a contract to sing *Tosca* with the company in which Muratore was already engaged as the leading tenor. Cavalieri and Muratore had returned to New York from Europe on November 1, 1921 on the White Star liner *Olympic*. They announced that they would be traveling on to Chicago as soon as possible in order to prepare for the opening production of the season, in which Muratore was to sing Saint-Saens's Samson. Garden claimed in her autobiography that Cavalieri had chosen her own role: "I sent word one day asking her what night she wanted to make her debut, what role she wanted it to be, and whom did she want to conduct. She sent back a reply that she wanted to sing Tosca with George Baklanoff and that Giorgio Polacco should conduct."[222] The planned performance, however, never took place. At midday on the day of the scheduled debut, the theater management received a message from Cavalieri's doctor saying that she was unwell and would not be able to appear. Garden claimed that she offered the indisposed singer an alternative date in the following week but that late in the afternoon on the performance day a similar doctor's message was received, and, once again, Cavalieri withdrew. Garden further recalled, "She had been engaged to sing at fifteen hundred dollars a night, but she never sang. I recall speaking to Baklanoff one day about Cavalieri. 'Mary, she'll never sing Tosca,' he said. 'But why? That's supposed to be one of her great successes.' 'She's afraid.'"[223]

Garden's memoirs are not particularly noted for their accuracy, and, in view of the ill feeling between the two singers occasioned so many years earlier by the *Thaïs* incident in New York, Garden would have had no compelling reason to paint her old rival in a favorable light. However, it seems entirely possible that Cavalieri was too frightened to risk a return to live performance and at such a high-profile venue, after so long an absence from the operatic stage.[224]

There is a revealing story behind Cavalieri's late association with Garden and the Chicago Opera. In January 1922, the *New York Times*, which had shown so avid

Opposite: **Cavalieri in the title role of Puccini's *Tosca* (photographs by Dupont, New York).**

an interest in the original *Thaïs* dispute between Garden and Cavalieri, announced that Muratore had decided to leave the Chicago company because he felt unable to continue working under the management of Garden. In an interview, he declared, "It is impossible to be a singer and a director at the same time.... Either artistic or business ability must be sacrificed."[225] He proceeded to state that there had been a heated debate between himself and Garden over the roles that he was contracted to perform. This, however, appeared to be only part of the problem. The *New York Times* article suggested very strongly that there had been "professional jealousy" between Cavalieri and Garden and that this had also "entered into the misunderstanding." It was stated that, in order to secure Muratore's services, the Chicago company had been obliged also to offer a contract to his wife, Cavalieri, although she had not actually appeared in the season. This accords, partially at least, with the version of the story told by Mary Garden. Muratore, however, denied this, adding, of Garden, "I do not like the way she spoke to me.... Miss Garden is too capricious. One day she is nice. Next day she will not even say good morning."[226] The report also suggested that friction had been caused between the management and Muratore over the extent of the tenor's expenses, which had included extravagant hotel bills for himself and Cavalieri, who had accompanied him to Chicago. In response, the company told Muratore that, in future, he would be paid only a flat, fully inclusive salary, to which he objected. There was also mention of ill feeling within the company that Muratore's contract included a clause that gave him the first choice of all of the leading tenor roles.

The day after this report was published, Muratore and Cavalieri departed for New York, where the tenor was scheduled to open the Chicago company's season at the Manhattan Opera House, singing opposite Marguerite D'Alvarez in *Samson and Delilah*. In spite of the threats, a spokesman for the company suggested that it was unlikely that Muratore would actually break his contract as he was being paid "$2,800 a performance ... the largest salary paid anywhere in the world to a grand opera star. It is $300 more ... than Caruso received from the Metropolitan."[227] Before leaving for New York, however, Muratore repeated his threat, saying that he was only waiting to hear if Mary Garden had been reengaged as director of the company for the forthcoming season. He showed a copy of his contract to the press. It stipulated that he would learn three new operas, which he had done. He claimed, however, that the first of these had been canceled, and the second and third given only a handful of performances. He told the *New York Times* that he had been offered contracts to sing in Buenos Aires and New York and confirmed that he would not accept the new contract offered by Garden, "Not for $5,000 a night with her as director."[228]

In any event, Muratore gave the scheduled performance as Samson on January 23 and was described as "singing with an impassioned fervour."[229] Garden, interviewed on the day after the opening, declared that she intended to remain in her post in Chicago and dismissed reports of a major rift with her star tenor. Shown a copy of an interview in which Muratore was said to have likened Garden to a frog, Garden responded, "Not me. I sink or I go to the top. I never float.... It says here that he detests publicity. Isn't that a pity."[230] When asked if she believed that Muratore would actually sing for the opening night, she replied, "I don't know. Lord help me from bossing a tenor."[231]

The Chicago Opera Company tour ended in Wichita, Kansas, on April 22, and Cavalieri and Muratore returned to New York. Three days after the end of the tour, it was announced that Garden had relinquished her directorial post with the Chicago Company: It was decided that, in future, the company would be managed by a committee, although Garden would remain with the company as one of its star performers. Muratore was quoted as saying, "I am not against her as an artist or as a woman ... but as a director."[232] He also claimed that Garden had said vindictive things about him behind his back: "when we sing together she hisses 'Pretty boy,' and when I am on stage she talks to other members of the company behind my back."[233] Two days later it was announced that Muratore had suffered a breakdown as a result of stress and that he might be compelled to take a lengthy break from performing. Muratore and Cavalieri returned to Paris, where, late in July, it appeared that, in spite of Garden's change of position, the Chicago controversy still burned: The tenor was quoted as saying that "I will beg the people of Chicago to be allowed to come and sing for them the day Mary Garden eventually leaves the Chicago Opera."[234]

At the end of July, the couple left Paris for a few days in Nice so that Muratore could spend time studying new roles in peace. He had been contracted by the Opéra Comique to sing in *Carmen*, *Werther* and Faure's *Penelope* in September. In November the couple moved on to Monte Carlo, and Muratore continued to accept only European engagements, refusing to sing for American companies while still in dispute with Garden. Cavalieri continued to travel with her husband, although the *New York Times* announced that she would not be undertaking any singing engagements during the 1922–1923 season. Lina Cavalieri's association with grand opera, a glamorous world which appeared so effectively to mirror her own extravagant life and beauty, was finally at an end.

V

THE FILM STAR

During the first two decades of the twentieth century, a strange progression occurred. A series of celebrated operatic performers began to appear in silent films. Although early experiments had been carried out by Oskar Messter, Leon Gaumont and others in the production of short opera films, with synchronized sound tracks supplied on gramophone records, often featuring the voices of distinguished singers of the day, these had failed to attract the personal appearances of actual operatic stars. The first to take the risk of appearing in the new medium, in the flesh as it were, was one who was accustomed to taking risks with her career, Lina Cavalieri. Making her moving picture debut in 1914, she set a precedent that was swiftly followed by Geraldine Farrar, Mary Garden, Feodor Chaliapin, and, finally, the great Enrico Caruso himself.

Cavalieri's excursion into the world of the cinema came at a time when movie studios all over the world were seeking new gimmicks, new stars, and most importantly of all, an association with the legitimate theater which would enable the new industry to graduate from the status of a fair ground novelty to that of a recognized art form in its own right. Cavalieri was to play a small but significant part in this important development, starring in a series of films both in America and in her native Italy. Her personal attitude toward the cinema appears to have been somewhat ambiguous. Writing in 1940, she stated, "Cinema means for me the end of my career as a beautiful woman, as an actress and as a singer. It is the last form of art in which I have expressed myself, and it is the only form of art in which I feel I can still perform."[1] Apparently, at this time, there was a possibility that a film of Cavalieri's own colorful life would be made, and she claimed that she would appear, presumably as herself, in the latter half of the film.

In the article, which was one of a series to appear in the Italian magazine *Film*, as well as outlining what she considered to be the shortcomings of filmmaking at this time, Cavalieri also noted that she was "proud to say I have worked in the period in which Italian cinema was one of the best in the world and produced films that are still considered milestones in the history of cinematography."[2] Certainly, by 1914, the year of Cavalieri's screen debut, the Italian film industry had already begun to establish an enviable reputation for the quality of its product, considered by many to be far superior to the majority of films being produced elsewhere. The Italian industry had also begun to establish a recognizable star system. One of the earliest identifiable Italian female stars of the silent screen, Francesca Bertini, had made her debut in a featured role in 1912, in the Cines production of *Rosa di Tebe* (*The Rose of Thebes*), playing opposite the highly distinguished theater actor Amleto Novelli. The film was an enormous success, and it made Bertini into a salable commodity as a screen performer. Tiber Studios bought out her contract for a single movie at a fee of two thousand lire a month. The film was so successful that Tiber refused to return her services to Cines, and a heated legal battle ensued which resulted in a level of publicity being given to the new star which foreshadowed the excesses of later Hollywood studio press offices. Bertini went on to make a series of highly successful features: These included versions of *King Lear* and *The Merchant of Venice* for the Film d'Arte Italiana Company and both also starring Novelli. She also made silent versions of the operatic subjects *Tosca* and *Fedora*. In 1919 she signed a contract to make a further eight films, for the then unprecedented fee of two million lire. After the third of these films, *La Fanciulla di Amalfi* (*The Girl from Amalfi*), which was completed in 1921, she suddenly announced her retirement from the movies.

A photograph taken in Italy (1914–1915), probably with Cavalieri's granddaughter (from the collection of Svetlana Vlasova).

For more than a decade, Bertini had reigned supreme as the queen of the Italian silent film industry, and few actresses were able to mount any kind of challenge to her dominance, but one who did was Lina Cavalieri, "whose statuesque beauty was in natural contrast to Bertini's slightly gamine vivacity.... Lina Cavalieri had reached such heights of popularity, abroad, as well as in Italy, that her films were sold in America not only unseen, but in at least two cases, before they were even made."[3] As early as August 1913, press reports had heralded the imminent appearance of Cavalieri before the moving picture cameras. *Musical America* stated that she would make her debut with her new husband, Lucien Muratore, in a silent film version of Riccardo Zandonai's opera *Francesca da Rimini*, in which, it was claimed, they would also perform together on stage in Boston. Neither the film nor the stage appearance materialized, however, becoming one of many unfulfilled promises at this stage of the singer's career.

In February 1914, the *New York Herald* announced that Cavalieri and Muratore had signed a contract with the Playgoers Film Company to make an unidentified six-reel feature film: it was suggested that the subject would be either *Tosca*, *Manon* or *Francesca da Rimini*. Speculation mounted in the popular press, and the *New York Telegraph* added fuel to this by reporting that the singer had asked for and been granted the highest fee ever recorded for a motion picture performer. *Vanity Fair* reported, inaccurately, that the subject for the film was to be Massenet's *Manon*, in which, as we have seen, Cavalieri had appeared on stage with much success. In fact, the planned film was to be based on Puccini's version of Abbe Prevost's novel, *Manon Lescaut*, and filming began at the Playgoers' studios in Yonkers. Cavalieri later recalled that, from the very beginning, she found the process of filming a difficult one: "I must confess right from the start that working for the cinema industry in that period was a real disaster, both in Italy and abroad. In that period, acting was ten times harder than it is now; suffice it to say that the studios at Cinecitta now have air conditioning systems and that the speed at which a scene is now edited is impressive.... When I worked, there were no diffuser scrims. We risked becoming blind, as happened to me: I could not see for a week, struck by conjunctivitis."[4]

The *New York Star* carried an unusual eyewitness description of part of the studio filming of the St. Sulpice scene in the opera adaptation. The correspondent noted that Cavalieri was obviously learning a new art in acting for the cameras: "And one of the things she learned to her sorrow was that to step back into a scene once one has made an exit is such a fatal move that the scene must be retaken in order to blot out one's mistake."[5] In spite of these learning difficulties the observer was also eager to express the obvious intensity of the acting: "The scene which I witnessed between Cavalieri and Muratore was spoken sotto voice ... but I realized, without knowing the story, just what the players sought to interpret, so well did their forms, faces and actions tell the tale of persuasion, sorrow and love that presents itself at just this point of the play."[6] In an interview published in *The New York Herald*, Cavalieri was asked if she missed the inspiration that music and the live reaction of a theater audience contributed to recreating emotional scenes in the very different atmosphere of the studio: "A little, but these things are not vital. Emotion is from the heart, and poor Manon is all heart, grace and delicacy."[7]

On April 8 the cast and crew sailed for France to complete location filming at a number of authentic sites before returning to the United States to finish the film in New Orleans, and *Manon Lescaut* finally received its New York premiere on June 13, 1914, at the Republic Theatre. In common with many other important movies at this time, in larger venues the film was screened with a live orchestral accompaniment appropriate to its operatic subject matter. For its run at Moore's Strand Theatre in Washington, D.C., it was noted that "The Strand orchestra of sixteen players plays the original operatic score of the production, which was especially arranged and adapted by Theodore Bendix."[8]

Manon Lescaut was promoted as an epic treatment of Abbe Prevost's romantic masterpiece. A souvenir program, published by the film's distributors, the Alco Film Corporation, exploited not only the lavish scale of the production, but also the glamorous reputation of its star: "The Incomparable Cavalieri, the World's Most Famous Beauty—and Lucien Muratore, the Great French Tenor and Lyric Actor—in a Superb Production ... 300 scenes, 300 people, 6 Acts."[9] An advertisement for the film, published in *Moving Picture World*, described the production as "The Six Act Picturization that will set a New Standard for the Art of Photoplay Production."[10]

The film was treated to a hitherto unprecedented level of publicity, less familiar to the studios of the time, than to Cavalieri, who had become accustomed to such interest since the earliest stages of her career. The advertising was described in *Musical America* as "billed throughout the city with huge lithographs bearing the likeness of the soprano with the heading—The Incomparable Cavalieri, The World's Most Famous Beauty."[11] The promotional campaign featured several highly exploitable aspects: not only the presence of the supremely glamorous Cavalieri, but here in partnership with her real-life partner, Muratore. An on-screen and off-screen romance combined, playing together in a story emanating from that most romantic and dramatic of sources, the world of grand opera. What more could any press office, audience or critic possibly desire?

In his review, H. W. De Long, writing in *The Moving Picture World*, made a point of mentioning the production itself before discussing the stars: "The scenes of the piece are portrayed in a lavish manner and the attention to details and historical correctness are manifested throughout."[12] Long also lavished praise on the director, Herbert Hall Winslow: "The photography is adequate in every respect and the whole ensemble evidences that a master-hand directed."[13] Considering the established celebrity of the film's two stars, De Long dealt with their contribution rather briefly, describing Cavalieri's performance as possessing "all the finesse that has made her world famous."[14] and Muratore as "at all times convincing."[15] The critic of the *New York Times* described the film as "staged in splendid style, and the cast supporting the two leading actors is an excellent one."[16] No specific assessment was offered of the performances of either Cavalieri or Muratore. An undated report in the *Chicago Herald*, commenting on the film's screening at that city's Ziegfield Theatre, where its popularity had caused the management to retain it for a further week, was far more emphatic and specific in allocating praise: "The grand opera stars make most other moving picture performers look tame by comparison."[17]

Since virtually every report of the film's screening in America notes the importance of the leading players and the significance of their origins in the world of grand opera, it may seem surprising that the critics were apparently so reluctant to comment on the qualities of their acting. The principal reason for this is simply that the power of the star name to sell a film, a phenomenon often considered so central to the cinema, dominated by the studio-imposed star system from the 1920s right up to the present day, was a far less significant aspect of marketing the product in 1914. As Richard de Cordova noted, prior to 1907 there was some doubt as to whether appearing before a movie camera actually constituted acting at all or rather if it equated to posing for a photograph, and therefore star acting, as such, was neither an issue nor a subject worthy of serious discussion. It was not until 1911 that screen credits came into common usage, and it was not possible to market feature films on the strengths of the acting if the actors themselves remained anonymous. Identifying individual actors in reviews and assessing their contribution was far less developed at this stage than, for example, in the area of theater or opera criticism where it was already a well-established practice.[18]

Uncharacteristically for this period, the *Variety* review of *Manon Lescaut* came much closer to addressing the real issue: the choice of starring partnership and how much influence that might have on the success of the feature: "With such famous names as Mme. Lina Cavalieri and Lucien Muratore featured, the Playgoers Film Co. anticipates a brisk demand for its recently exploited four-part picturized version of Abbe Prevost's immortal love story, *Manon Lescaut*. The story as film is nothing out of the ordinary, and for a feature does not come up to expectations, although Cavalieri and Muratore may be sufficiently strong to maintain a vigorous market circulation.... Just how this feature will succeed depends wholly on Cavalieri's fame on this side of the water.... One must remember that a fancy figure was paid for the photoplay services of Cavalieri and Muratore.... The picture has interest through Cavalieri's connection. Otherwise it misses fire."[19]

Manon Lescaut should probably be considered a relatively unremarkable feature then, given interest by the casting of its remarkable star. But how remarkable was Cavalieri's acting in front of the movie cameras? This question was also addressed in *Variety*: "Cavalieri does well as a movie actress, though at times she appears to have forgotten that for the moment she is enacting a pantomime role instead of a stage character with which her voice has been half the battle. She makes Manon attractive. Especially sweet and sympathetic does she appear in the last two parts.... In the woods death scene Cavalieri moves several times when she is supposed to be very dead."[20]

As a performer who had enjoyed success in several of the major opera houses of the world and who now stood at the beginning of a film career of some evident promise, Cavalieri had a very specific idea of how varied her career could be. In her view it should not be confined either to singing or silent movie acting: In an extensive interview she stated that "Paul Hervieu, the French author who has written several plays for the Theatre Français ... says that he will write me a piece if I will act in it. But the ideal condition, which I am afraid, will never come, would be to dance one evening, sing the next, and act the next. They are all my life, and I would then be able to express myself in what I am now limited in expressing. I feel that I have something that I want to give and cannot give to audiences when I merely sing."[21]

Cavalieri's partner, both on screen and off, Lucien Muratore, whose costarring role as Des Grieux received far less attention from the press, was certainly one of the finest French tenors of his generation, but he was also an accomplished actor. He had appeared at the Varieties in Paris and the Casino in Monte Carlo before joining Mme. Rejane's company at the Paris Odéon. He had made his operatic debut with the Opéra Comique and built a repertoire with the company that included the leading tenor roles in *Carmen*, *Werther* and *Mignon*, singing with Calvé, Dufresne and Fougères. Muratore made his debut with the Paris Opéra in Gluck's *Armide* and sang many leading roles with the company including *Faust* and *Romeo et Juliette*. He also created the leading tenor roles in the Paris premieres of several operas including *Bacchus*, *Roma*, *Monna Vanna*, *Salome*, and *Francesca da Rimini*. He came to America for the first time when Cleofonte Campanini contracted him to sing with the Chicago Opera, where he became a favorite artist for many seasons, often singing with Mary Garden.

One of his many interests as a performer, probably inherited from his training as an actor, was a concern for the correct appearance of the characters that he created. Richard Savage, in a profile of the singer, remarked, "Muratore is noted for his visual presentment and his varied characterizations. He has an extensive library of works on the apparel of all peoples at all times, with many rare plates illustrating not only these varied habiliments, but the ornaments, weapons and insignia that go with them. For each new role he designs his own costumes."[22] Perhaps this interest in period style accounts, in part at least, for the sense of scenographic accuracy noted by De Long in his review, as one of the outstanding features of the production. Much later in his career, after his separation from Cavalieri, Muratore was to make three sound features in France: *Le Chanteur Inconnu*, was made in 1931, was directed by Victor Tourjansky, and co-starred Simone Simon and Simone Cerdon. In 1933 he made two further films; in the first, *Le Chant du Destin*, for Pan Films, he played a Venetian gondolier. The film, directed by Jean-Rene Legrand and costarring Jica Helda and Suzanne Stanley, was notable for a score cowritten by Bronislaw Kaper. His final film, *La Voix sans Visage*, was made for Vander-Film and directed by Leo Mittler. In it, Muratore played Pierre Saltare, a singer accused of murder. His costars included Vera Korene and Simone Bourday.

Cavalieri made her second film with Muratore on location in Paris and Rome in 1915: *La Sposa della Morte* (*The Bride of Death*), for the Italian company Tiber Studios. Giorgio Vecchietti later stated that she was paid "with a quota of the proceeds—a good percentage."[23] The budget for the production must have been relatively generous as it was announced that all of Cavalieri's costumes were made by Paquin. The direction of this film is credited to Emilio Ghione, with a scenario provided by Ghione and Muratore, but the review in *Variety* of the film's American release suggests that it was Muratore who actually supervised the making of the film. The critic went on to state, "If that is the case, Mons. Muratore had best stick to grand opera, for there will be little or no chance for him as a movie director."[24]

The film was released in the United States by Pathé under the title *The Shadow of Her Past* in July 1916 and received its New York premiere in the following month, but it was not well received. The somewhat improbable story is of the adventures of two young students in Rome. The girl, Elyane Chalmers, played by Cavalieri, is studying the piano at the Villa Medici and starts a romance with an art student called Pierre Marsant, played by Muratore; she then falls victim to the advances of a predatory duke, played by Alberto Collo, who takes her away to Paris with him. Ghione devoted a whole scene to their journey aboard the new luxury train, the Express de Paris. The young man, played by Muratore, follows her and fights a duel with the nobleman, which results in his sustaining a serious injury. The two young lovers are reunited and reconciled, but, unable to face the truth of her past, the girl commits suicide, leaving the message—"Pierre, only in death can I be your wife."

It was suggested that the presence of Cavalieri in the cast was probably the only reason that the film was made. The review in *Variety* continued, "As to its direction and the acting, the least said the better. Lina Cavalieri looks as handsome as ever and wears clothes very well indeed and at one point in the picture does a very graceful dance. Mons. Muratore was at his best in the duelling scene, where his actions after being shot resembled a man swimming, and it was one of the best laughs in the picture, although not intended for comedy."[25] Margaret McDonald, writing in *The Moving Picture World*, praised "the beauty of photography, richness of setting and grace of posture"[26] but tempered her praise by adding that the film suffered from a "lack of dramatic fitness."[27] *The Chicago News*, however, saw fit to comment on the operatic quality of the film; opening its review with the headline "Quality of Cavalieri saves Movie Opera," it was noted that at the Fine Arts Theatre in Chicago, the film was accompanied by specially arranged extracts from operatic scores.[28]

Perhaps in deference to the enormous popularity that she had enjoyed in the country, a single copy of the film was transported to Russia in January 1916, where it premiered at the Art Electric Theatre in Moscow. Much was made of the fact that this was an exclusive presentation, and the publicity for the release made extravagant claims: "The most beautiful woman in the world and the queen of diamonds, Lina Cavalieri debuts in the film, The Bride of Death, a cine-drama in 5 acts with a prologue.... The scene of the story is laid in Rome in the present day. The outstanding staging. The luxurious shooting. The heroine's costumes are the latest Paris models by Paquin."[29] Initially the film played three times a day, but so great was the demand to see Cavalieri on the screen that all discounts and advanced bookings were suspended, and the film had to be screened five times a day to cope with the sheer numbers of the audience.

The Moscow Leaflet carried the following report: "There is a crowd at the door of the Art Electric Theatre. But the whole crowd is not admitted into the theatre because all tickets for all three performances are sold. But what has called the attention of so many people? The name of Lina Cavalieri did.... Yesterday she appeared before the Muscovites in a new phase of her career: on the screen. Impression? In the first place we can say that the woman on the screen has not aged: Lina Cavalieri, yesterday, was an effulgent beauty.... Her acting is also excellent. In her performance she gives the full scale of feelings and affections."[30] *The Theatre* noted that the line outside the cinema to see Cavalieri's film was hardly shorter than the line outside the opera house to hear Chaliapin sing in Zimine's latest season.

The Time devoted a long article to discussing Cavalieri's new choice of career: "The movie house is besieged.... The film she appears in could not be less interesting than what is going on outside the movie theatre. The street is crowded with automobiles.... All pavements, all gaps between the carriages are densely crowded. The movie! The public forces the doors. 'Let me in! I have a ticket!...' New crowds arrive. Time is moving on.... The public leaving [the performance] cannot get out."[31] The Biochrom Company, who licensed the rights of the film for Russia, soon made prints available to other theaters, and within a few weeks of the initial opening, it was being shown in movie theaters large and small. At Moscow's European Theatre the film was accompanied by a military school orchestra.

Some of the more serious critics took exception to the fact that the film's distributors had so blatantly exploited the fashion aspect of the production; one suggested that the film was so obviously simply a promotional tool for the fashion industry that they might just as well supply the audiences with the price lists of the Paris couture houses. *The Pegasus* added, "Lina Cavalieri is a very bad actress but she executes superbly the role of a Paquin model. She turns slowly and gracefully, allowing us to discern all of her costumes in detail."[32] In spite of such criticism, it was obvious that Cavalieri's first appearance on Russian movie screens was an enormous success and that *The Bride of Death* was one of the most popular films to have been released for some considerable time.

One month later, the film appeared in St. Petersburg (now renamed Petrograd). It opened simultaneously at four leading movie theaters, and the advertising that appeared in *The Theatre Review* was as extravagant as it had been in Moscow: "The rich psychological subject. The luxurious scenery. On screen will be featured the personal villa of the reigning beauty of Rome and of the world, three strings of pearls worth two million francs and a chinchilla mantel valued at 250,000 francs."[33] In their actual review, the same paper stated that the story of the film was of little interest compared to the splendid production and to the presence of Cavalieri herself on the screen, although they also commented that the star "doesn't play, she just poses."[34] The film enjoyed the same degree of success in Petrograd as it had in Moscow, and within a short time, Biochrom had licensed the film for release in Kharkov, Odessa, Kiev, Minsk and many other towns and cities, even to Irkutsk and Vladivostok.

Cavalieri's second feature film for the Tiber Studio, *La Rosa di Granata*, was made in 1916. The film was released in the United States by Paramount-Artcraft in 1919 under the title *House of Granada* (also known as *The Rose of Granada*). It had a melodramatic plot the equal of Cavalieri's previous movie; this involved a young monk forced to leave the monastery, a beautiful girl impelled to seek solace in a convent, mysterious and unexplained deaths, gunshots and sea voyages. The film became notable principally through its very notoriety: On its release, the Italian censors "cut 2.5 metres of the original film in which the protagonist, after having opened the shawl that covers her shoulders, stands before a bed at the back of the room."[35] Such a shot was considered entirely unacceptable. In view of the somewhat revealing poses in which the star had appeared in some of the many thousands of photographs that had been published of her earlier in her career, this judgment might seem somewhat redundant.

Even though Cavalieri had not appeared on a Russian stage for more than three years, Russian audiences eagerly awaited a second chance to see her on screen. Her new film release was announced in Petrograd, and a screening was promised in the near future, but there is no evidence that the film was ever shown there. When new films starring the great actresses Bernhardt and Duse appeared in Petrograd, the critic of *The Theatre Review* was quick to point out to readers, incorrectly, that Cavalieri had been the first to act in the medium: "The film with Italy's first actress [*Cenere* with Elenora Duse] appeared only two weeks ago in Petrograd cinemas, yet it already disappears from the horizon. Cavalieri made full houses in dozens of cinema theatres and for many months."[36]

Cavalieri resumed her American film career in May 1917, when Paramount Studios, one of the leading producers of the time, announced that they had signed an exclusive contact with her to make two features. The value to the studios of securing the services of such a prominent personality was highlighted in the press: "The acquisition of Mme. Cavalieri is an important one both for Paramount and its exhibitors, because she is one of the best known women in the professional world, her reputation being international and her beauty having been the source of almost

A studio still issued as a publicity shot: Cavalieri and Muratore in *The Rose of Granada* (Paramount Pictures).

endless newspaper and magazine comment for the past several years."[37]

Cavalieri's first film under the new contract was *The Eternal Temptress*, made for Famous Players, for the reputed salary of $4,600 a week. The film, made at the studios in Fort Lee, costarred Alan Hale and Elliott Dexter. It was directed by Emile Chautard, with a scenario by Eve Unsell and a screenplay by Cavalieri's friend Madame Frederick De Gresac, wife of the distinguished French baritone Victor Maurel. The story was set in Venice and, appropriately enough for the period, was a tale of espionage. Cavalieri played the Princess Cordelia Sanzio, who has captured the affections of a young American, Althrop, played by Elliott Dexter. He falls madly in love with the princess and puts himself deeply into debt in order to impress her. In an attempt to extricate himself from his financial problems, he is enticed into an espionage plot against his own country. The princess realizes what is going on, and while returning some stolen papers which would incriminate Althrop, she murders an Austrian secret service agent, played by Alan Hale. In total remorse for her actions she commits suicide and dies in the arms of the young American admirer for whom she has sacrificed herself.

Interviewed by Aileen St. John-Brenon prior to beginning her work with Famous Players, Cavalieri expressed the hope that she might be cast in a contemporary story. "I want my play to be modern.... I want a subject that is at once plausible, dramatic and up to date. Costume productions have small appeal for the picture public as it is today.... They want to see on the screen human beings. They want real people with whom they can sympathise.... The public of today wants realism."[38] After dealing with the novelty of witnessing an operatic star on screen, an experience thus far restricted primarily to the films of Geraldine Farrar, St. John-Brenon noted that, of all such performers who might wish to make the transition to this new medium, Cavalieri certainly possessed the necessary physical attributes: "Mme. Cavalieri has beauty, personality and charm, all of which are strong factors on the right side. She is not one of the fifty-seven varieties of operatic 'heavies' who nightly warble the tuneful melodies of Verdi or the difficult arias of Wagner."[39] Her personality appeared to lack all of the worst attributes of what might widely be identified as star temperament, a quality also noted by her director, Chautard, who described his star as "an artist with whom it is a pleasure to work. She is amenable to every suggestion ... and she is so animated, so full of enthusiasm for her work that it is a joy to direct her."[40]

In America, Cavalieri was reunited with the comedian Max Linder, who was developing a very successful career as a comedy actor, in direct competition with Charlie Chaplin. They had first worked together many years earlier at the Folies Bergère in Paris, where Linder was performing as an acrobatic dancer. Cavalieri was later to recall, "He had a very spectacular number: he skated on the set making the public breathless when he pretended he was about to jump off the stage. Max Linder was as good and as popular as Charlot (Chaplin) if one considers his specific abilities."[41] Linder's rivalry with Chaplin was exploited by the studios in a series of publicity stunts in which Linder, accompanied by Cavalieri, in the guises of king of comedy and queen of the opera, were subjected to a mock kidnapping and photographed in comic poses in strange locations all over Los Angeles. The published photographs served to keep the fictional battle between the two great screen clowns on the front pages of the popular press for several weeks.

The distributors of Cavalieri's new film, Paramount Pictures, also exploited this increased exposure for their star. They took out a full-page advertisement on the opening page of *The Dramatic Mirror* to promote the release of this new picture. Once again, Cavalieri's appearance in the cast and her fame as a star of the operatic stage and as a great beauty were considered the most profitable selling points: "The majority of the crowds that packed the Metropolitan Opera House on Cavalieri nights went to see her—her glorious voice was secondary to her marvellous physical beauty, her powerful personality, and her gripping dramatic power. The name, fame and ability of Mme. Cavalieri are international by-words.... Mme. Cavalieri, in her greatest dramatic triumphs, has never reached the heights she attains in this picture."[42] Perhaps the copywriters were anticipating one of the major criticisms that was to be leveled at the films made by both Enrico Caruso and Mary Garden by some commentators in the near future; without their voices, what was there to enjoy? Much, in the case of Cavalieri, as the studio had the admirable good sense to strongly suggest—emphasizing her beauty, her personality, her celebrity, or perhaps notoriety, and her effective acting as far more important than the sound of her voice.[43]

In many respects, their promotional gamble paid off. *The Bioscope* noted exactly those aspects of Cavalieri, the film actress, that Paramount had attempted to emphasize: "Wonderful for her beauty is Lina Cavalieri, rare for her grace, and as the heroine of this story, a miracle."[44] In *Variety*, the reviewer began by noting the significance of Cavalieri appearing in a Paramount release, presumably interpreting this development as a consolidation of her new career. Though no specific comments are made on Cavalieri's performance, the film itself is described as "thrilling and beautiful, with a strong plot and exceptional direction.... Seldom has the atmosphere of the Latin country been better simulated: the settings are gorgeous or sordid as the case may be, but in every case the exotic effect is maintained.... The picture is a distinct triumph in artistry and worthy of its beautiful star."[45]

In 1918 Cavalieri made *Love's Conquest* for Famous Players-Lasky. The film, directed by Edward Jose, with a scenario by Charles Whittaker, was based on Victorien Sardou's play *Gismonda*, which had first been seen in Paris in 1894, and was a stage success for Bernhardt. *Gismonda* was also originally planned to be the title of the film. The adaptation must rank as one of the most unusual of an operatic subject. The film was released in June 1918, some seven months before Henri Fevrier's opera based on the same story received its premiere, at the Sullivan Auditorium in Chicago on January 14, 1919, with Mary Garden playing the title role.[46] It was seen in New York shortly after in a production by the Boston Opera Company. The advance publicity for the film claimed that $5,000 had been spent on Mme. Cavalieri's costumes alone. With a clearly stated proviso that essentially all costume dramas should be action films, the critic of *Variety* felt that although the film "drags in spots, there are many things to be said for the picture, first and foremost the unusual beauty and grace of Cavalieri, and also the magnificence of the production, both setting and costumes."[47] The direction of Edward Jose also came in for special praise, as did the standard of photography. In conclusion, the *Variety* reviewer noted that "Cavalieri fulfils every demand as Gismonda, both in appearance and in acting."[48]

The *Theatre Magazine* made a comparison between the effectiveness of one scene in the stage and film versions of the story: "There is supposed to be a lion.... In the stage version one saw a lion's pit—indicated by a stone wall down which the actors peered interestedly while the tap drum man roared from the orchestra with his roaring machine. In the picture a real and very fierce lion was obtained. Lina Cavalieri ... told me that she prayed for that picture to be finished before any serious accident happened because of the lion. In fact, one keeper was severely attacked."[49] Cavalieri later recalled the incident with the lion very vividly, in one of a series of articles which she wrote for the Italian magazine *Film*: "The plot stated that one of my cousins who loved me had to throw my baby into the lion's den, and a brave tamer would save him. The lion was really in the den, but fortunately the baby was not. The tamer would have to move through a tunnel to get into the cage and save the innocent child. However, the lion did not like the lights, or the scenery, and refused to be tamed. With a sudden leap, he jumped over the tamer and bit him. The tamer started to scream, but nobody had the courage to get close to him, and the lion escaped from the cage. Luckily, two gaffers who had heavy hammers with them had the courage to kill the lion, saving the whole cast and crew. The poor tamer died in hospital and the lion was replaced by another, who had his claws removed."[50]

In an interview published two months after the film's release, Cavalieri compared the challenges of acting on stage with those of acting for the camera: "There is difficulty in assuming a character before the camera that is not found on stage.

Film scenes are of such short duration that the artiste who wishes to get herself into the proper temperamental spirit of the part finds that just as she is working herself into the frame of mind required, the scene is over. But I like this new artistic procedure ... because it gives scope to energetic imagination and more quickly labels the true artist of being worthy of her calling."[51]

A Woman of Impulse, Cavalieri's next film, was also made for Famous Players-Lasky, directed by Edward Jose and distributed by Paramount. Released in September 1918 and based on the play by Louis Anspacher that had been seen on Broadway earlier that same year, the cast included Gertrude Robinson, Raymond Bloomer and Robert Cain. The film included some autobiographical elements for its star. The daughter of a poor Italian family is unable to afford singing lessons until she and her sister are adopted by a wealthy American couple. She later wins fame on the operatic stage in Paris and is falsely accused of murdering her rejected suitor. In this almost ideal vehicle, Cavalieri's performance was well received, which gave further indication

A publicity photograph of Cavalieri in the garden of her summer home in Waterford, Connecticut, 1917. It was released to promote her forthcoming film *A Woman of Impulse*.

that she was developing well as a dramatic actress, although perhaps the vehicles generally chosen for her were not giving these talents a real opportunity to thrive. In *Variety*, the opening sentence of the review declared that the film proved that she was "an actress as well as merely a beautiful woman. It is a part well suited to her temperament and talents.... While the picture is cut to fit Cavalieri, and does fit her, she is capable of doing bigger and heavier things."[52]

Interestingly, the film also captured Cavalieri in several stage roles, though these were naturally adapted to fit the narrative of the film. The only extended operatic scene was a staged excerpt from *Carmen*, in which she was partnered with Muratore as Don Jose. The filming of this sequence was subsequently described in a feature article published in *Pictures and Picturegoer*: "[A]n entire opera company took part in a scene from *Carmen* before the camera.... One of the largest theatres in America was hired to give realism to this camera opera. The seats were occupied by a well dressed audience of extras who were naturally delighted at being paid to sit and listen to the famous pair, to hear whom, thousands of people have paid gold for gallery seats!"[53]

The promise suggested by her three previous features was not to be maintained in *The Two Brides*, her final film for Famous Players-Lasky, with scenario by Margaret Turnbull and, once again, directed by Edward Jose. The film was released in February 1919 but was very coolly received. A weak and convoluted plot concerning the love affair of the daughter of a sculptor who lives with her father on a small island and acts as his model failed to draw any encouraging comments from *Variety*: "The picture will never start anything anywhere. Cavalieri is always beautiful and interesting. As a model she may be worth the price of admission. Her support is capable, but the story is not, and the direction is careless."[54]

It seems that just as Cavalieri's film career was being consolidated, it fell apart again through poor choice of material. The reviewers were astute enough to know that a film career based simply on physical appearance had a finite and restricted future. What was lacking was the input of a producer who could develop material that would nurture this new career and give it a life beyond the mere exploitation of a beautiful face and figure. In her previous career as an opera star it had been possible to sustain an impressive number of engagements utilizing a relatively small and carefully chosen repertoire. The international nature of the movies and their very immediacy, which meant that a film could potentially be seen by hundreds of audiences on exactly the same day, required a faster and more varied turnover of material.

In this respect, the ultimate failure of Cavalieri's career in the cinema had much in common with that of her contemporary at the Metropolitan Opera, Geraldine Farrars, although it is fair to note that the latter had considerably more natural acting ability. The frustration expressed by Farrar in the poor quality of material being offered to her in the latter stages of her film career must also have been acutely felt by Cavalieri. They were of a similar age and both unable to continue playing the glamorous leading ladies for very much longer. Even though Cavalieri was slightly the older of the two stars, her natural physical advantages were not enough to save her movie career from entering a rapid decline after the making of *The Two Brides*.

In 1921 she made one further feature in Italy, *Amore che ritorna*, for the Libertas company. No record of a finished release has been found, and the film appears not to have been reviewed, and it is possible, therefore, that it was not completed. Cavalieri now spent the majority of her time either at her home in the south of France or accompanying her husband on his operatic engagements. In March 1921, *Musical America* published an announcement that she and her husband had formed the Cavalieri-Muratore Company and that they had made their first feature film on location near their French home. A second release was promised for later that same year. The film was *L'Idole brisée*, released in the United States in 1922 as *The Crushed Idol*. Although the article claimed that the film was directed by Muratore, Maurice Mariaud is credited in the titles. The film was released by Comptoir-Cinelocation Gaumont but failed to make any impact at the box office, and it signaled the end of Cavalieri's film career.

The conclusion of Cavalieri's movie career is clouded with the same inaccuracies as its beginning: She claimed in her autobiography that the adaptation of *Gismonda* marked her last screen appearance. Her stated reason for quitting films, however, is believable enough. She said that she "could not stand the projectors' [camera] lights and ... often suffered a severe form of conjunctivitis."[55] This problem was not uncommon among early film actors. She also recorded that she had left the cinema while her services as a film actress were still in demand. Discounting the disappointing nature of her last two film assignments, this is certainly true; her career appeared to suffer from a lack of suitable material rather than a lack of potential or ability: "I gave a silent farewell to the public when I still had all my vocal, artistic and aesthetic faculties. The farewell was meant to be only temporary, but it wasn't. I totally withdrew from the artistic scene.... Leaving cinema when the audience can still sigh, saying 'What an artist she has been!'—seems very wise to me and this satisfies both my pride and my ambition.... I withdrew without any fuss, perhaps after too sensational a career."[56] In a later article she added, "I would be wrong if I did not say that cinema actually was a satisfactory employment and I am grateful for the opportunities it has given me, but nothing could make me forget the lyric theatre,"[57] A medium to which Cavalieri was never to return.

Her final exit on the movie screen was to mark her effective exit from public life. For more than twenty-five years Lina Cavalieri had enjoyed being in the gaze of a largely adoring international public. Undoubtedly, with clever management, she could have extended her stage career. She chose not to. She certainly displayed evidence of having the ability to make a respectable career before the movie cameras but chose not to try to pursue this either beyond its natural lifespan.

It seems likely that Cavalieri, the professional celebrity, would have taken the much-quoted advice offered by the old vaudeville entertainer, "Always leave them wanting more."

VI

ENDINGS

Over the next few years, Lina Cavalieri seemed finally to lose the interest of the media as she continued to travel with her husband or live in relative obscurity either in Paris or New York. She had formed a particular affection for the town of Onano, the birthplace of her mother, Teonilla Peconi. She visited the town many times and chose as her first private secretary a young Onano man, Romeo Giuliani. In 1912, while visiting her brother Nino, who had a house on the Via Della Porta Nuova, she donated two of her elaborate stage costumes from *Thaïs* to be converted into costumes for the statues of the Vergine del Rosario and the Madonna Addolorata in the church of the Frati di Onano.[1] Apparently, Cavalieri's final visit to Onano came in the 1930s when she visited her mother, who was dying of pneumonia.

Cavalieri's devotion to the church in Onano is noted by several local historians, including Scalabrella and Bonafede Mancini, who also noted the many local stories pertaining to the singer's visits to the area:[2] "There are still a lot of unedited anecdotes about the visits.... They also tell about her cosmetic beauty face packs made with steaks of fresh meat that she applied to her face and how the whole family waited for the occasion, after this, to cook some meat for dinner. They tell about the diffusion of the records of her singing from a gramophone set up on a car, which drove through the streets and across the countryside.... The little beggar children, who, seeing Lina and her mother Teonilla parading their luxurious dresses on the streets, had a habit of putting large pebbles on the elegant trains of their dresses and shawls.... The little girls ... used to present the diva with small bunches of flowers from the fields to be remunerated with some denaro coins."[3]

Not every aspect of Cavalieri's life, however, proved to be so tranquil. It seemed that her marriage to Muratore was in some difficulties. Late in 1926 an unusual story appeared in *The New York Times*, which, in retrospect may have been symptomatic of increasing marital problems. In 1924 the French courts had judged that Ariane Rouvier was the natural daughter of the dancer Marcelline Rouvier and Lucien Muratore. The courts now overturned that decision on the basis that, at the time of the child's birth, Muratore had been married to Cavalieri. The new action had been taken by the girl's mother in an attempt to prevent Muratore from taking his eighteen-year-old "daughter" to Italy, where, it was suggested, he had intended to arrange a marriage between the girl and Cavalieri's son.[4] Perhaps unsurprisingly in July of the following year the couple was divorced in Paris. "Mme. Cavalieri charged that her husband had abandoned her and had refused her entreaties to resume married life together." The *New York Times* speculated, rather fancifully, that a major cause of the breakdown had been Muratore's disapproval of Cavalieri's increasing admiration for Benito Mussolini and his fascist regime. Whatever the real cause, Muratore seemed to recover very quickly, and in the spring of 1928, while living in Blot, near Nice, he married a twenty-three-year-old Parisian woman called Marie Louise Brivaud.

Cavalieri retired to her villa at Fiesole near Florence. In 1926 she returned to the beauty products industry with which she had been associated almost twenty years earlier. She founded an institut de beauté in Paris, which sold products of her own invention. She was also married again, for the last time, to Giovanni Campari, a wine dealer with a fondness for racing cars.

Cavalieri's death was as dramatic as many episodes in her life had been. The United Press reported on February 8, 1944, that she was killed during an Allied air raid when a stray bomb hit her house on the outskirts of Florence. A story circulated for some time that she had returned to her house from the air-raid shelter in order to rescue her jewelry. *Il Messagero* confirmed the manner of her death, noting her celebrity: "She also wrote a curious book of memoirs which had many readers at the time; the book is interesting not only for its own relevance, but also for the description of the ambience of fashionable society at the end of the 19th century when the beauty and adventures of Lina Cavalieri were so famous."[5]

Even in the report of her death, Cavalieri could not escape controversy. The brief obituary published by the *New York Times*, after noting her operatic career and her marital adventures, added, almost as a footnote, "She was reputedly an admirer of the former Duce, Benito Mussolini."[6]

In the notes to *My Parabola*, the autobiography of the baritone Titta Ruffo, who had sung with Cavalieri in *Fedora* in 1905, the singer's son adds the following account of Cavalieri's demise: "Lina Cavalieri also came to live in that city [Florence], in a villa she purchased at Poggio Imperiale.... Linked by an old friendship, the two colleagues got together frequently. Cavalieri had invited TR and some others to dinner in her villa on February 7. TR, after having accepted with pleasure the evening before, was suddenly struck by a fit of depression, and telephoned her to excuse himself from the invitation: he was upset by the lack of news of his family in Rome; the 8th February was my birthday, and in short, he preferred to be alone rather than to inflict his melancholy on someone else. The next day, at about the dinner hour, Cavalieri's villa was hit by an aerial bombardment which buried the hostess and her guests under rubble."[7]

Lina Cavalieri was buried in the Cimetero Verano in Rome.

In Russia, where Cavalieri had enjoyed such celebrity, her death passed unmarked. Although she had achieved cult status to rival the daughter of the tsar, there were few people who now remembered her and even fewer who had known her personally. Petersburg as a city of grand dukes no longer existed. That city which Cavalieri loved so much for its opulence and sumptuousness, for its style and refinement, and for its attraction to the beauty of women had even been renamed Leningrad, after the very man who had led the destruction of the old world of which she had been a part. On January 27, 1944, Leningrad celebrated the defeat of the invading Nazi army and the lifting of the 900-day siege of the city. During this period of the worst possible deprivations, the old city gave the last of its possessions to keep the new generation alive: Precious parquet floors, antique furniture, books, diaries, the correspondence of generations and albums of postcards and photographs were all burned in an effort to ward off the penetrating cold of the Leningrad winter. But not everything fed the fires. Lina Cavalieri, the subject of so many countless postcard photographs, still has a presence today in the antique shops of modern St. Petersburg. After the 1917 revolution, however, the Soviet authorities apparently considered her to be a bourgeois figure whose life and activities were a poor example to the new proletariat. The memoirs of the many Russian aristocrats who had fled from the new regime were inaccessible and have only recently become available in Russia. However, for those who wanted to rediscover this glittering figure of a past age, the Russian newspapers of her time provided as much detail of her activities as those of the most prominent politicians and often much more.

Many significant singers, musicians and composers of the nineteenth and twentieth centuries have been memorialized on screen: A highly fictionalized version of Enrico Caruso's life, *The Great Caruso*, was to become one of the most popular and influential musical features of all time. Lina Cavalieri, however, was to live on more vividly, as the subject of both theater and film, than did many of her contemporaries who survived her professionally.

The American playwright Edward Sheldon based one of his most popular characters on the soprano. The latter's play, titled *Romance*, was to score an immense international success and was adapted for two screen versions and as a Broadway musical comedy.[8] Sheldon's greatest attribute as a writer for the stage appears to have been the theatricality of his work, about which Barrett Clark wrote: "Even before the advent of O'Neill, he was aware that no matter what a writer has to say, or how subtly he may want to say it, the theatre's power depends on the writer's ability to use broad and striking effects."[9] Such a sense of theatricality would seem to recommend Sheldon as a perfect candidate to dramatize a life as full of this commodity as that of Lina Cavalieri. Sheldon, who had apparently been obsessed by the figure of Cavalieri from childhood, thinly disguised the identity of his heroine under the fictitious name of Rita Cavallini. He began working on his script, originally titled *When All Is Said*, in 1909, describing it as his "Catholic play."[10] The work was completed during a visit to Italy in 1912 and retitled *Romance*, possibly as a tribute to the actress Doris Keane, to whom Sheldon was engaged at this time and for whom the role of Rita Cavallini was created.[11]

The plot is based very loosely on Cavalieri's life story and concerns a priest who, in later life, recounts an early love affair with an operatic diva, an affair that alters the entire course of his life. Loren Ruff suggests that one of the most interesting and original aspects of the play was its construction: "Sheldon employed a relatively new device for the American theatre, when he used the flashback technique to begin his play."[12] The priest, now a bishop, is advising a young man who is about to marry and tells him the sad story of his own early romance. This narrative, seen in flashback, then becomes the main structure of the plot, and the play ends with a return to the present: As the bishop listens to a gramophone record of the voice of Rita Cavallini, he is informed by his niece that the singer had died that same day.

After a preview in Albany, *Romance* received its Broadway premiere at the Maxine Elliot Theatre in February 1913, produced by the Shubert organization. Although Cavalieri was singing in the United States throughout the spring of 1913, it is not recorded whether she attended the play, or, if she did, what her reaction was. Acton Davies, reviewing the production for *The New York Evening Sun*, stated that "Edward Sheldon produced one of the most engrossing ... dramas which has been shown in a long, long time.... It is a play which fascinates."[13] In keeping with Cavalieri's reputation for a glamorous stage persona, Sheldon went to great lengths to dress his star appropriately, hunting through antique shops in Paris to find the right jewelry: according to Eric Barnes, "Everything pointed up the personality of the diva ... a gown of black velvet ... a long string of pearls and a jewelled crucifix."[14] A portrait of Keane in the role of Cavallini, wearing this very same costume, can be seen in the theater collection of the Museum of the City of New York.

After a long and successful Broadway run, in which Doris Keane scored great personal success, Charles Dillingham produced an extensive American tour. In 1915 *Romance* opened in London and after an inauspicious start enjoyed a run of 1,049 performances, including a command performance before Queen Mary. Productions were mounted all over the world: The first Russian staging, in a translation by Matveev, was seen at the Saburov Theatre in St. Petersburg in December 1916, with Elena Granovskaya in the leading role. During the season the play was given seventy-eight times and always to a full house. Madame Maria Andreeva, Maxim Gorky's common law wife, also enjoyed great success in the leading role, in which she toured for more than five years.

In 1920, Keane repeated her role for the film cameras in an adaptation of the play coauthored by Sheldon and Wells Hastings. This seven-reel silent film version costarred Basil Sydney and Norman Trevor, was directed by Chester Withey and produced by D. W. Griffith.[15] In this way, Cavalieri enjoyed the most unusual distinction of being portrayed as a fictional character on film at the same time as appearing on screen herself.[16]

In 1930, MGM returned to Sheldon's play as a vehicle for Greta Garbo. Bess Meredith and Edwin Mayer adapted the film, and it was directed by Clarence Brown, who had already directed Garbo in *Flesh and the Devil* (1927), *Woman of Affairs* (1929) and *Anna Christie* (1930).[17] Though not an outstanding production,[18] the film was distinguished by Garbo's performance as Cavallini, for which she was nominated, jointly with *Anna Christie*, for an Academy Award.[19] An otherwise static and "stage-bound" production which makes little attempt to disguise its theatrical origins, the film itself suggests that there was little if any attempt on the part of the director or the star to reproduce any of the subject's (Cavalieri's) physical presence or performance style. On the contrary, it is possible to suggest that Garbo's screen performance, framed by an entirely theatrical production, is notably nontheatrical and, furthermore, may be considered representative of what might be called early modern naturalistic screen acting. By direct comparison, the limited extant film footage of Cavalieri suggests a performer whose technique could be described as both "operatic" and "theatrical." Garbo appears to be nonoperatic in her portrayal and, in any event, is not given the opportunity to portray an operatic performance: The film includes some staged operatic performance scenes, but for these, Clarence Brown employed a stand-in for Garbo, Geraldine de Vorak, seen only in long shots, with her singing voice dubbed by the soprano Diana Gaylen.

Romance reappeared in yet another guise at New York's Shubert Theatre in October 1948, when the play reemerged in a musical adaptation under the title *My Romance*, starring Ann Jeffreys and Charles Fredericks, with a score by Sigmund Romberg and lyrics by Rowland Leigh. Although hardly accountable as a success — it ran for less than three months — *My Romance* was significant for two other reasons. It was Romberg's last stage show produced during his lifetime, and it was the last operetta produced on the Broadway stage by the Shuberts. Brooks Atkinson, writing in the *New York Times*, dismissed *My Romance* as "pretentious fiddle-faddle ... standard operetta with standard routines and situations that have not changed through the years."[20]

The representation of Cavalieri on film did not end there. In 1955, Robert Z. Leonard directed a cast including Gina Lollabrigida, Vittorio Gasmann and Robert Alda in a highly fictionalized Italian film about Cavalieri under the title *La Donna Piu Bella del Mondo* (*The Most Beautiful Woman in the World*), released in the United States as *Beautiful but Dangerous*. The film's main source of interest is the representation of Lollabrigida in the joint roles of actress and opera singer — she recorded her own vocal track, which includes an adequate, if undistinguished, version of "Vissi d'arte."[21]

The film became the subject of a legal case when Cavalieri's brother Oreste petitioned the Rome courts to recall all copies so that certain offending scenes could be removed: These were a scene with Cavalieri's foster mother, a scene in which Lina fought a duel with the actress Manolita (a thinly disguised portrayal of Caroline Otero), and a love scene between Lina and the character of Prince Bariatinsky. An article in *Il Messagero* suggested that "Prince Wassili d'Angio-Durazzo ... intervened to settle the argument, but in vain. The prince had been connected with the Italian artiste [Cavalieri] by ties of the closest affection and friendship for more than five years. Being at the time an Imperial Guard sub-lieutenant of 18, he had assisted in the production of *La Traviata* in St. Petersburg. He was so taken with her that he had the whole route from the theatre to her hotel covered with a carpet of fresh red roses."[22] By the time of the film's release, the brief fashion for operatic biopics had begun to wane, yet it seems highly appropriate that the first major opera star to appear on the movie screen also became the last, from this era at least, to have her life story represented in this way.

Much was written of Lina Cavalieri in her lifetime, yet few of the facts of her life have been properly corroborated in the years since her death. The singer herself, of course, orchestrated some elements of the mystery, for mystery inevitably lends enchantment. In many ways, she retains her fascination because of what we do not know about her. Interviewed by Richard Fletcher while she was singing in London, Cavalieri outlined her ambitions: "Nothing means so much to me as arousing the sympathy of an audience. Applause in an opera house is my food and drink. Give me a success with my audience, and I ask for nothing else. There is nothing quite like the pleasure one feels when listening thousands are attuned to every note— every movement of the hand.... I wanted to be a prima donna, and when I want a thing."[23]

Interviewed in 1908, she was asked, "'How does it feel to be a beautiful woman?' ... 'That does not interest me in the least,' was her quick, decisive answer, 'I am much more pleased if people speak well of me as an artist.'"[24]

On her death, the writer Felix Soloni recorded, "Lino d'Ambra called her 'the last of the fatal women. Too much beauty was her fault.'"[25] But this same beauty was also her greatest asset and, combined with a well-documented skill as an effective if somewhat inconsistent and flamboyant actress, made her an ideal candidate to join the earliest ranks of the world's new glamorous elite, as leading film performers.

The discrepancies between the facts and the myths of her life and career were recognized by Cavalieri herself in the last of a series of articles which she wrote for the Italian magazine *Film*, which she titled "Verità e leggende sulla mia vita" [Truth and Legend about my Life]. Writing only four years before her death, Cavalieri provided her own fitting epitaph to one of the most intriguing and colorful careers to bridge the gap between opera and film: "I finally reached my goal.... I was able to create art.... Today, Hollywood divas live as in a legend and nothing can be known of their lives before.... I never felt the need to say that I have never worked in a florist's shop or that I never sold newspapers.... The profession of a woman, whatever it might be, is never shameful if her aim is art."[26]

Chronology of Operatic Roles and Appearances

1894	**Rome, Grande Orfeo**
1895	**Naples, Salone Marguerita**
	Vienna English Garden
1896–1897	
Winter	**Paris Folies Bergère**
1896–1900	**Paris, Folies Bergère**
1897	
May 25–June 11	**London, Empire Theatre**
July 3–19	**Saint Petersburg, Krestovsky Theatre**
September/October	**Paris, Folies Bergere**
December 26–31	**Moscow, Aumont Theatre**
1898	
January 1–February 11	**Moscow, Aumont Theatre**
January 1–2	**Moscow, International Theatre (Aumont)**
January 29	**Moscow, Shelaputin Theatre (Aumont)**
August 2–September 12	**Saint Petersburg, Aquarium**
1899	
January 11	**Saint Petersburg, Pavlova Hall (concert)**
January 14	**Saint Petersburg, Kononov Hall (concert)**
July	**Paris, Ambassadeur**

(In November 1899, Cavalieri announced that she would retire from the variety stage)

1900	
January 29	**Lisbon, Teatro San-Carlo**
	I Pagliacci (operatic debut)—with Garulli, Sammarco, DeLucia, Daddi
March 4	**Naples, Teatro San-Carlo**
	La Bohème—Bonci, Casini, Bozzoli, Nicolay, conductor Mingardi

1901

January 4   **Warsaw, Bolshoi Theatre**
                     La Bohème—with Hofman, Khodakovski, Sillikh, Skulskaia
January 11   *I Pagliacci*—with Sammarco, Cornuber
January 14   *La Traviata*—with Hofman, Sammarco
January 21   *I Pagliacci*—with Sammarco, Cornuber
January 23   *La Traviata*—with Florianski, Sammarco
January 29   *Faust*—with Cornuber, Sammarco, Sillikh
January 31   Charity concert in the Redoubt Hall, Warsaw
February 4   *I Pagliacci*—with Sammarco, Cornuber
February 7   *La Traviata*—with Florianski, Grombchevski
February 9   *La Traviata* –with Florianski, Sammarco

March ?   **Ravenna, Teatro Mariani**
                     La Bohème—with Romieri, Isalberti, conductor Nini Bellucci

April 15   **Palermo, Teatro Massimo**
                     La Bohème—Bonci, Martelli, Angelini-Fornari,
                        conductor Ferrari
                     (three performances)

May 29   **Saint Petersburg, Theatre Alexandroff Aquarium**
                     (under the management of Raoul Gunsbourg)
                     La Traviata—with Garret, Soulacroix, conductor Grelinger
May 31   *La Traviata*—with Garret, Soulacroix
June 2   *La Traviata*—with Garret, Soulacroix
June 7   *Faust*—with Garret, Soulacroix, Bouxman
June 9   *Faust*—with Garret, Soulacroix, Bouxman
June 12   *La Traviata*—with Garret, Soulacroix
June 14   *Faust*—with Garret, Soulacroix, Bouxman
June 19   *La Traviata*—with Garret, Soulacroix
June 25   *La Bohème*—with Delmas, Soulacroix, Bouxman,
                        conductor Zardo
June 27   *La Bohème*—with Delmas, Soulacroix, Bouxman
June 29   *La Bohème*—with Delmas, Soulacroix, Bouxman
June 30   *La Traviata*—with Garret, Soulacroix
July 2   *La Traviata*—with Garret, Soulacroix
July 4   *Faust*—with Garret, Soulacroix, Bouxman
July 6   *La Traviata*—with Garret, Soulacroix
                     (Benefit performance for Cavalieri)
July 7   *La Bohème*—with Delmas, Soulacroix, Bouxman
                     (Benefit performance for Red Cross Society)
July 9   *La Traviata*—with Garret, Soulacroix

October 3   **Florence, Teatro Verdi**
                     La Traviata—with Bassi

1902

February 18   **Florence, Teatro Verdi**
                     Manon—with Ventura
March 19   *Fedora*—with Ventura

May 10   **Milan, Teatro Dal Verme**
                     Manon—with Ravazzolo, Rapisardi, Montico,
                        conductor Zuccani

October 18	**Florence, Teatro Verdi**
	Andrea Chenier
November 15	*Fedora*—with Angelini

1903
April 23	**Milan, Teatro Lirico**
	Fedora—with Biolchi, Ventura, Sottolano, conductor Zuccani (eight performances)
June 1	**Performance in Paris (?)**
October 17	**Milano, Theatro Lirico**
	Thäis—with Quadri, Bonini, Brancaleoni, conductor Ferrari

1904
January 5	**Genoa, Teatro Carlo Felice**
	Fedora—with Cassandro, Innocenti, Stacciari, conductor Perosio
February 4	**Trieste, Teatro Il Comunale**
	Manon—with Mannucci, D'Albore, conductor Mingardi
February 25/March 1	**Monte Carlo, Casino**
	Les Contes de Hoffmann—with Deschamps, Renaud, Alvarez, conductor Jehin
March 9	**Saint Petersburg, Conservatory Theatre (Italian Opera Company)**
	Manon—with Paganelli, Anselmi, Kashman, Navarini, conductor Pagani
March 10	*Manon*—with Paganelli, Anselmi, Kashman, Navarini
March 20	*La Traviata*—with Anselmi, Kashman
March 21	*Manon*—with Paganelli, Anselmi, Kashman, Navarini
March 24	*La Traviata*—with Anselmi, Kashman
March 27	*La Traviata*—with Anselmi, Kashman
March 31	*La Traviata*—with Tomars, Kashman (Benefit performance for Cavalieri)
April 1	*Manon*—with Paganelli, Anselmi, Kashman, Navarini
April 2	Benefit concert in the D. Poliakov house
April 14	**Paris, Theatre Sarah Bernardt**
	(Monte Carlo Opera Company, under the management of Raoul Gunsbourg)
	Benefit performance for the Russian hospital train of Grand Duchess Maria Pavlovna
	Rigoletto –with Caruso, Renaud, Thevenet, Arimondi, conductor Vigna

1905
February 14	**Monte Carlo, Theatre Casino**
	Cherubin (world premiere) with Garden, Carre, Renaud, conductor Jehin.
February 16	*Cherubin*—(cast as above)
February 18	*Cherubin*—(cast as above)
February 19	*Cherubin*—(cast as above)
March 21	**Saint Petersburg, Theatre Maly (Italian Opera Company)**
	Manon—with Anselmi, Brombara, Navarini

March 25	*La Traviata*—with Anselmi, Battistini
March 26	*Manon*—with Anselmi, Brombara
March 31	*La Traviata*—with Anselmi, Battistini
April 9	*La Bohème*—with Antonini, Anselmi, Brombara, Navarini
	(Benefit performance for Cavalieri)
April 12	*Manon*—with Anselmi, Brombara, Navarini
April 14	*La Bohème*—with Antonini, Anselmi, Brombara, Navarini
April 16	*La Traviata*—with Anselmi, Battistini
April 18	*La Bohème*—with Antonini, Anselmi, Brombara, Navarini
April 20	*La Traviata*—with Anselmi, Battistini
April 21	*La Traviata*—with Constantino, Battistini

May 13	**Paris, Theatre de Sarah Bernardt (Sonzogno Company)**
	Fedora—with Caruso, Ruffo
May 15	*Fedora*—(cast as above)

August 6	**Orange (France), Theatre Antique**
	Mefistofele—with Chaliapin, Girerd, Bassi, Mary,
	conductor Colonne

October 18	**Genova, Theatre Politeama Genovese**
	Thäis—with Giusoni, Simeoli, Peteani, Trucchi,
	conductor Baroni
November 8	*Mademoiselle de Belle Isle*—with Veccia, Bassi, Maurizio Renaud

1906

February 6/8	**Monte Carlo, Casino**
	Mademoiselle de Belle Isle—with Bassi, Renaud,
	conductor Baroni
February 11	*Mademoiselle de Belle Isle*—(cast as above)
March 1	*Mefistofele*—with Chaliapin, De Marchi, Armand,
	conductor Jehin
March 4	*Mefistofele*—(cast as above)
March 6	*Mefistofele*—(cast as above)

March 11	**Saint Petersburg, Maly Theatre (Italian Opera Company)**
	Manon—with Anselmi, Brombara, Navarini
March 25	*La Traviata*—with N. Figner, Battistini
March 27	*Thäis* (Russian premiere)—with Battistini
March 28	*Thäis*—with Battistini
March 30	*Thäis*—with Battistini
March 31	*La Traviata*—with N. Figner, Battistini
April 2	*Thäis*—with Battistini
April 3	*Manon*
April 5	*Thäis* –with Battistini
	(Benefit performance for Cavalieri)

April 16	**Moscow, Opera of Sergei Zimine**
	Manon—with Giorgini, conductor Ippolitov-Ivanov
April 18	*La Traviata*—with Raiski, Battistini
April 19	*La Bohème*—with Raiski
April 21	*Manon* –with Giorgini
April 22	*La Traviata*—with Raiski, Battistini
April 25	*Faust*—with Raiski
April 26	*La Traviata*—with Giorgini, Vekov

April 30	**Kiev, Opera Theatre**
	La Traviata –with Shpiller, Bocharov, Gavrilov
May 2	*La Bohème*—with Losski, Akimov, Bocharov
May 3	*Faust* –with Egorov, Zelinski, Kovalevski, Rostovsky
May 8	*La Bohème*—(cast as above)
May 9	*La Traviata*—(cast as above)
May 11	**Kharkov, Opera Theatre**
	Manon—with Giorgini, Sergeev, Romanov
May 12	*La Traviata*—with Giorgini, Obraztsov, Sergeev, conductor Margulian
May 14	*La Traviata*—with Giorgini, Obraztsov, Sergeev
May 18	**Moscow, Sokolnichi Krug Garden**
	The first concert performance, conductor Gurevich
	Program included an aria from *Mefistofele* and some Italian songs
May 22	The second concert performance
December 5	**New York, Metropolitan Opera**
	Fedora (debut/U.S. premiere)—with Caruso, Scotti, Alten, conductor Vigna
December 9	Sunday evening concert
December 15	*Fedora*—(cast as above)
December 24	*Fedora*—(cast as above)
December 27	**Philadelphia Academy of Music (Metropolitan Opera)**
	Fedora (cast as above)
December 30	New York, Metropolitan Opera
	Sunday evening Concert

1907

January 4	*Fedora* (cast as above)
January 18	*Manon Lescaut* (Met. premiere)—with Caruso, Scotti, Simerli, Rossi, conductor Vigna
January 21	Gala performance—*Mefistofele* (one aria)
January 25	*Tosca*—with Caruso, Scotti, Rossi, conductor Vigna
January 27	Concert—*Cherubin* (one aria), *La Bohème* (one aria)
January 28	*La Bohème*—with Dipplel, Alten, Scotti, Journet, conductor Vigna
January 31	**Philadelphia Academy of Music (Metropolitan Opera)**
	La Bohème (cast as above)
February 5	**Philadelphia Academy of Music (Metropolitan Opera)**
	Pagliacci—with Rousseliere, Scotti, conductor Vigna
February 7	Private musicale for Mrs. J. Pulitzer
February 8	**New York, Metropolitan Opera**
	Pagliacci—with Rousseliere, Scotti, conductor Vigna
February 17	**New York, Metropolitan**
	Concert—*Manon* (one aria), *Mefistofele* (one duet, with Jacoby)
February 21	**Philadelphia Academy of Music (Metropolitan Opera)**
	Manon Lescaut (cast as above)
February 25	**New York, Metropolitan Opera**
	Manon Lescaut (cast as above)

February 28	*La Bohème*—with Caruso, Alten, Stracciari, Journet, conductor Vigna
March 2	*Manon Lescaut*—(cast as above)

March 25 **Saint Petersburg, Conservatory Theatre (Italian Opera Company)**
Thäis—with Battistini, Brombara, conductor Polacco.

March 26	*Thäis*—(cast as above)
March 28	*Thäis*—(cast as above)
March 29	*Manon*—with Anselmi
April 1	*La Bohème*—with Anselmi, conductor Polacco
April 3	*Thäis*—(cast as above)
April 4	*La Traviata*—with Anselmi, Battistini, conductor Polacco
April 5	*La Traviata*—(cast as above) (Benefit performance for Cavalieri)

June 17 **Paris, Grand Opera**
Thäis—with Delmas, Dubois, Delpouget, conductor Vidal

June 26	*Thäis*—(cast as above)
July 5	*Thäis*—(cast as above)
July 10	*Thäis*—(cast as above)
July 17	*Thäis*—(cast as above)
July 26	*Thäis*—(cast as above)
August 2	*Thäis*—(cast as above)

November 18 **New York, Metropolitan Opera**
Adriana Lecouvreur (Met. premiere)—with Caruso, Scotti, Jacoby, Journet, conductor Ferrari

November 29	*Adriana Lecouvreur*—(cast as above)

December 2 **Chicago**
Concert for Steinway and Sons

December 19 **New York, Metropolitan Opera**
Fedora—with Caruso, Alten, Scotti, conductor Ferrari

December 22	Sunday evening Concert
December 23	*Fedora*—(cast as above)
December 28	*Fedora*—(cast as above)

1908

January 4	*Pagliacci*—with Martin, Stracciari, conductor Ferrari

January 14 **Philadelphia Academy of Music (Metropolitan Opera)**
Adriana Lecouvreur—(cast as above)

January 19 **New York, Metropolitan Opera**
Sunday evening Concert

January 25	*Manon Lescaut*—(cast as above)
January 28	*Musicale for Payne Whitney*
January 29	*Manon Lescaut*—(cast as above)
February 15	*Pagliacci*—with Caruso
February 17	*Manon Lescaut*—(cast as above)
February 22	*La Bohème*—with Bonci, Barocchi, Scotti, conductor Ferrari

February 25 **Philadelphia Academy of Music (Metropolitan Opera)**
La Bohème—(cast as above)

March 4	**New York, Metropolitan Opera**
	Musicale for Mrs. Emma Gary
March 5	*Manon Lescaut*—(cast as above)
March 8	Sunday evening concert—*Carmen* (one aria)
March 14	*Manon Lescaut*—with Martin
April 10	**Boston (Metropolitan Opera)**
	Manon Lescaut—(cast as above)
April 13	**Baltimore (Metropolitan Opera)**
	Manon Lescaut—(cast as above)
April 27	**Saint Petersburg, Maly Theatre (Italian Opera Company)**
	Manon—with Sobinov
April 29	*Manon*—with Sobinov
May 1	*Thäis*—with Nani
May 3	*La Traviata*—with Sobinov
May 4	*Thäis*—with Nani
May 6	*Thäis*—with Nani
May 7	*Manon*—with Sobinov
May 9	*La Traviata*—with Sobinov
	(Benefit performance for Cavalieri)
May 10	*Thäis*—with Nani
May 12	*Faust*—with Sobinov
May 19	**Warsaw, Opera Theatre (Bolshoj)**
	Manon—with Lovchinski, Ostrovski, Grombchevski,
	conductor Sledzinski
May 21	*La Traviata*
May 23	*La Traviata*
May 26	*La Bohème*—with Dygas, Tartsikevich, Grombchevski,
	conductor Sledzinski
June 18	**London, Covent Garden**
	Manon Lescaut (debut)—with Zenatello, Scotti, Gianoli,
	Zucchi, conductor Panizza
June 24	*Manon Lescaut*—(cast as above)
July 3	*Manon Lescaut*—(cast as above)
July 7	*Fedora*—with Scotti, Garbin, Lejeune, Marcoux,
	Crabbe, Zucchi
July 18	*Tosca*—with Scotti, Garbin, Gianoli, Gillibert, Zucchi,
	conductor Campanini
July 28	*Tosca*—(cast as above)

1909

January 25	**New York, Manhattan Opera**
	Tosca (debut)—Zenatello, Sammarco, Gilibert,
	conductor Campanini
January 28	**Philadelphia, Opera House (Manhattan Opera Co.)**
	Faust—with Constantino, Arimondi, Polese, Zeppilli,
	conductor Sturani
February 2	*Tosca*—with Zenatello, Renaud, de Grazia, conductor Sturani

February 6   **New York, Manhattan Opera**
                      La Bohème—with Constantino, Zeppilli, DeSegurola,
                          Sammarco, conductor Campanini

February 13   **Philadelphia, Opera House (Manhattan Opera Co.)**
                      Faust—(cast as above) conductor Sturani

February 17   **New York, Manhattan Opera**
                      La Bohème—(cast as above)

March 7   **Saint Petersburg, Conservatory Theatre**
                      Thäis—with Battistini, conductor Truffi
March 10   *La Traviata*—with Pintucci, Battistini, conductor Truffi
March 11   *Thäis*—with Battistini
March 12   Concert in honor of jubilee of Alexis Suvorin (owner of the
                          newspaper *Novoje Vremia* [New Time]
March 20   Benefit concert in the French Embassy
March 22   *Manon*—with Carpi, Brombara
March 24   *La Bohème*—with Isalberti, Brombara, Navarini
March 26   *Manon*—with Carpi, Brombara, Rusconi
March 27   *Manon*—(cast as above)
March 30   *Thäis*—with Battistini
March 31   Concert in honor of jubilee of the impresario of Italian
                          Opera Company in St. Petersburg, Carlo Guidi
April 1   *Tosca* with Isalberti, Nani
April 2   Benefit concert in the house of the governor of St. Petersburg

May/June   **Paris, Grand Opera**
                      Thäis.—with Laute-Brun, Jeanne Durif, Campredon,
                          Goulancourt, Delmas, Dubois, Delpouget

                      New York, Manhattan Opera
November 8   *Herodiade*—with Dalmores, Renaud, Gerville-Reache,
                          Vallier, Nicolay, conductor de la Fuente

November 11   **Philadelphia, Opera House (Manhattan Opera Co.)**
                      Herodiade—with Gerville-Reache, Dalmores, Renaud,
                          conductor Nicosia

November 13   **New York, Manhattan Opera**
                      Pagliacci—with Zenatello, Sammarco, Venturini,
                          conductor Anselmi

November 16   **Philadelphia, Opera House (Manhattan Opera Co.)**
                      Herodiade—(cast as above)

November 20   **New York, Manhattan Opera**
                      Herodiade—with Doria, Duffault, conductor de la Fuente
November 24   *Herodiade*—(cast as November 8)
November 25   *Carmen*—with Zenatello, Miranda, Dufranne, Gentle,
                          Nicolay, conductor de la Fuente

November 30   **Philadelphia, Opera House (Manhattan Opera Co.)**
                      Carmen—with Zenatello, Miranda, Crabbe, conductor Nicosia

December 3   **New York, Manhattan Opera**
                      Herodiade—with Dalmores, Duffault, conductor de la Fuente

December 11   **Philadelphia, Opera House (Manhattan Opera Co.)**
                   Herodiade—with Gerville-Reache, Dalmores, Renaud,
                       conductor Nicosia

December 24   **New York, Manhattan Opera**
                   Carmen—with Carasa, Vicarino, Laskin,
                       conductor de la Fuente
December 25   *Les contes de Hoffman*—(as Giulietta), with Dalmores, Trentini,
                       Renaud, Gentle, Gilibert, conductor de la Fuente
December 27   *Carmen*—with Zenatello, Vicarino, Laskin,
                       conductor de la Fuente
December 29   *Les contes de Hoffman*—(as Giulietta), with Lucas, Trentini,
                       Renaud, conductor de la Fuente

1910
January 1   *Herodiade*—with Dalmores, D'Alvarez, Duffault,
                       conductor de la Fuente

January 11   **Philadelphia, Opera House (Manhattan Opera Co.)**
                   Pagliacci—with Zenatello, Polese, Zerola, conductor Anselmi
January 18   *Les contes de Hoffman*—(as Giulietta)—with Trentini, Lucas,
                       Gentle, Renaud, conductor Nicosia

January 21   **New York, Manhattan Opera**
                   Les contes de Hoffman—(as Giulietta), with Lucas, Trentini,
                       Renaud, conductor de la Fuente

January 29   **Philadelphia, Opera House (Manhattan Opera Co.)**
                   Les contes de Hoffman—(as Giulietta)—with Lucas, Trentini,
                       Renaud, conductor Nicosia

January 31   **New York, Manhattan Opera**
                   Les contes de Hoffman—(as Giulietta), cast as above
February 7   Gala concert—*Tosca* (Act II only)—with McCormack, Renaud,
                       conductor de la Fuente
February 18   *Pagliacci*—with Harold, Crabbe, conductor Anselmi
February 19   *Carmen*—with Dalmores, Trentini, Duchene, Dufranne,
                       Gilibert, conductor de la Fuente
February 22   *Les contes de Hoffman*—(as Giulietta), with Devries, Trentini,
                       Renaud, conductor de la Fuente
February 28   *Pagliacci*—with Harold, Crabbe, conductor Anselmi

March 5   **Philadelphia Opera House (Manhattan Opera Co.)**
                   Les contes de Hoffman—(as Giulietta), with Lucas, Gentle,
                       Trentini, Renaud, conductor Charlier

March 12   **New York, Manhattan Opera**
                   Carmen—with Devries, Crabbe, Trentini,
                       conductor de la Fuente
March 19   *Les contes de Hoffman*—(as Giulietta), with Devries, Trentini,
                       Renaud, conductor de la Fuente
March 25   Gala concert—*Les Contes d'Hoffmann* (Act II only)—with
                       Devries, Gentle, Renaud, conductor Charlier
                   Herodiade (Act I only)—with D'Alvarez, Lucas, Renaud,
                       conductor Nicosia

March 26	**Philadelphia, Opera House (Manhattan Opera Co.)**
	Gala concert (closing night of the season) –
	Les Contes d'Hoffmann (Act II only)—with Devries, Gentle,
	   Renaud, conductor Sturani
	Herodiade (Act I only)—with D'Alvarez, Lucas, Renaud,
	   conductor Nicosia

May 4	**Saint Petersburg, Conservatory Grand Hall** **(Italian Opera Company)** *Thäis*—with Battistini
May 7	*Carmen*—with Cicolinin, Parvis
May 9	*Thäis*—with Battistini
May 11	*Thäis*—with Battistini (Benefit performance of Cavalieri)
October 20	**Paris, Grand Opera** *Fedora* (second act)—with De Lucia, Heilbronner, Vours, conductor Giordano
November	*Thäis*

1911

February 1	**Saint Petersburg, Winter Palace, the White Hall** Concert of artists of Italian opera in Saint Petersburg
February 3	**Saint Petersburg, Conservatory Grand Hall** *Thäis*—with Battistini
February 7	*Thäis*—with Battistini
February 10	*Carmen*—with Pintucci, Navarini, Moretti
February 12	*Thäis*—with Battistini
February 13	*Carmen*—with Pintucci, Navarini, Moretti
February 16	*Thäis*—with Battistini (Benefit performance for Cavalieri)
February 17	Concert in honor of the impresario of Italian opera in St. Petersburg, A. Ughetti
February 19	Concert, Academy of Arts, St. Petersburg
June 6	**Paris, Grand Opera** General repetition of "Siberia"
June 9	*Siberia* (French premiere)—with Muratore
June 12	*Siberia*—(cast as above)
June 21	*Siberia*—(cast as above)
June 28	*Siberia* –(cast as above)
July 25	**Rome, Quirino** *Zaza*—with Schipa, De Ferrari, Reversi, conductor Rubino (Several more performances in July/August)
	London, London Opera House
December 15	*Herodiade*—with D'Alvarez. Renaud, Auber, Weldon, Bozzano, conductor Cherubini
December 26	*Les contes de Hoffmann*—with Lyne, Fer, Ratti, Renaud, Pollock, conductor Merola
December 27	*Herodiade*—with D'Alvarez, Danse, Auber, Weldon, Bozzano
December 29	*Les contes de Hoffmann*—(cast as above)

1912

January 2	*Les contes de Hoffmann*—(cast as above)
January 3	*Herodiade*—(cast as above)
January 6	*Les contes de Hoffmann*—(cast as above)

February 3	**Saint Petersburg, Conservatory Grand Hall**
	(Italian Opera Co.).
	Thäis—with Battistini
February 5	*Tosca*—with Garbin, Battistini
February 6	*Thäis*—with Battistini
February 8	*Manon*—with Garbin, Arimondi
February 15	*Thäis*—with Battistini
	(Benefit performance for Cavalieri)
February 16	*Tosca*—with Garbin, Battistini

1913

February through April	Concert tour with Muratore: Dates included Boston, Rochester, Cleveland, Fort Wayne, Philadelphia, Providence, New Haven, Hartford, Bridgeport, Pittsburgh, Youngstown, Toledo, Detroit, Kansas City

March 9	**New York, Hippodrome Theatre**
	Concert with Lucien Muratore, conductor Nathan Franko
	Program included extracts from *Werther*, *Manon Lescaut*, *Mefistofele*

June 27	**Paris, Grand Opera**
	Thäis—with Vanni Marcoux

August 12	**San Sebastian, Grand Teatro Circo**
	Pagliacci—with Ruffo, Ibos, Gaudenz [performance cannot be verified]

1916

	Milano, Theatro Carcano
	La Traviata (last verified stage performance)

1920

April 1/3	**Lecce, Politeama Greco**
	La Traviata—with Volpi, Bartolini, conductor Sabastiani [performance cannot be verified]

FILMOGRAPHY

Manon Lescaut (1914)
Playgoers Film Co. (U.S.)
Director—Herbert Hall Winslow
Scenario—based on the novel by Abbe Prevost
Cast—Lina Cavalieri, Lucien Muratore, Frank H. Westerton, Dorothy Arthur

Sposa nella Morte (*The Bride of Death*) (1915)
Tiber Film, Rome (Italy)
Director—Emilio Ghione
Scenario—Emilio Ghione and Lucien Muratore
Cast—Lina Cavalieri, Lucien Muratore, Ida Carloni Talli, Albert Collo, Luigi Scotto
(Released in the United States as *The Shadow of Her Past*)
Archive—Filmoteca de la Generalitat, Valencia (incomplete—approx. 22 minutes, with Spanish intertitles—damaged but restored), Cineteca del Commune di Bologna, Bologna, Italy (same version as above)

La Rosa di Granata (1916)
Tiber Film, Rome (Italy)
Director—Emilio Ghione
Scenario—Emilio Ghione and Lucien Muratore
Cast—Lina Cavalieri, Lucien Muratore, Diomira Jacobini, Ida Carloni Talli, Kally Sambucini
(Released in the United States as *The House of Granada*)

The Eternal Temptress (1917)
Famous Players Film Co. (Distributed by Paramount Pictures) (U.S.)
Director—Emile Chautard
Scenario—Eve Unsell, based on a story by Mme. De Gresac
Cast—Lina Cavalieri, Elliot Dexter, Alan Hale, Edward Fielding, Hallen Mostyn
(Released in Italy, 1920, as *L'eterna Tentatrice*)

Love's Conquest (1918)
Famous Players—Lasky Corp. (U.S.)
Director—Edward Jose
Scenario—Charles E. Whittaker (based on *Gismonda*, by Victorien Sardou)
Cast—Lina Cavalieri, Courtenay Foote, Fred Radcliffe, Frank Lee, Isabelle Berwin
(The original title for the film was *Gismonda*)

A Woman of Impulse (1918)
Famous Players—Lasky Corp. (U.S.)
Director—Edward Jose

179

Scenario—Eve Unsell (based on the play by Louis Anspacher)
Cast—Lina Cavalieri, Gertrude Robinson, Raymond Bloomer, Robert Cain, Ida Waterman
(The film included scenes from *Carmen*, which feature Lucien Muratore)
(Released in Italy, 1920, as *Unna donna impulsiva*)

The Two Brides (1919)
Famous Players—Lasky Corp. (U.S.)
Director—Edward Jose
Scenario—Margaret Turnbull (from a story by Alicia Ramsey)
Cast—Lina Cavalieri, Courtenay Foote, Hal Reid, Warburton Gamble
(Released in Italy, 1920, as *La donna e la statua*)

L'Idole brisée (1920)
Comptoir-Cinelocation Gaumont, Paris (France)
Dir. Maurice Mariaud
Scenario—Albert Dieudonne
Cast—Lina Cavalieri, Lucien Leubas, Herbert Langley, Alice Garreray, Henri Bandin
(Released in Italy in 1922; released in the United States as *The Crushed Idol*)

Amore che Ritorna (1921)
This film, although listed in Cavalieri's biography, appears not to have been completed

DISCOGRAPHY

American Columbia

February 1910
A5172

Puccini *La Bohème*—Mi Chiamano Mimi
Boito *Mefistofele*—L'Altra Notte

February 24, 1910
A5178

Puccini *Tosca*—Vissi D'Arte
Puccini *Manon Lescaut*—In Quelle Trine Morbide

February/March 1910
A5179

Bizet *Carmen*—Habañera
Di Capua—Mari, Mari

March 1913
A1434

Di Capua—O Sole Mio
Tosti—Mattinata

American Pathé

Date ?
62030

Bizet *Carmen*—Habañera
Massenet *Herodiade*—Il est doux

NOTES

Chapter I

1. Erté, *My Life, My Art*, New York: E. P. Dutton, 1989.

2. See Erté, op. cit, p. 19.

3. Marvin Lyons, letter to Olga Usova, Dec.11, 2000.

4. Rupert Christiansen, *Prima Donna*, London: Penguin Books Ltd., 1986, pp. 195–196.

5. Sergei Levik, trans. Edward Morgan, *The Levik Memoirs*, London: Symposium Records, 1995, pp. 115–116.

6. See Sergei Levik, op. cit, p. 116.

7. See Sergei Levik, op. cit., p. 116.

8. See Sergei Levik, op. cit., p. 116.

9. See Sergei Levik, op. cit., p. 116.

10. William Armstrong, "Lina Cavalieri, the Famous Beauty of the Operatic Stage", in *Munsey's Magazine*, April 1908, pp. 77–78.

11. Jarro (G. Piccini), *Viaggio Umoristico nei Teatri*, Florence: R. Bemporad e figlio editori, 1903, pp. 20–21.

12. *The Petersburg Newspaper*, 01.04.1902.

13. Lina Cavalieri and Paolo D'Arvanni, *Le Mie Verita*, Rome: Poligrafica Italiana, 1936, p. 163.

14. This event is recorded in the baptismal book, 1875–1880, page 59 (historic archives of the Rome vicariate).

15. M. Dell'Arco, *Café chantant di Roma*, Rome, 1970, p. 27.

16. See Rupert Christiansen, p. 195.

17. M. Illari, "Lina Cavalier nel cinquantesimo della morte," in *Lazio ieri e oggi*, no. 10, 1994, p. 298.

18. Lina Cavalieri and Paulo D'Arvanni, *Le Mie Verita*, Rome: Polygrafica Italiana, 1936, p. 69

19. See Cavalieri and D'Arvanni, op. cit., p. 22.

Chapter II

1. Paolo Guzzi, *Café-chantant a Roma: Il Caffè-concerto tra canzoni e "varietà" da Lina Cavalieri alla Bella Otero, da Fregoli a Petrolini*, Roma: Rendina Editori, 1995, p. 8.

2. See Cavalieri and D'Arvanni, *Le Mie Verità*, p. 20.

3. O. Taburi, *Gloria e Bellezza di Lina Cavalieri*, Rome: Studio Editoriale Italiano, pp. 20–21.

4. V. Paliotti, *Salone Margherita. Una storia napoletana: Il primo café-chantant d'Italia dalle follie della belle époque all'avanspettacolo e oltre*. Naples: Altrastampa Edizioni, 2001, p. 88.

5. See Cavalieri and D'Arvanni, p. 30.

6. See Cavalieri and D'Arvanni, p. 30

7. Lina Cavalieri, "Le Memorie di Lina Cavalieri: Il Tempo dei giuochi è finito," in *Film*, no. 51, 1939, p. 5.

8. See Cavalieri and D'Arvanni, p. 69.

9. Yuri Belayev, *Actors and Plays*, St. Petersburg, 1902, p. 191.

10. Anastasia Tsvetayeva, *Memoirs*, Moscow: Soviet Writer, 1983, p. 117–118.

11. M. A. Rostovtsev, *Pages of Life*, Leningrad: Academic Small Opera Theater Edition, 1939, p. 95.

12. V. Yureneva, *Memoirs of an actress*, Moscow-Leningrad, 1946, p. 11.

13. Leonid Sobinov, letter to E. Korneva, dated June 20, 1901, in Leonid Sobinov, *Letters, Volume 1*, Moscow: Iskusstvo, 1970, pp. 115–116.

14. "Some Pretty Parisians," in *The Sketch*, April 19, 1899, p. 544.

15. To avoid unnecessary complications and confusions, we have adopted the new calendar for all future date references.

16. *Playbills of the Imperial Theatre*, St. Petersburg, June 8, 1897.

17. *The Petersburg Newspaper*, no. 159, 13 (June 6, 1897).

18. *The Petersburg Leaflet*, no. 168, June 22, 1897.

19. *The Playbills of the Imperial Theatres*, June 21,.1897.

20. *The Petersburg Newspaper*, no. 170, June 24, 1897.

21. *The Petersburg Newspaper*, July 10, 1897.

22. *The Petersburg Newspaper*, May 7, 1898.

23. Otero was born Dec. 20, 1868, and died April 12, 1965.

24. *The Moscow Leaflet*, Dec. 14 1897.

25. *The News of the Season*, Dec. 15–16, 1897.

26. *The Moscow Leaflet*, Jan. 18, 1898.

27. Marcel Edrich, *The Mysterious Coco Chanel*, Moscow, 1994, p. 109.

28. *The Petersburg Newspaper*, July 22, 1898.

29. *The Petersburg Leaflet*, July 24, 1898.

30. *The Petersburg Newspaper*, Aug. 3, 1898.

31. *The Petersburg Leaflet*, Aug. 16, 1898.

32. *The Petersburg Leaflet*, Aug. 26, 1898.

33. *The Petersburg Leaflet*, Feb. 2, 1899.

34. *The Petersburg Newspaper*, Jan. 31, 1899.

35. *The Petersburg Leaflet*, Feb. 8, 1899.

36. *The Petersburg Leaflet*, March 4, 1899.

37. *The Petersburg Leaflet*, Sept. 9, 1899.

38. *The Petersburg Newspaper*, Dec. 6, 1899.

39. See Cavalieri and D'Arvanni, p. 65.

40. *The International Dictionary of Opera, vol. 1.*, London, 1993, p. 227.

41. *The International Dictionary of Opera, vol. 1.*, London, 1993, p. 227.

Chapter III

1. Lina Cavalieri, "Una dedica di Gabriele D'Annunzio," from "Le Memorie di Lina Cavalieri," in *Film*, no. 3, Rome, January 1940, p. 6.

2. See Lina Cavalieri, "Una dedica di Gabriele D'Annunzio," p. 6.

3. Robert Tuggle, *The Golden Age of Opera*, New York: Holt, Rinehart and Winston, 1983, p. 120.

4. De Segurola's memory of this is somewhat suspect: Thomas Kaufman's chronology of Caruso's stage appearances (in Enrico Caruso Jr. and Andrew Farkas, *Enrico Caruso: My Father and My Family*, Portland, Ore.: Amadeus Press, 1990) places Caruso in St. Petersburg in January 1900 and confirms his Lisbon debut as February 1903.

5. Andreas De Segurola, *Through My Monocle*, Steubenville, Ohio: Crest Publishing Co., 1990, p. 77.

6. At this early stage in her career, it seems certain that her sponsor was Prince Bariatinsky. She remained with him until July 1901, and in October of that year he married.

7. See Andreas De Segurola, op. cit., pp. 77–78.

8. See Andreas De Segurola, op. cit., p.78.

9. *The Petersburg Leaflet*, Dec. 29, 1900

10. *The New York Sun*, Oct. 27, 1909.

11. "Cavalieri talks of her operatic ambitions," in *Theatre Magazine*, Feb. 1910, p. 58.

12. See Lina Cavalieri, "Una dedica di Gabriele D'Annunzio," p. 6.

13. *The Petersburg Newspaper*, April 6, 1900.

14. *Il Mattino*, April 8–9, 1900.

15. *Il Mattino*, April 8–9, 1900, op. cit.

16. "Cavalieri without Puritans," in *Il Pungolo*, April 8–9, 1900.

17. See "Cavalieri without Puritans," op. cit.

18. Jerome Shorey, "The Romance of Cavalieri and Muratore," in *Photoplay*, March 1919, p. 34.

19. Lina Cavalieri, "La fatica di essere bella," from "Le Memorie di Lina Cavalieri," in *Film*, no. 4, Rome, January 1940, p. 8.

20. The Ravenna performance, at the Teatro Mariani, took place in March 1901 and was followed by three performances at the Teatro Massimo in Palermo in April, in which she was partnered by Alessandro Bonci.

21. Matilde Serao, in *Il Mattino*, op. cit.

22. *The Warsaw Journal*, Oct. 11, 1900.

23. *The Petersburg Newspaper*, Nov. 7, 1900.

24. *The Warsaw Journal*, Dec. 23, 1900.

25. See *The Warsaw Journal*, Dec. 23, 1900, op. cit.

26. See *The Warsaw Journal*, Dec. 23, 1900, op. cit.

27. See *The Warsaw Journal*, Dec. 23, 1900, op. cit.

28. *The Warsaw Journal*, Dec. 27, 1900.

29. *The Petersburg News*, Nov. 7, 1900.

30. *The Warsaw Journal*, Dec. 31, 1900.

31. See *The Warsaw Journal*, Dec. 31, 1900, op. cit.

32. *The Warsaw Journal*, Jan. 3, 1901

33. *The Warsaw Journal*, Jan. 12, 1901

34. See *The Warsaw Journal*, Jan. 12, 1901, op. cit.

35. See *The Warsaw Journal*, Jan. 12, 1901, op. cit.

36. *The Warsaw Journal*, Jan. 18, 1901.

37. *The Warsaw Journal*, Jan. 28, 1901.

38. James Harding, *Massenet*, New York: St. Martin's Press, 1970, p. 121.

39. See Lina Cavalieri, "La fatica di essere bella," p. 8.

40. Buyanov, "Diary" in *The Petersburg Leaflet*, May 13, 1901.

41. *The Petersburg Newspaper*, May 17, 1901.

42. See, *The Petersburg Newspaper*, May 17, 1901, op. cit.

43. *The Petersburg Leaflet*, May 17, 1901.

44. *The St. Petersburg Gazette*, May 17, 1901.

45. See *The Petersburg Leaflet*, May 17, 1901, op. cit.

46. See *The St. Petersburg Gazette*, May 17, 1901, op. cit.

47. See *The St. Petersburg Gazette*, May 17, 1901, op. cit.

48. N. Soloviev, *The Exchange Gazette*, May 18, 1901.

49. *The New Time*, no. 9053, May 20, 1901.

50. "Spectator," in *The Petersburg Newspaper*, May 20, 1901.

51. See *The Petersburg Newspaper*, op. cit. May 20, 1901.

52. See *The Petersburg Newspaper*, op. cit. May 20, 1901.

53. *The St. Petersburg Gazette*, May 27, 1901.

54. See *The St. Petersburg Gazette*, op. cit., May 27, 1901.

55. See *The St. Petersburg Gazette*, op. cit., May 27, 1901.

56. *The News and Bourse Newspaper*, May 27, 1901.

57. See *The News and Bourse Newspaper*, May 27, 1901, op. cit.

58. See *The News and Bourse Newspaper*, May 27, 1901, op. cit.

59. *The Petersburg Leaflet*, May 30, 1901.

60. *The Petersburg Newspaper*, June 3, 1901.

61. *The Petersburg Newspaper*, June 13, 1901.

62. *The News and Exchange*, June 16, 1901.

63. Leonid Sobinov, letter to E. Korneva, June 20, 1901, in, Leonid Sobinov, *Letters*, vol. 1, Moscow: Iskusstvo, 1970, pp. 115–116.

64. *The New Time*, June 27, 1901.

65. *The Petersburg Leaflet*, June 28, 1901.

66. *The Petersburg Leaflet*, July 15, 1901.

67. *The Theatre and Art*, no. 35, Aug. 25, 1901.

68. Vialtseva had been born in 1871 and made her debut as a chorus member in Kiev in 1887. She first appeared at the Aquarium in Moscow in 1893 and for the next four years performed mostly as an operetta singer before incorporating popular gypsy romances into her repertoire. As an opera singer she appeared in both St. Petersburg and Moscow, dying in 1913.

69. See Lina Cavalieri, "La fatica di essere bella," p. 8.

70. James Harding, *Massenet*, New York: St. Martin's Press, 1970, p. 121.

71. Sobinov's fees for the 1904 season reached 1,700 rubles per performance; Cavalieri's fees were estimated at 1,500 rubles and Arnoldson's at 1,000.

72. Quoted by T. J. Walsh, *Monte Carlo Opera, 1879–1909*, Ireland: Gill and Macmillan, 1975, p. 183.

73. Leonid Sobinov, letter to M. Ostrovskaya, Feb. 16, 1904, in Leonid Sobinov, *Letters*, vol. 1, Moscow: Iskusstvo, 1970, pp. 226–227.

74. *The Petersburg Leaflet*, Feb. 25, 1904.

75. See *The Petersburg Leaflet*, op. cit., Feb. 25, 1904.

76. *The Petersburg Newspaper*, Feb. 25, 1904.

77. *The Petersburg Newspaper*, Feb. 2, 1904.

78. Ossip Dymov, in *The Exchange Gazette*, March 7, 1904.

79. See, Ossip Dymov, op. cit., March 7, 1904

80. E. A. Stark, in *The St. Petersburg Journal*, Feb. 26, 1904

81. See *The St. Petersburg Journal*, Feb. 26, 1904.

82. *The Exchange Gazette*, Feb. 26, 1904.

83. *The New Time*, Feb. 26, 1904.

84. M. Nesterov, *Theatre and Art*, Feb. 29, 1904.

85. *The Petersburg Newspaper*, March 1, 1904.

86. Y. Beliayev, *New Time*, March 7, 1904.

87. *The Petersburg Newspaper*, March 9, 1904.

88. *The Petersburg Newspaper*, March 8, 1904.

89. See *The Petersburg Newspaper*, op. cit., March 8, 1904.

90. Yuri Beliayev, *The New Time*, March 9, 1904.

91. *The Petersburg Diary*, which reported this event, also noted that in February and March alone, 70,000 postcards had been sold in St. Petersburg featuring portraits of Cavalieri.

92. *Le Monde Illustré*, no. 2645, April 16, 1904.

93. Pierre Key, *Enrico Caruso: A Biography*, London: Hurst and Blackett, Ltd., 1923, pp. 196–197.

94. *The Petersburg Newspaper*, March 23, 1904.

95. See *Le Monde Illustré*, April 16, 1904, op. cit.

96. *Le Journal de Monte Carlo*, April 19, 1904.

97. *Le Journal de Monte Carlo*, Feb. 21, 1905.

98. André Charlot, in *Le Monde Illustré*, no. 2500, Feb. 25, 1905.

99. *The Petersburg Theatregoers Diary*, Oct. 2, 1904.

100. *The Petersburg Leaflet*, March 22, 1905.

101. Yuri Beliaev, *The New Time*, March 27, 1905.

102. *The Petersburg Leaflet*, April 2, 1905.

103. *The Petersburg Newspaper*, Jan. 7, 1906.

104. *The Petersburg Newspaper*, Jan. 22, 1906.

105. *The Petersburg Newspaper*, Sept. 14, 1905.

106. Victor Abaza, *The Petersburg Theatregoers' Diary*, April 23, 1905.

107. Yuri Elets, *The Petersburg Theatregoers' Diary*, May 7, 1905.

108. *The Petersburg Newspaper*, April 16, 1905.

109. Nicola Daspuro (trans. Arrigo Anitua), *Enrico Caruso*, Mexico City: Ediciones Coli, 1943.

110. T. R. Ybarra, *Caruso: The Man of Naples and the Voice of God*, New York: Harcourt, Brace and Company, 1953, p. 123.

111. Frances Alda, *Men, Women and Tenors*, New York: AMS Press, 1971, p. 132.

112. See Frances Alda, p. 132.

113. The libretto for Giordano's opera was written by Arturo Colautti. The opera was premiered at the Teatro Lirico, Milan, in November 1889.

114. The play *Fedora*, which had opened at the Vaudeville in Paris in December 1882, was the first of seven vehicles which Sardou wrote for Bernhardt; the others were to include *La Tosca* (1887) and *Gismonda* (1894), both of which were also to be memorably adapted for the operatic stage.

115. See Lina Cavalieri, "La fatica di essere bella," p. 8.

116. A. Boisard, in *Le Monde Illustré*, no. 2513, May 27, 1905.

117. Nina Froud and James Hanley (eds.), *Chaliapin: An Autobiography as Told to Maxim Gorky*, London: MacDonald, 1967, p. 180.

118. See Lina Cavalieri, *Le Mie Verità*, op. cit., pp. 94–96.

119. See Lina Cavalieri, *Le Mie Verità*, op. cit., pp. 94–96.

120. See Lina Cavalieri, *Le Mie Verità*, op. cit., pp. 94–96.

121. Spiro Samara (Spiros Samaras) was born in Corfu in 1863. He studied at the Athens Conservatoire and later in Paris with Delibes and Massenet. A pioneer of the verismo style, his first opera, *Flora Mirabilis*, was premiered at the Teatro Carcano Milan in 1886. His work found favor with Sonzogno, who staged Samara's opera *La Martire* as the opening production of his Teatro Lirico in Milan in 1894. His opera *Medge*, staged at the Costanzi in Rome in 1888, featured Calve in the title role, and in 1896 he composed a hymn in celebration of the modern Olympic movement. He died in 1917.

122. The work later enjoyed a respectable success in Milan, Constantinople and Berlin.

123. See Lina Cavalieri, *Le Mie Verità*, op. cit., pp. 94–96.

124. "The Artistic Life," in *Le Journal de Monte Carlo*, Feb. 13, 1906.

125. Fernand Platy, "The Artistic Life," in *Le Journal de Monte Carlo*, March 6, 1906.

126. *The Petersburg Newspaper*, March 12, 1906

127. Yuri Beliaev, *The New Time*, March 13, 1906.

128. A. Ossovski, *The Word*, no. 398, March 14, 1906.

129. *The Word*, March 27, 1906.

130. The New Time, no. 10776, March 28, 1906.

131. *The Petersburg Newspaper*, March 28, 1906.

132. *The New Time*, March 29, 1906.

133. See *The New Time*, op. cit.

134. *The Exchange Gazette*, April 4, 1906.

135. *The New Time*, no. 10785, April 6, 1906.

136. *The Moscow Leaflet*, March 30, 1906.

137. A. Less, *Titta Ruffo: Life and Work*, Moscow: Soviet Composer, 1983, pp. 33–34.

138. *The Muscovite*, April 18, 1906

139. *The Daily News*, April 18, 1906

140. *The Daily News*, April 20, 1906

141. *The Daily News*, April 20, 1906.

142. Ilya Schneider, *Sketchbook of an Old Muscovite*, Moscow, 1970, pp. 63–66.

143. *Life Echoes*, March 29, 1906.

144. *The Kiev Citizen*, no. 97, April 22, 1906.

145. *Kievskaya Zarya*, no. 26, May 1, 1906.

146. V. Chechott, *Kievskaya Zarya*, no. 27, May 2, 1906.

147. B. Yanovsky, *Echoes of Life*, no. 81, May 3, 1906.

148. V. Chechott, *Kiev Dawn*, no. 35, May 10, 1906.

149. *Kharkov Life*, no. 60, May 5, 1906.

150. *The Day Before*, no. 44, May 13, 1906.

151. *The Day Before*, May 13, 1906.

152. *The Kharkov Gazette*, no. 95, May 13, 1906

153. "Music Notes," in *South Country*, no. 8775, May 14, 1906.

154. *The Moscow Gazette*, no. 119, May 19, 1906.

155. See *The Moscow Gazette*, op. cit., May 19, 1906

156. *The Moscow Gazette*, no. 122, May 24, 1906

Chapter IV

1. Records in the archives at the Metropolitan Opera confirm that in the 1906–1907 season, Emma Eames was the highest paid singer, receiving $1,500 per performance: Caruso was the second highest, at $1,440, followed by Marcella Sembrich at $1,200. All of the other principal artists on the Met's roster received fees lower than Cavalieri's: Gadski ($1,000), and Farrar ($700), Fremstad and Schumann-Heink ($500).

2. "La Cavalieri Signs Conried's Contract," handwritten transcript of press report, no publication, no date (Metropolitan Opera archives, New York).

3. Mary Jane Matz, "Manon Incarnate: The Story of Lina Cavalieri," in *Opera News*, March 26, 1956, p. 8.

4. Pay book for 1906–1907 season, Metropolitan Opera archives, New York.

5. See pay book for 1906–1907 season, op. cit.

6 Lina Cavalieri and Paulo D'Arvanni, *Le Mie Verità*, Rome: Polygrafica Italiana, 1936, p. 106.

7. See Michael Aspinall, p. 47.

8. See Lina Cavalieri and Paulo D'Arvanni, p. 107.

9. W. J. Henderson, quoted by Irving Kolodin, *The Story of the Metropolitan Opera*, New York: 1966, p. 182.

10. "Lina Cavalier Sings as Fedora," in *The New York Telegraph*, Dec. 6, 1906, no page number.

11. See Robert Tuggle, p. 120.

12. Puccini, letter to Tito Ricordi, January 19, 1907, in Mosco Carner (ed.), *Letters of Giacomo Puccini*, London: Harrap, 1974, p. 86.

13. "Conried Produces Manon Lescaut," in *Musical America*, Jan. 26, 1907, p. 3.

14. See "Conried Produces Manon Lescaut," op. cit. p.3.

15. "Manon Lescaut," in *The New York Globe*, Jan. 19, 1907, no page number.

16. "Mlle. Cavalieri's Success as Mimi," in *The New York Herald*, no publication date, no page number (Robinson Locke scrapbook, vol. 108, NYPL Perf. Arts).

17. "Puccini Operas at Metropolitan," in *The New York Telegraph*, March 3, 1907, no page number.

18. Although the *Theatre Review* (Feb. 7, 1907) mentioned that Cavalieri was studying this role in Rubinstein's opera, she never actually performed it on stage.

19. A. Koptiayev, "Cavalieri in Thaïs," in *The Exchange Gazette*, March 26, 1907

20. *The Exchange Gazette*, April 2, 1907.

21. *The Petersburg Leaflet*, no. 77, April 7, 1907.

22. Mathilda Kshessinskaya, *Memoirs*, Moscow, 1992, pp. 118–119.

23. Edmond Stoullig, *Les Annales du Theatre et de la Musique*, 1907.

24. "Cavalieri to Sing Carmen," in *The New York Times*, Oct. 30, 1907, p. 4.

25. See "Cavalieri to Sing Carmen," op. cit.

26. Pay book, 1907–1908 season, Metropolitan Opera archives, New York.

27. "Metropolitan Opens with Italian Opera," in *Musical America*, Nov. 23, 1907, p. 1.

28. "Brilliant Audience Attends Opening of Metropolitan Opera House," in *Musical America*, Nov. 23, 1907, p. 3.

29. See "Brilliant Audience Attends Opening of Metropolitan Opera House," op. cit.

30. See "Brilliant Audience Attends Opening of Metropolitan Opera House," op. cit.

31. "Adriana Lecouvreur at the Metropolitan Opera House," no publication, Nov. 19, 1907, no page number (Robinson Locke scrapbook, vol. 108, NYPL Perf. Arts).

32. "The Metropolitan Opening," in *The Musical Leader*, Nov. 21, 1907, no page number.

33. "Lina Cavalieri Sings for Chicago Society," in *Musical America*, Dec. 14, 1907, p. 18.

34. See "Lina Cavalieri Sings for Chicago Society," op. cit.

35. Quaintance Eaton, *Opera Caravan*, New York: Da Capo Press, 1978, p. 128.

36. *The Petersburg Leaflet*, April 28, 1908.

37. *The New Time*, April 29, 1908.

38. *The New Time*, May 4, 1908.

39. *The Exchange Journal*, 4.05.1908.

40. According to the Italian newspaper *L'Espresso* (March 25, 1956), her son, Alessandro, was born as the consequence of a liaison that the 22-year-old Lina had with the Marquis Carlo di Rudini.

41. Serge Oblenski, *One Man in His Time*, New York, 1958, pp. 164–165.

42. Ivan Nikolaevich Perestiani, *Seventy-Five Years of My Life in Art*, Moscow: Iskusstvo, 1962, p. 186.

43. *The Warsaw Diary*, no. 129, May 23, 1908.

44. *The Warsaw Diary*, no. 134, May 28, 1908.

45. See *The Warsaw Diary*, no. 134, op. cit.

46. *The Petersburg Newspaper*, no. 152, June 18, 1908.

47. *The Petersburg Newspaper*, no. 131, May 27, 1908.

48. Harold Rosenthal, *Two Centuries of Opera at Covent Garden*, pp. 332–333.

49. See Harold Rosenthal, op. cit., p. 333.

50. "Opera at Covent Garden," in *The London Musical Courier*, May 9, 1908, p. 245.

51. See "Opera at Covent Garden," op. cit., p. 245.

52. James Mapelson (1830–1901) produced several seasons of Italian opera in London at theaters, including Covent Garden and Drury Lane, between 1861 and 1889. He also produced seasons at the Academy of Music in New York and extensive tours with leading artists such as Adelina Patti. His colorful, if sometimes inaccurate, memoirs have been published (Harold Rosenthal, ed., *The Mapelson Memoirs*, London: Putnam, 1966).

53. "Mlle. Cavalieri's Romantic Story," in *The Tatler*, no. 306, May 20, 1908, p. 198.

54. *The Tatler*, July 1, 1908, p. 18.

55. See *The Tatler*, op. cit., p. 18.

56. See *The Tatler*, op. cit., p. 18.

57. See *The Tatler*, op. cit., p. 18.

58. "Manon Lescaut," in *The Times*, June 19, 1908, p. 11.

59. "A New Singer," in *The Daily Telegraph*, June 19, 1908, p. 9.

60. See "A New Singer," in *The Daily Telegraph*, op. cit. p. 9.

61. See "A New Singer," in *The Daily Telegraph*, op. cit. p. 9.

62. See "A New Singer," in *The Daily Telegraph*, op. cit. p. 9.

63. Michael Aspinall, "La Voce della Donna piu Bella del Mondo," in *Musica*, no. 88, 1994, p. 49.

64. This was the first London revival for Giordano's opera: It had been staged at Covent Garden in 1906, with Giachetti, Caruso's mistress, in the title role, supported by Zenatello and Sammarco.

65. "Fedora," in *The Musical News*, July 18, 1908, p. 55.

66. *The Times*, July 8, 1908, p. 11.

67. See "Fedora," in *The Musical News*, op. cit., p. 55.

68. *The Daily Telegraph*, July 8, 1908, p. 12.

69. "La Tosca at Covent Garden," in *The Daily Graphic*, July 20, 1908, p. 5.

70. *The Times*, July 20, 1908, p. 6.

71. *The Musical News*, Aug. 8, 1908, p. 125.

72. *The Petersburg Newspaper*, no. 320, Dec. 3, 1908.

73. This incident is dealt with in detail later in this chapter.

74. Garden was not the original creator of the role. That privilege had fallen to her friend and former benefactress, the American Sybil Sanderson, at the Paris Opera in 1894.

75. She sang *Manon* at the Paris Opéra Comique in 1901; *Griselidis* at Aix the following year; later, in 1905, she was to score a personal triumph at Monte Carlo, creating the title role in *Cherubin*, with Cavalieri as L'Ensoleillad, which she repeated in Paris three months later. In November 1908, Garden created Jean for the New York premiere of *Le Jongleur de Notre Dame* and a year

later sang *Sapho* for Hammerstein in Philadelphia. The year 1911 saw her add the prince in *Cendrillon* to her growing repertoire, and she was the first New York Dulcinée in *Don Quichotte* in 1914. She sang *Cleopatre* in Chicago in 1919 and later in her career gave a few performances of Charlotte in *Werther* and Anita in *La Navarraise*.

76. Mary Garden and Louis Biancolli, *Mary Garden's Story*, London: Michael Joseph, 1952, p. 131.

77. See Mary Garden and Louis Biancolli, op. cit., p. 105–106.

78. "Mary Garden as Thaïs" in *The New York Times*, Dec. 14, 1907, no page number.

79. "Massenet Thaïs at the Manhattan" in *The New York Times*, Nov. 12, 1908, no page number.

80. See "Massenet Thaïs at the Manhattan" in *The New York Times*, Nov. 12, 1908, no page number.

81. "Lina Cavalieri for the Manhattan" in *The New York Times*, Jan. 19, 1909, no page number.

82. See Mary Garden and Louis Biancolli, op. cit., p. 114.

83. Unpublished manuscript of Mary Garden's autobiography, p. 60. Royal College of Music, London.

84. See unpublished manuscript, op. cit., p. 61.

85. Jules Massenet, *My Recollections*, Westport, Conn.: Greenwood Press, 1970, p. 202.

86. Demar Irvine, *Massenet: A Chronicle of His Life*, Portland, Ore.: Amadeus Press, 1994, p. xviii.

87. "Mary Garden Will Have No New Thaïs," in *The New York Times*, Jan. 20, 1909, no page number.

88. "Miss Garden Wins Fight over Thaïs," in *The New York Times*, Jan. 21, 1909, no page number.

89. See *The New York Times*, Jan. 21, 1909.

90. See *The New York Times*, Jan. 21, 1909.

91. See *The New York Times*, Jan. 21, 1909.

92. See *The New York Times*, Jan. 21, 1909.

93. See *The New York Times*, Jan. 21, 1909.

94. See *The New York Times*, Jan. 21, 1909

95. "Mary Garden Gives out the Letters," in *The New York Times*, Jan. 23, 1909, no page number.

96. See *The New York Times*, Jan. 21, 1909.

97. "Mary Garden Back in Manhattan fold," in *The New York Times*, Jan. 22, 1909, no page number.

98. See *The New York Times*, Jan. 23, 1909.

99. See *The New York Times*, Jan. 23, 1909.

100. See *The New York Times*, Jan. 23, 1909.

101. "Massenet's Sapho Is Disappointing," in *The New York Times*, Nov. 18, 1909, no page number.

102. "Griselidis Charms at the Manhattan," in *The New York Times*, Jan. 20, 1910, no page number.

103. "Mme. Mazarin's Great Opera Feat," in *The New York Times*, Feb. 13, 1910, no page number.

104. See unpublished manuscript, p. 62.

105. Michael Turnbull, *Mary Garden*, Aldershot: The Scholar Press, 1997, p. 92.

106. See Michael Turnbull, op. cit., p. 92.

107. "M. Cavalieri as Tosca" in *The New York Times*, Jan. 26, 1909, p. 9.

108. See "M.Cavalieri as Tosca," op. cit.

109. "Cavalieri's Debut at the Manhattan," in *Musical America*, Jan. 30, 1909.

110. See "Cavalieri's Debut at the Manhattan," op. cit.

111. "Cavalieri in Business" in *The New York Times*, Dec. 25, 1908, p. 7.

112. See "Cavalieri in Business," op. cit., p. 7.

113. The Petersburg Newspaper, no. 356, Jan. 9, 1909.

114. See Mary Jane Matz, p. 30.

115. "Salome Continues to Attract Crowds," in *Musical America*, Feb. 12, 1909, p. 8.

116. "La Bohème," in *Variety*, Feb. 13, 1909, no page number.

117. Andreas De Segurola, *Through My Monocle*, Steubenville, Ohio: Crest Publishing Co., 1991, p. 261.

118. Rodolfo Celletti, *Le Grandi Voci*, Rome: 1964, p. 157.

119. "Cavalieri to Sing Thaïs," in *The New York Times*, March 7, 1909, p. C1.

120. See "Cavalieri to Sing Thaïs," op. cit., p. C1.

121. F. Koptiaev, in *The Exchange Journal*, March 8, 1909.

122. *The Petersburg Newspaper*, March 8, 1909.

123. *The Speech*, March 9, 1909.

124. *The Exchange Gazette*, March 13, 1909.

125. *The Petersburg Leaflet*, March 23, 1909.

126. *The Speech*, no. 68, March 24, 1909.

127. *The Petersburg Leaflet*, April 2, 1909.

128. *The Speech*, April 3, 1909.

129. See *The Speech*, op. cit., April 3, 1909.

130. "Mme Cavalieri Arrives," in *The New York Times*, Oct. 27, 1909, p. 11.

131. See "Mme Cavalieri Arrives," op. cit., p. 11.

132. "Opera Season Opens," in *The New York Journal*, no publication date, no page number (Robinson Locke scrapbooks, vol. 108, NYPL Perf. Arts).

133. "Herodiade Opens Manhattan Opera," in *Musical America*, Nov. 10, 1909, no page number.

134. "A New Salome Opens Season at Manhattan," in *Musical America*, Nov. 13, 1090, pp. 1–3.

135. See "A New Salome Opens Season at Manhattan," op. cit., p. 1.

136. See "A New Salome Opens Season at Manhattan," op. cit., p. 1–3.

137. "Opera Season Opens at the Manhattan," in *The New York Times*, Nov. 9, 1909, p. 3.

138. "Cavalieri Gay in Role of Carmen," in *Musical America*, Dec. 4, 1909, p. 8.

139. See *Musical America*, op. cit., p. 8.

140. See *Musical America*, op. cit., p. 8.

141. "Hoffmann revived at the Manhattan," in *Musical America*, Jan. 1, 1910, p. 37.

142. "Mlle Cavalieri in Hoffman Tales," in *The New York Times*, Dec. 26, 1909, p. 6.

143. "Elektra Again at Manhattan Opera," in *Musical America*, Feb. 26, 1910, p. 37.

144. Harvey O'Connor, *The Astors*, New York: Alfred A. Knopf, 1941, p. 293.

145. See Quaintance Eaton, p. 128.

146. *The Petersburg Newspaper*, May 6, 1910.

147. See *The Petersburg Newspaper*, op. cit., May 6, 1910

148. A. Koptiayev, *The Exchange Gazette*, May 5, 1910.

149. *The Petersburg Leaflet*, May 5, 1910.

150. *The Petersburg Newspaper*, May 8, 1910.

151. *The Exchange Gazette*, no. 11681, May 9, 1910.

152. *The New Time*, no. 12156, May 10, 1910.

153. *Manon Lescaut* was premiered at the Teatro Regio, Turin, in February 1893. It was first performed at Covent Garden a year later.

154. See Quaintance Eaton, p. 155.

155. Quaintance Eaton, *The Boston Opera Company*, New York: Appleton-Century, 1965, p. 194.

156. News reports published in July and August suggest very strongly that Cavalieri and Chanler were still living together although this cannot be substantiated.

157. Lina Cavalieri, "Rubacuori, mestiere difficile," from "Le memorie di Lina Cavalieri," in *Film*, no. 6, Rome, February 1940, p. 8.

158. Harvey O'Connor, *The Astors*, New York: Alfred A Knopf, 1941, p. 308.

159. "Chanler gave up all to wed Cavalieri," in *The New York Times*, Sept. 17, 1910, p. 1.

160. "Cavalieri Explains Again," in *The New York Times*, Dec. 4, 1910, p. C3.

161. See "Cavalieri Explains Again," op. cit.

162. "Cavalieri Ponders Divorcing Chanler," in *The New York Times*, April 2, 1911, p. C3.

163. See "Cavalieri Ponders Divorcing Chanler," op. cit.

164. "Cavalieri Holds on to Chanler Fortune," in *The New York Times*, Sept. 16, 1911, p. 2.

165. See "Cavalieri Holds on to Chanler Fortune," op. cit.

166. "Cavalieri's $80,000 Raised by Chanler," in *The New York Times*, Dec. 12, 1911, p. 11.

167. "Cavalieri Gets Divorce," in *The New York Times*, Jan. 4, 1912, p. 3.

168. See Lina Cavalieri, "Rubacuori, mestiere difficile," p. 8.

169. In 1927, it was reported that Chanler was engaged to marry the dancer Isadora Duncan, who died in a famous car accident the day following the announcement. Chanler, who had been seriously injured in an accident himself, retired to Woodstock, where he died in 1930.

170. This story was reported widely by the popular press and included in several of Cavalieri's obituary notices in 1944. It is also repeated in Harvey O'Connor's book, *The Astors*, p. 308, op. cit.

171. *The Petersburg Newspaper*, Jan. 19, 1911.

172. See *The Petersburg Newspaper*, op. cit., Jan. 19, 1911

173. *The New Time*, 4.2.1911.

174. *The Petersburg Leaflet*, Feb. 4, 1911.

175. *The Theatre Review*, no. 1301, Feb. 7, 1911.

176. *The Speech*, no. 33, Feb. 15, 1911.

177. *The Theatre Review*, no. 1415, June 16, 1911.

178. This later became known as the Stoll Theatre and was demolished in 1957.

179. Unidentified press report, London, December 1911.

180. Columbia Records advertisement, in *The London Musical Courier*, Sept. 30, 1911, p. 231.

181. "Columbia Grand Opera Records," in *Music*, no. 11, vol. XVI, September 1911, p. 27.

182. See, "Columbia Grand Opera Records," op. cit., p. 27.

183. "London Opera House," in *Music*, no. 1, vol. XVII, November 1911, pp. 5–6.

184. See "London Opera House," in *Music*, no. 1, vol. XVII, November 1911, pp. 5–6.

185. "Hammerstein Opera Opens London's Eyes," in *Musical America*, 18.11.1911, pp. 1–4.

186. See "Hammerstein Opera Opens London's Eyes," op. cit.

187. See "Hammerstein Opera Opens London's Eyes," op. cit.

188. *The Daily Telegraph*, Nov. 14, 1911, no page number.

189. One critic noted that when the opera had first been staged at Covent Garden, the Lord Chamberlain's office had required a number of changes to be made to the libretto: Herod became the King of Ethiopia and Herodias was renamed Hesatoad. For this new production, the description of John as "the" prophet was changed to "a" prophet.

190. "Herodiade" in *Musical News*, Dec. 23, 1911, p. 6.

191. Vincent Sheean, *Oscar Hammerstein I*, New York: Simon and Schuster, 1956, pp. 322–323.

192. "Gives London Its First Herodiade," in *Musical America*, Dec. 23, 1911, p. 4

193. "London Opera House: Herodiade," no publication, Dec. 15, 1911.

194. "London Opera House: Herodiade and Lucia," no publication, Dec. 15, 1911.

195. "London Opera House: Herodiade," in *The Daily Graphic*, Dec. 16, 1911.

196. "London Opera House: Herodiade Triumphant," in *The Daily Telegraph*, Dec. 16, 1911, p. 15.

197. "Sumptuous Spectacle," in *The Daily Graphic*, Dec. 16, 1911, p. 6.

198. See "London Opera House: Herodiade and Lucia," op. cit.

199. *The Times*, Jan. 3, 1912, p. 7.

200. "The Tales of Hoffmann," in *The Daily Graphic*, Dec. 27, 1911.

201. "London Opera House," no publication, Dec. 27, 1911.

202. See "London Opera House," op. cit.

203. *The Times*, Dec. 27, 1911, p. 8.

204. *Musical News*, Jan. 6, 1912, p. 7.

205. *The Times*, Dec. 27, 1911, p. 8.

206. *Musical News*, Jan. 6, 1912, p. 7.

207. *The Petersburg Leaflet*, Jan. 28, 1912.

208. *The Exchange Gazette*, No 12751, Feb. 6, 1912.

209. "Cavalieri to Wed Again," in *The New York Times*, April 9, 1912, p. 3.

210. Zandonai's opera premiered at the Teatro Regio, Turin, in February 1914. The U.S. premiere was given at the Metropolitan two years later with Frances Alda and Giovanni Martinelli.

211. *The Theatre Review*, no. 1955, Jan. 13, 1913.

212. "Miss Lina Cavalieri to return and give series of recitals," in *The New York Herald*, Jan. 26, 1913.

213. Charles Henry Meltzer, "Lina Cavalieri as Charming as Ever, Here for Concerts," in *The New York American*, Feb. 13, 1913, no page number.

214. "Jewels bedeck Lina Cavalieri," unidentified publication, Feb. 20, 1913, no page number (Robinson Locke scrapbook, vol. 108, NYPL Perf. Arts).

215. *The Theatre Review*, May 27–28, 1914

216. Glenn Dillard Gunn, "Miss Cavalieri Sings in Opera Caricatures," in *The Chicago Tribune*, 31.3.1913, no page number.

217. *Vanity Fair*, May 1916, p. 68.

218. *The Theatre Review*, no. 2242, Nov. 6, 1913.

219. See Cavalieri and D'Arvanni, *Le Mie Verita*, p. 157.

220. *The News of the Season*, no. 2961, Oct. 2–3, 1914.

221. Geraldine Farrar, *Such Sweet Compulsion*, New York: The Greystone Press, 1938, p. 236.

222. Mary Garden and Louis Biancolli, *Mary Garden's Story*, London: Michael Joseph, 1952, p. 226.

223. See Mary Garden and Louis Biancolli, op. cit, p. 226.

224. In his biography of Garden, Michael Turnbull tells a story that rather appropriately illustrates the sense of ill feeling that existed between the two singers. Garden was being sued by a Paris milliner for the nonpayment of a $150 bill. "When the milliner won her case, Lina Cavalieri was said to have commented: 'How bourgeois! A bagatelle! I would never wear such cheap hats.'" (Michael Turnbull, *Mary Garden*, Aldershot: Scholar Press, 1997, p. 102).

225. "Muratore to Quit the Chicago Opera," in *The New York Times*, Jan. 19, 1922, p. 8.

226. See "Muratore to Quit the Chicago Opera," op. cit., p. 8.

227. See "Muratore to Quit the Chicago Opera," op. cit., p. 8.

228. "Says Mary Garden Struck at Polacco," in *The New York Times*, Jan. 20, 1922, p. 13.

229. "Chicago Opera Gets a Warm Reception," in *The New York Times*, Jan. 24, 1922, p. 15.

230. "Mary Garden here in indulgent mood," in *The New York Times*, Jan. 24, 1922, p. 15.

231. "Mary Garden here in indulgent mood," in *The New York Times*, Jan. 24, 1922, p. 15.

232. "Mary Garden's place will not be filled," in *The New York Times*, April 25, 1922, p. 17.

233. See "Mary Garden's place will not be filled," op. cit., p. 17.

234. "Muratore Pleads to sing in Chicago Opera," in *The New York Times*, July 28, 1922, p. 8.

Chapter V

1. Lina Cavalieri, "Le Memorie di Lina Cavalieri: I miei film," in *Film*, no. 8, February 1940.

2. See Lina Cavalieri, "I miei film," op. cit.

3. Vernon Jarratt, *The Italian Cinema*, London: Falcon Press, 1951, p. 22.

4. See Lina Cavalieri, "I miei film," op. cit.

5. "Wig-Wag at the Movies—Watching Cavalieri Pose," in *The New York Star*, April 11, 1914, no page number.

6. See "Wig-Wag at the Movies—Watching Cavalieri Pose."

7. "Mme Cavalieri Helps to Put Manon Lescaut into Movies," in *The New York Herald*, April 1914, no page number.

8. "Strand—Lina Cavalieri in Films," in *The Washington Star*, Oct. 6, 1914, no page number.

9. Alco Film Corporation Souvenir Program for the Playgoers Film Company production of *Manon Lescaut* (Metropolitan Opera archives, New York).

10. Promotional advertisement for the release of *Manon Lescaut*, in *Moving Picture World*, May 16, 1914.

11. "Cavalieri and Muratore in Film Version of Manon," in *Musical America*, June 20, 1914, no page number.

12. H. W. De Long, "Manon Lescaut," in *The Moving Picture World*, June 27, 1914, p. 1858.

13. See H. W. De Long, p. 1858.

14. See H. W. De Long, p. 1858.

15. See H. W. De Long, p. 1858.

16. "Manon Lescaut," in *The New York Times*, June 14, 1914, p. 15.

17. "Lina Cavalieri as Manon," in *The Chicago Herald*, no date, no page number (Robinson Locke scrapbooks, vol. 108, NYPL Perf. Arts).

18. This matter is covered in considerable detail by Richard de Cordova, in *Picture Personalities: The Emergence of the Star System in America*, Chicago: University of Illinois Press, 1990.

19. "Manon Lescaut," in *Variety*, June 19, 1914, p. 21.

20. See "Manon Lescaut," in *Variety*, p. 21.

21. "Lina the Beautiful," no publication, no date (Robinson Locke scrapbook, New York Public Library for the Performing Arts).

22. Richard Savage, "Lucien Muratore: A Singing Actor," no publication, no date (New York Public Library for the Performing Arts).

23. See Giorgio Vecchietti, p. 924.

24. "The Shadow of her Past," in *Variety*, July 21, 1916, p. 19.

25. See "The Shadow of Her Past," in *Variety*, p. 19.

26. Margaret McDonald, "The Shadow of Her Past," in *The Moving Picture World*, Aug. 5, 1916, no page number.

27. See Margaret McDonald, "The Shadow of Her Past."

28. *The Chicago News*, Aug. 8, 1916.

29. Playbill for the Art Electric Theatre, Moscow, January 1916.

30. "News of the Screen—Lina Cavalieri on the Screen," in *The Moscow Leaflet*, Jan. 21, 1916.

31. *The Time*, no. 491, Jan. 26, 1916.

32. *The Pegasus*, no. 2, February 1916.

33. *The Theatre Review*, March 11–12, 1916.

34. *The Theatre Review*, March 15, 1916.

35. See Giorgio Vecchietti, p. 924.

36. *The Theatre Review*, June 21, 1917.

37. "Famous Players Signs Cavalieri, Noted Diva," no publication, no date (Robinson Locke scrapbooks, NYPL Perf. Arts).

38. Aileen St. John-Brenon, "Lina Cavalieri wants to play human role," in *The New York Telegraph*, Aug. 12, 1917, no page number.

39. See Aileen St. John-Brenon, "Lina Cavalieri wants to play human role."

40. "Operatic Star in Paramount studio," in *The New York Mirror*, Sept. 29, 1917, no page number.

41. Lina Cavalieri, "I miei film" from "Le Memorie di Lina Cavalieri," in *Film*, no. 8, Rome, February 1940, no page number.

42. "Lina Cavalieri in the Eternal Temptress," promotional advertisement in *The Dramatic Mirror*, Nov. 17, 1917.

43. This matter had been raised in an article titled "Opera in Moving Pictures," in an unidentified publication from August 1914, which commented on the release of *Manon Lescaut*. "It is the old story of a musical play given without music and thereby degenerating into a series of more or less inconsequential incidents without the dramatic fire necessary to hold the attention of an audience.... If other operas are to be put into the moving picture category, they will require special study and care.... In the case of *Manon Lescaut* it is apparently a plan to draw the public, through the medium of the two principal actors" (Robinson Locke scrapbooks, vol. 108, NYPL Perf. Arts).

44. "The Eternal Temptress," in *The Bioscope*, June 13, 1918, p. 79.

45. "The Eternal Temptress," in *Variety*, Dec. 14, 1917, p. 45.

46. Fevrier (1873–1957) had studied composition with Faure, Massenet and Messager. His setting of *Gismonda* was written to a libretto by Cain and Payen. Garden had scored a great success with one of his earlier operas, *Monna Vanna*, in 1909.

47. "Love's Conquest," in *Variety*, July 5, 1918, p. 29.

48. See "Loves Conquest," in *Variety*, p. 29.

49. "Are Movies Popularising Opera?," in *Theatre Magazine*, May 1919, p. 297.

50. Lina Cavalieri, "I miei film," from "Le Memorie di Lina Cavalieri," in *Film*, no. 8, Rome, February 1940, no page number.

51. "A Prima Donna in Pictures," in *Pictures and Picturegoer*, Aug. 17, 1918, p. 179.

52. "A Woman of Impulse," in *Variety*, Sept. 27, 1918, p. 43.

53. "A Prima Donna in Pictures," in *Pictures and Picturegoer*, Aug. 17, 1918, p. 179.

54. "The Two Brides," in *Variety*, April 25, 1919, p. 81.

55. See Lina Cavalieri and Paulo D'Arvanni, p. 163.

56. See Lina Cavalieri and Paulo D'Arvanni, p. 166.

57. See Lina Cavalieri, "I miei film," op. cit.

Chapter VI

1. This custom of donating clothes for the statues has a long tradition in Onano, dating back to the 16th century.

2. D. Scalabrella, *La Chiesina del Piano nella Storia di Onano*, Onano: 1969.

3. Bonafede Mancini, "La Communita," in *Pio XII—Eugenio Pacelli e Onano*, Grote di Castro: Ceccarelli, 1998, p. 31.

4. A certain mystery surrounds this case: If the girl was eighteen years old in 1926, she would have been born in 1908, and Cavalieri and Muratore were certainly not married at this time.

5. "Lina Cavalieri, a victim of an air raid," in *Il Messagero*, Feb. 10, 1944.

6. "Lina Cavalieri Killed by Bomb, Rome Reports," in *The New York Times*, Feb. 9, 1944.

7. Titta Ruffo, notes on Titta Ruffo (trans. Connie DeCaro), *My Parabola*, Dallas: Baskerville Publishers Inc., 1995, pp. 371–372.

8. Sheldon was born in 1886 "into a wealthy Chicago family…. At 18 he enrolled at Harvard, where he attended George Pierce Baker's play writing class…. After his graduation he began work on *Salvation Nell*, a daring, realistic drama…. With Minnie Maddern Fiske in the title role, it opened in New York on November 17, 1908, and established Sheldon as a force to be reckoned with" (Michael A. Morrison, *John Barrymore: Shakespearean Actor*, Cambridge: Cambridge University Press, 1997, p. 48). In 1911, the actor John Barrymore played the leading role in Sheldon's light romantic comedy, *The Princess Zim-Zim*, which began a friendship and professional association which was later to influence Barrymore to develop his skills as a great classical actor. Later in life, when Barrymore's poor health incapacitated him almost completely, Don B. Wilmeth states that "he served as a play doctor to the likes of Sidney Howard and Charles MacArthur, and probably O'Neill" (Don B. Wilmeth, e-mail to the author, Dec. 22, 1998).

9. Barrett H. Clark, *Intimate Portraits*, New York: Dramatists Play Service, 1951, p. 54.

10. Loren K. Ruff, *Edward Sheldon*, Boston: Twayne Publishers, 1982, p. 118.

11. Though the romantic association between Sheldon and Keane had ended even before the play opened, the author was later to give the actress both the motion picture rights to the work and half of the royalties on all stage productions.

12. See Loren K. Ruff, op. cit., p. 121.

13. Acton Davies quoted by Eric. W. Barnes, *The High Room*, London: W. H. Allen, 1957, p. 76.

14. See Eric W. Barnes, op. cit., p. 67.

15. Griffith's name does not appear in the film's credits.

16. In 1921 *Romance* was revived in New York and Chicago, again with Doris Keane in the leading role. It was seen in Paris in 1921 and again in 1928 and revived in London in 1926. During this decade productions were mounted in Norway, Sweden, Spain, Egypt and India.

17. "Clarence Brown Filmography," in Allen Estrin, *The Hollywood Professionals, Volume 6*, New York: A. S. Barnes & Co., 1980, pp. 180–187.

18. The supporting cast included Lewis Stone, Gavin Gordon and Elliott Nugent—although Garbo had apparently made it very clear that she wanted Gary Cooper as her costar—and the elegant settings were provided by Cedric Gibbons, with costumes by Adrian.

19. Garbo did not win the Oscar. It was awarded to Norma Shearer.

20. Brooks Atkinson quoted by Brooks McNamara, *The Shuberts of Broadway*, Oxford: Oxford University Press, 1990, p. 206.

21. Greater vocal interest is supplied by the presence in the film of the tenor Mario del Monaco, who dubbed the singing voice of an apparently fictional character represented as one of Cavalieri's lovers.

22. C. Matteini, "Due vagoni di rose rosse furono tappeto per Lina Cavalieri," in *Il Messagero*, Dec. 1, 1955, p. 3.

23. Richard Fletcher, "The Beauty Who sings," no publication, no date, pp. 736–737 (Robinson Locke Scrapbooks, New York Public Library for Performing Arts).

24. See William Armstrong, p. 81.

25. Felix Soloni, "A Prince's Tragic Wish Comes True," no publication, copyrighted 1944.

26. Lina Cavalieri, "Verità e leggende sulla mia vita," from "Le Memorie di Lina Cavalieri," in *Film*, no. 9, Rome, March 1940, no page number.

BIBLIOGRAPHY

Adami, G., and M. Carner. *Letters of Puccini*. London: Harrap, 1974.

Alda, Frances. *Men, Women and Tenors*. New York: AMS Press, 1971.

Armstrong, William. "Lina Cavalieri: The Famous Beauty of the Operatic Stage," in *Munsey's Magazine*, April 1908, pp. 74–81.

Aspinall, Michael. "La Voce della Donna Piu Bella del Mondo," in *Musica*, no. 88, 1994, pp. 44–50.

Barnes, Eric. *The High Room: The Biography of Edward Sheldon*. London: 1957.

Beliayev, Yuri. *Actors and Plays: Impressions*, Saint Petersburg: 1902.

Bell, Archie. "Lina the Beautiful," in *The Green Book Magazine*, November 1913, pp. 807–812.

Cavalieri, Lina. "Capricci, Prepotenze e Papere di Corte," in *Film*, Rome, no. 5, February 1940, p. 8.

_____. "Come Fu Rapita la Cavalieri," in *Il Progresso Italo-Americano*, November 10, 1940, p. 4.

_____. "Costumes: Presenting a Truthful Stage Appearance," no publication, no date (Margaret Herrick Library).

_____. "Dalle Nebbie di Londra al gelo di Pietroburgo," in *Film*, Rome, no. 2, January 1940, p. 6.

_____. "La Fatica di Essere Bella," in *Film*, Rome, no. 4, January 1940, p. 8.

_____. "I Miei Film," in *Film*, Rome, no. 8, February 1940, p. 9.

_____. *My Secrets of Beauty*. New York: 1914.

_____. "Notte d'Avventura a Londra," in *Film*, Rome, no. 1, January 1940, p. 6.

_____. "Quand'ero la Principessa Linotchka," in *Film*, Rome, no. 3, January 1940, p. 6.

_____. "Quando presi a Pugni la Bella Otero," in *Film*, Rome, no. 52, December 1939, p. 4.

_____. "Ricette di Bellezza," in *Film*, Rome, no. 7, February 1940, p. 8.

_____. "Rubacuori, Mestiere Difficile," in *Film*, Rome, no. 6, February 1940, p. 8.

_____. "Il Tempo dei Giuochi e Finito," in *Film*, Rome, no. 51, December 1939, p. 5.

_____. "Verità e Leggende Sulla Mia Vita," in *Film*, Rome, no. 9, March 1940, p. 8.

_____, and D'Arvanni, P. *Le Mie Verità*, Rome: 1936.

Celletti, R. *Le Grandi Voci*. Rome: Instituto per la collaborazione culturale, 1964.

_____. "Lina Cavalieri," in *Enciclopedia Dello Spettacolo*, vol. III, Rome, Le Maschere, 1956, pp. 259–260.

Chaliapin, Fiodor Ivanovich. *Literary Heritage: Letters*. vol. I, Moscow: 1976.

Christiansen, Rupert. *Prima Donna*. London: Penguin, 1984.

Cone, J. F. *Oscar Hammerstein's Manhattan Opera Company*. Norman: University of Oklahoma Press, 1966.

Curzon, Henri de. "Madame Lina Cavalieri." In *Le Théâtre*, Paris, no. 259, October 1909, pp. 9–10.

Dell'Arco, M. *Café Chantant di Roma*. Rome: 1970.

De Segurola, A. *Through My Monocle: Memoirs of the Great Basso*. Parsons, W. Va.: McClain Printing Co., 1991.

Dymov, O. "Cavalieri and Komissarjevskaya." In *Exchange Gazette*, St. Petersburg, no. 122, March 7, 1904, p. 3.

Eaton, Quaintance. *The Miracle of the Met*. Westport, Conn.: Greenwood Press, 1976.

_____. *Opera Caravan*. New York: Farrar, Straus, and Cudahy, 1978.

Erté. *My Life, My Act*. New York: E. P. Dutton, 1989.

Essays in the History of the Russian Theatre Critic. End of the XIXth to the Beginning of the XXth Century. Leningrad: 1979.

Farrar, Geraldine. *Such Sweet Compulsion*. New York: Greystone Press, 1938.

Froud, Nina, and James Hanley (eds.). *Chaliapin: A Biography as Told to Maxim Gorky*. London: Stein and Day, 1967.

Garden, Mary, and Louis Biancolli. *Mary Garden's Story*. London: Oxford University Press, 1952.

Guzzi, P. *Café Chantant a Roma*. Rome: Rendina Editori, 1995.

Harding, James. *Massenet*. New York: St. Martin's Press, 1970.

Ilari, M. "Lina Cavalieri nel cinquantesimo della morte," *Lazio Ieri e Oggi*, 1994, no. 10, pp. 298–305.

Ilyin, Yuri, and S. Mikheev. *The Great Caruso*. St. Petersburg: Glagol, 1995.

Irvine, Demar. *Massenet: A Chronicle of His Life*. Portland: Amadeus Press, 1994.

Jarratt, Vernon. *The Italian Cinema*. London: Falcon Press, 1951.

Jarro (G. Piccini). *Viaggio Umoristico nei Teatri*. Florence: 1903.

Key, Pierre. *Enrico Caruso: A Biography*. London: 1923.

Kolodin, Irving. *The Metropolitan Opera*. Oxford: Oxford University Press, 1940.

Kshessinskaya, M. *Memoirs*. Moscow: 1992.

Kutsch, K., and L. Riemens. *Concise Biographical Dictionary of Singers*. Philadelphia: Chilton Book Co., 1969.

_____, and _____. *Grosses Sängerlexikon*, vol. 1. Bern: Francke, 1978–1991.

Lauri-Volpi, G. *Vocal Parallels*. Leningrad: Musyka, 1972.

Less, A. *Titta Ruffo: Life and Creativity*. Moscow: 1983.

Levik, Sergei. *Commentaries of an Opera Singer*. Moscow: Iskusstvo,1962.

_____ (trans. Edward Morgan). *The Levik Memoirs*. London: Symposium, 1995.

Martinelli, V. "L'Avventura Cinematografica di Lina Cavalieri," in *Il Territorio*, 1986, pp. 285–299.

Marwick, Arthur. *Beauty in History*. London: Thames and Hudson, 1988.

Massenet, J. *My Recollections*. Westport, Conn.: Greenwood Press, 1970.

Matz, Mary Jane. "Manon Incarnate," in *Opera News*, March 26, 1956, pp. 7, 8, 29, 30.

Moore, Edward. *Forty Years of Opera in Chicago*. New York: 1977.

Musicians since 1900: Performers in Concerts. New York: 1978.

Obolensky, S. *One Man in His Time*. New York: McDowell, Obolensky, 1958.

O'Connor, Harvey. *The Astors*. New York: Knopf, 1941.

Ossovsky, A. V. *Musical Critical Essays (1894–1912)*. Leningrad: Musyka, 1971.

P., Kr. *M. N. Kuznetsova and Lina Cavalieri*. Saint Petersburg: 1910.

Paliotti, Vittorio. *Salone Margherita*. Naples: Altrastampa Edizioni, 2001.

Palmegiani, F. *Mattia Battistini*. Moscow-Leningrad: Musyka, 1966.

Perestiani, I. N. *Seventy-five Years of My Life in Art*. Moscow: 1962.

Poplavsky, G.V. *Sobinov in Petersburg-Petrograd-Leningrad*. Leningrad: Lenizdat, 1990.

Rosenthal, Harold. *Two Centuries of Opera at Covent Garden*. London: Putnam, 1958.

Rostovtsev, M. A. *Pages of Life*. Leningrad: State Academic Maly Opera Theatre, 1939.

Ruff, Loren K. *Edward Sheldon*. Boston: Twayne Publishers, 1982.

Ruffo, Titta. *My Parabola*. Dallas: Baskerville, 1995.

Sadoul, Georges. *The Universal History of Cinema*, vol. 1. Moscow: 1958.

Schneider, I. *Sketchbook of an old Muscovite*. Moscow: Soviet Russia, 1970.

Seligman, Vincent. *Puccini among Friends*. London: Macmillan, 1938.

Seltsam, W .H. *The Metropolitan Opera Annals*. New York: Wilson, 1947.

Sheean, Vincent. *Oscar Hammerstein I*. New York: Simon and Schuster, 1956.

Shorey, Jerome. "The Romance of Cavalieri and Muratore," in *Photoplay*, March 1919, p. 34.

Sobinov, L. *Letters to L. Sobinov. Memories of L. Sobinov*, vol. 1, *Letters*. vol. 2, *Articles. Speeches*. Moscow: Iskusstvo, 1970.

Taburi, O. *Gloria e Bellezza di Lina Cavalieri*. Rome (no publication date).

Theatre Encyclopedia. Moscow: 1963.

Tortorelli, V. *Enrico Caruso*. Moscow: Musyka, 1965.

Tsvetaeva, A. *Memoirs*. Moscow: 1983.

Tuggle, Robert. *The Golden Age of Opera*. New York: Henry Holt, 1983.

Turnbull, Michael. *Mary Garden*. Aldershot: Scolar Press, 1997.

Usova, O. "La Belle Cavalieri. " In *Natalie*, St. Petersburg, 1999, no. 6, pp. 16–17, 31.

Walsh, T. J. *The Monte Carlo Opera*. London: Gil and Macmillan, 1975.

Yuriev, Y. *Memoirs,* vol. 2. Leningrad: Iskusstvo, 1945.

Yussupov, F. *Memoirs*. Moscow: Vagrius, 1998.

INDEX